THE HIDDEN HALF

Studies of Plains Indian Women

Patricia Albers
University of Utah

Beatrice Medicine
University of California—Northridge

UNIVERSITY
PRESS OF
AMERICA

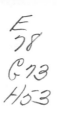

Copyright © 1983 by

University Press of America, Inc.

P.O. Box 19101, Washington, D.C. 20036

TABLE OF CONTENTS

PREFACE

This volume contains a collection of papers which are concerned with research and analyses on Plains Indian women. All of the papers (with the exception of Albers and Medicine, pp. 123-140) were presented originally at a symposium entitled "The Role and Status of Women in Plains Indian Cultures," held in 1977 at the Plains Conference in Lincoln, Nebraska.

The symposium had two major aims. On the one hand, it involved a review and critique of past evaluations of the role and status of Plains Indian women. And on the other, it included a reassessment of the position of these women in the light of recent empirical and theoretical developments in anthropology and women's studies. Of the ten original participants in the symposium, eight have contributed papers to this volume.

It must be pointed out that while the articles in this book cover a range of topics and tribal groups, the volume is not intended to be comprehensive in its scope. From a topical standpoint, the volume presents a selection of case studies which focus on particular aspects of the female condition in Plains Indian societies. The data used in these studies are drawn from ethnological, ethnohistorical, and contemporary field research. Geographically, most of the articles concentrate on tribal groups in the northern Plains region of the United States and Canada. This orientation coincides with the research interests and experiences of the contributors. Finally, the book is primarily historical in focus, dealing with the conditions of Plains Indian women in the pre-reservation period. Two contributions, however, are concerned with the role and status of women in the modern reservation era.

The articles which appear in this volume were revised and finalized at different times between 1978 and 1982. Consequently, there is some lag in references to more recent studies which have been published on subjects covered in this volume. Although these omissions are regrettable, it would have been impractical to revise articles continually to include many of these newer references. Indeed, the literature pertaining to women in anthropology and other disciplines has been growing at such an enormous and rapid rate that it has become nearly impossible to keep articles entirely up-to-date.

In organizing and editing this book, we are indebted to many different people. First, we wish to thank the contributors for their patience and support in seeing us through this effort. We owe considerable gratitude to William James for his major efforts in the editing of the final manuscript. Ursula Hanly, who typed the final, camera-ready manuscript, is to be given special mention for her careful and conscientious work. Finally, we would like to extend our appreciation to the many American Indian women who have given us their encouragement in this undertaking. In particular, we wish to acknowledge Anna Grace (Gabe) Medicine whose life example has been an inspiration to both of us, and it is to her memory that we dedicate this book.

CHAPTER 1

INTRODUCTION:
NEW PERSPECTIVES ON PLAINS INDIAN WOMEN

Patricia C. Albers
University of Utah

Since the end of the nineteenth century, the cultures of the Teton, Blackfeet, Comanche, Pawnee, and other native peoples of the Great Plains have formed the basis for popular stereotyping of Indian life in the United States and Canada. For most Americans and Europeans, the Plains Indian is the quintessential symbol of "Indianness" (Ewers 1968a: 187-203; Price 1973:153-154; Berkhofer 1978:96-103). Indeed, this association is so pervasive that even today when White people think of Indian culture, they identify it with the equestrian, buffalo-hunting life of the nineteenth century Plains Indian.

The Plains Indians qua American Indians that figure most predominately in popular stereotyping are men. Chiefs constitute the most dominant symbol in this image-making. Commonly shown wearing a Plains Indian costume of fringed buckskin and a full-feathered headdress, the chief has dominated classic characterizations of Indians in the mass media. Scores of factual and fictional accounts have focused on the lives of such well-known men as Sitting Bull, Quanah Parker, Red Cloud, and Geronimo. Photographs and paintings of these and lesser known Indian men fill the pages of coffee-table picture books on Native Americans, and they are printed on widely distributed posters, greeting cards, and post cards. Not far behind the chiefs in popularity are the warriors. In Hollywood movies and Western dime novels, the warrior is portrayed clashing with the U.S. cavalry, swooping down on wagon trains, or fighting off the attacks of enemy tribes. The image of the warrior appears as an emblem in advertizing, as a mascot for sports teams, and as a major subject in the bronze statuary of city parks and squares. Equally popular in media myth-making are the hunters. Whether depicted surrounding herds of buffalo or stalking the lone antelope, the hunter shares equal billing with the warrior in the creation of popular symbols and myths.

The side of Plains Indian life most often seen by the American public is the male half. It is the male-dominated universe of native diplomacy, warfare, and hunting that has captured the attention of national image-makers in Hollywood, New York, and Toronto. That the symbolism of the Plains Indian is masculine is reinforced in a number of recent review articles on the subject (Ewers 1968a; Friar and Friar 1972; Price 1973; Berkhofer 1978). In discussing the role played by Plains Indians in the development of the Western genre of novels and movies, John Ewers (1968b) and Robert Berkhofer, Jr. (1978) hardly mention the female-side of Plains Indian imagery. Equally interesting, neither of them use the feminine gender when referring to Plains Indians in singular or plural form. The very fact that women are largely omitted in discussions of Plains Indian imagery testifies to their secondary place in popular myth and stereotypes.

Where are Plains Indian women in the mass media? They are present but hidden in the background of popu-lar images. In most Hollywood movies (with the recent exception of Walks Far Woman), Plains Indian women are mere backdrops on stages dominated by the actions and dialogue of men. They are seen fleeing burning tipis while the men are fighting off the U.S. cavalry. Women are located on the sidelines scraping hides or gathering roots as the camera focuses in on a line of warriors returning from battle. Inside the tipi, women sit in the background making moccasins or cooking a meal while the debates of an all male coun-cil dominate the picture. Rarely do native women carry on conversations in Western films. When they do, it is usually in response to a request or command of some male--a fur trader, U.S. soldier, or a man from their own tribe. The important point is that in most films Indian women are not portrayed autono-mously, as having skills, conversations, and par-

2

ticipating in areas of life that exist in partial independence of those of men.

In the few films and novels where Indian women occupy a prominent role, they act as counterpoints to the advances and interests of men. Typically, the native woman is portrayed as a "Princess" (chief's daughter) who mediates the conflict between Redmen and Whitemen, or else she is cast as a "Squaw" who has been used and abandoned by a philandering trader or soldier (Friar and Friar 1972:229-245). Whether glorified in the figure of the "Princess" or denigrated in the image of the "Squaw," native women are shrouded in the arabesques of female models that have existed in European myths since Classical times (Green 1975). In the entire genre of Western novels and films, the life experiences of Plains Indian women have been ignored or concealed by images that are indisputably European.

Even outside the realm of fiction, Plains Indian women are described in a European mode. In keeping with the pervasive European idea that women constitute the passive, inferior, and hidden side of humanity, Plains Indian women are rarely visible as individuals or a category of people in the early journals of traders, missionaries, explorers, and government agents (see Weist in this volume). Often, these journalistic accounts ignore the experiences of women, considering them too insignificant to merit special treatment. Or else, such writings denigrate and trivialize female activity. Some early writers went as far as portraying Plains Indian women as chattel, enslaved as beasts of burden and beaten into submission by over-bearing male masters. The sensationalized accounts of men like E.D. Neill (1872), Thaddeus Culbertson (1952), and Pierre-Antoine Tabeau (1939) were extreme even during the time they were written. Unfortunately, it has been these views, rather than the more balanced and sensitive portrayals of observers like Edwin Denig (1961) or Samuel Pond (1908), that have generated the most publicity and that have had the most enduring impact on the popular image of Plains Indian women.

The general neglect of Plains Indian women is also evident in the twentieth century writings of historians and anthropologists. Katherine Weist (1980) and Margot Liberty (1981) have recently reviewed the

3

state of the literature on Plains Indian women, and both reach the conclusion that the more recent writings on this subject are meager. In the writings of historians, native women rarely appear in descriptions of diplomatic and trade negotiations between Whites and Indians, nor are they usually present in discussions of military encounters. Except for the now mythologized figure of Sacajawea, women are conspicuous by their absence in the historical literature on the Native Plains. In the ethnographic writings of anthropologists, Plains Indian women are also generally ignored. With few exceptions (Grinnell 1923; Mead 1932; Deloria 1944; Hilger 1952; Ewers 1955; Flannery 1953; Hassrick 1964; Weltfish 1965), the contributions of Plains Indian women rarely receive more than passing reference in ethnographies devoted to the more 'vital' and 'valorous' accomplishments of men. In this century, only a handful of books and articles have been written about Plains Indian women, and most of these are autobiographical (Grinnell 1904; Lowie 1922; Michelson 1932, 1933; Hebard 1933; Lewis 1941; Anderson 1956; Ewers 1968b, 1980; Kehoe 1970, 1976; Wilson, G. 1971; Linderman 1972; Jones 1972; Crary 1973; Wilson, D. 1974; Bysiewicz and Van de Mark 1977; Maynard 1979; Hungry Wolf 1980). Aside from a few studies (Lewis 1941; Anderson 1956; Kehoe 1970; Jones 1972; Marriott and Rachlin 1977; Schneider 1979; Weist 1979; Powers 1980), the bulk of writings that deal with Plains Indian women do not involve the kind of sustained scrutiny or sophisticated analysis apparent in much of the literature on male activities and roles.

Not only is the literature on Plains Indian women sparse and fragmentary, but much of it is biased. The biases found in the work of anthropologists and historians may not be as prejudicial nor as blatant as those appearing in the accounts of earlier observers; nonetheless, they are distortions just the same. Many ethnographic descriptions, for example, portray the work of Plains Indian women as menial and monotonous--a view clearly originating from Euro-American ideas on the value of household labor (see Kehoe in this volume). Another widely held notion is that the place of Plains Indian women in the household is not as important as her male counterpart's position in the community at large. This idea is based on the assumption that everywhere domestic life is separated from and subordinated by a public sector;

4

but while this state of affairs is obvious in the organization of European societies, it is questionable whether it applies to many native communities in the Great Plains and elsewhere (Reiter 1975; Leacock 1978; Etienne and Leacock 1980). In either case, these views tell us more about the attitudes of the Euro-Americans who studied Plains Indians than about the actual conditions under which these people lived.

Whether by omission or misrepresentation, the life experiences of Plains Indian women remain hidden from view. This kind of situation, however, has not been unique to the popular and scholarly literature on Plains Indians. In most conventional writings by scholars in the humanities and social sciences, female views and activities rarely penetrated descriptions of a world purportedly controlled by men. Everywhere, the position and role of women was regarded as inferior. Their accomplishments were denigrated and their influence denied. For the vast majority of scholars, society and its transformations were envisioned as the primary, if not exclusive, result of the labor, power, and ideas of men. Ultimately, this led to a very one-sided and distorted vision of society; one in which only the male half of the populace counted. As a general rule, interpretations of indigenous societies in the Great Plains did not deviate, one iota, from this one-sided view.

It has only been within the last decade that scholars have begun to take a more serious look at the conditions of women in our own and other societies. Current research is filling in the empirical gaps created by the customary exclusion of data on women in the historic and social scientific record. Through the gathering of new information and the reinterpretation of old data, scholars are beginning to remedy the oversights and prejudices of their predecessors by incorporating women into the analysis of total social formations. Today, models of society and history are being reconstructed in which women occupy a more visible and vital place.

The mercurial rise of interest in women's issues has been apparent in most academic disciplines within the humanities and social sciences. Anthropology, a discipline straddling both areas, has witnessed a virtual explosion of writings on women's subjects (Rosaldo and Lamphere 1974; Matthiasson 1974; Friedl

1975; Martin and Voorheis 1975; Raphael 1975; Reiter 1975; Rohrlich-Leavitt 1975; Ardener 1975; McCormack 1976; Schlegel 1977; McElroy and Matthiasson 1979; Bourguignon 1980; Sanday 1981). Not only have many theoretical treatises appeared on the broad characteristics of women's role, status, and identity cross-culturally, but scores of descriptive studies have been published on various aspects of women's lives in particular cultural settings (Quinn 1977). The experiences of women in nearly every major world area have been the subject of one or more volumes of collected works. Volumes of this kind have been devoted, for example, to the women of Latin America (Pescatello 1973; Nash and Safa 1976; Latin American Perspectives 1979), the Middle East (Fernea and Bezirgan 1977; Beck and Keddie 1978), Africa (Paulume 1963; Hafkin and Bay 1976), and Oceania (Brown and Buchbinder 1976).

Despite the recent surge of publications on women in different cultures, writings on American Indian women have lagged behind. Since the late sixties, when the Feminist Movement spurred an interest in Women's Studies, the literature on American Indian women has not been comparable either in size or quality to the writings being published on women of other ethnic origins. The bulk of recently published literature on native women continues to be auto-biographical in focus, and many writings appear as reprints of work originally published more than a decade ago (Lurie 1966; Reichard 1968; Udall 1969; Shipek 1970; Landes 1971; Barnett and Sterling 1975; Niethammer 1977; Underhill 1979).[1] Those studies that are not autobiographical are largely descriptive, and even though a few involve innovative approaches (Briggs 1970, 1974; Brown, J.A. 1970, 1975; McElroy 1975, 1979; Klein 1976, 1980; Leacock and Goodman 1976; Medicine 1975, 1978; Green 1980), the vast majority employ outmoded concepts and frameworks when analyzing the life experiences of Native American women. With few exceptions (Schlegel 1972; Lamphere 1974; Nelson 1976; Rothenberg 1976, 1980; Leacock 1978, 1980; Brown, J.S. 1980; Greemet 1980), recent theoretical and analytical developments in women's studies have not been applied to the Native American data.

The moribund state of the literature on American Indian women does not necessarily indicate a lack of interest on the part of scholars. Instead, it seems to

6

reflect a general pessimism about the possibility of doing significant research on the conditions of American Indian women in past or present times. The reasons for this pessimism are many but two stand out.

The first, which pertains largely to studies on native women in historic times, is founded on the widely held notion that data necessary for sound research are either lacking or inaccessible. There is no question that primary source materials on American Indian women are sparse and difficult to find. Most of these materials are buried in obscure and widely scattered accounts, ethnographic as well as historical, and uncovering them is a laborious task. It is also clear that much of the available data are heavily biased by the preconceptions of Euro-American observers. Since it is not always easy to separate the valid interpretations from the false ones, conclusive and unequivocal statements about the experiences of native American women are hard to make. But no matter how meager or distorted existing records may be, they must be uncovered, reinterpreted, and systematized if a more complete and reliable picture of historic American Indian women is ever to emerge.

The second reason for pessimism has to do with the problems scholars now encounter in conducting research among contemporary American Indian groups. In recent times, American Indians have questioned the objectives and implications of much research taking place in their midst. Increasingly, they are monitoring research and insisting that studies have direct relevance to the pressing needs of their own communities. Generalized studies on the role and status of modern women, for example, would not be considered a research priority when poverty, unemployment, and resource development are issues requiring immediate attention. Consequently, it is often difficult for outsiders, male or female, to carry on a study unless it corresponds with an Indian community's own research interests.

Not only are non-Indians finding it difficult to justify general descriptive or theoretical research in American Indian communities, but Native Americans, themselves, are facing similar problems. For most American Indians, women as well as men, gender is not the central focus in research on health, education, employment, and resource development. Rather, class

and ethnic variables take priority over sex-linked
ones in the analysis of critical problems in native
communities. While it is recognized that men and
women have been impacted in different ways by such
problems as poverty and unemployment, most American
Indians maintain that their problems must be tackled
through the united efforts and interests of men as
well as women.

Today, most educated Indian women tend to study
and deal with problems with the interests of both
sexes in mind. This does not mean, however, that they
are adverse to thoughtful studies on the conditions of
native women. As a matter of fact, many American
Indian women, who cannot do so themselves because of
other obligations and priorities, encourage and support research that will offer a more accurate
appraisal of their past and present situation. This
is the case, especially if such an evaluation can lead
to an improvement in their conditions and those of
their people as a whole.

Notwithstanding the many difficulties involved in
studying American Indian women, either in the past or
present, important work has been done, as demonstrated
by the articles in this volume. These articles indicate that it is possible to explore and make significant insights on a wide range of issues that bear upon
the historic and modern conditions of American Indian
women. Although the contributors to this volume are
concerned primarily with the situation of American
Indian women from the Great Plains region of the
United States and Canada, they deal with problems that
are applicable to the study of all native women.

The articles in this book cover a wide range of
subjects, and they approach these from different philosophical and theoretical viewpoints. Yet, underlying this variation, there are four basic themes
which dominate each of the articles in this book.

CRITICISM

It is a truism that much of the conventional
literature is filled with myth and stereotypes which
obscure fundamental realities about women's status and
role. Underlying the received wisdom of generations

8

of scholarship is an ideological bedrock resting on sexist and racist interpretations of women in society and history. Identifying the nature and workings of those academic as well as popular ideologies which distort the place of women has become a central theme in many feminist writings (Fee 1974, 1976; Reiter 1975; Leacock 1978). The extensive attention, if not preoccupation, with criticism in these writings not only involves dissecting the character of prevailing ideologies. It is equally concerned with discovering the philosophical and social roots of these ideologies. Disclaiming and dismantling false perceptions from the past has been a necessary step in developing a more accurate awareness of women's present conditions and their place in history.

Criticism of received opinion on the subject of women is also a major theme in this book. The theme is particularly central to the essays contained in the section on imagery. The articles by Katherine Weist and Alice Kehoe identify the kinds of biases that have prevailed in writings on Plains Indian women, and they trace these biases to the philosophical and social heritages of Euro-American observers. Weist's work is concerned primarily with biases that dominated the accounts of pre-twentieth century observers, notably, fur-traders, missionaries, and government agents, whereas Kehoe's study is aimed at uncovering and explaining biased images in the writings of American anthropologists. What is interesting about these two articles is that although they deal with image-making in very different historical contexts, they demonstrate striking continuities in the character of dominant stereotypes over time.

Other authors in this volume also critique distorted images of Plains Indian women as these impinge on the subject matter of their articles. Janet Spector and Mary Jane Schneider draw attention to biases inherent in writings on the character and organization of women's work from the prehistoric to the modern period. The essay by Patricia Albers and Beatrice Medicine speaks to the vexing problems of developing accurate characterizations of female contributions in ceremonial art. Beatrice Medicine's work makes the important point that the varieties of women's experiences in the native Plains have been glossed over in a literature seeking to discover "ideal" or "modal" feminine personality types.

9

Finally, Raymond DeMallie's discussion of feminine and masculine imagery among the Teton stresses the need to pay closer attention to the native point of view.

Although some may argue that the criticism in these essays is overstated in certain places, we believe the criticism is justified. If a critical review of the literature does nothing more than impress upon the reader a need for rethinking past portrayals of American Indian women, it has served an important function. We have no intention of avoiding controversies that may emerge over the critical issues contained in this book. Indeed, we cultivate controversy in order to force the development of more serious thought on the role and status of Plains Indian women.

METHOD

Along with its emphasis on criticism, the recent literature on women has taken an interest in expanding and revising the empirical record on such topics as women's role, status, and identity. To this end, scholars are raising questions that have not been asked before. They are uncovering data not previously used, and they are developing novel concepts and approaches better suited to the nature of their inquiry. Since many of the concepts and methods customarily used in the humanities and social sciences have been biased by unsubstantiated assumptions about the place of women, as Alice Kehoe so carefully argues, it has been necessary for scholars in women's studies to develop their own conceptual frameworks.

Janet Spector's article speaks directly to certain methodological problems in studies of women's work. She proposes a novel technique for understanding aspects of women's labor in the archeological record. The points Spector makes are not only relevant for archeological evidence but are pertinent in retrieving and interpreting ethnographic and historical materials as well.

From the articles by Mary Jane Schneider and Raymond DeMallie, it is apparent that anthropologists have not fully exploited available data on Plains Indian women. With some effort and ingenuity in tracking down information, Mary Jane Schneider demonstrates that the Plains Indian literature contains very revealing data on female contributions in the industrial and decorative arts. Through his careful culling of ethnohistoric and ethnographic sources, Raymond DeMallie illustrates the richness of primary sources on Teton attitudes towards male and female. It is clear from these articles, as well as others in this volume, that significant data on Plains Indian women are available, and that more effort is needed in uncovering, organizing, and interpreting the materials that exist.

Data relevant to interpreting the place of women in Plains societies are not always self-evident, however. Only when scholars ask the right questions of the empirical record will the data become significant in understanding the conditions of Plains Indian women in historic and modern times. This point is forcefully made in Beatrice Medicine's study of warrior women. As Medicine argues, if we assume a standard role modality for women, our questions are going to be very different from those that presume variation in female roles. From this, it logically follows that the kinds of data gleaned from the literature will be different, and ultimately, interpretations of that literature will diverge. Similarly, Patricia Albers and Beatrice Medicine's analysis of the role of Sioux women in quilt production suggests that the form our questions take will influence the interpretive results. More specifically, they argue that misrepresentations of women's artistic contributions have been a product of inappropriate or biased frames of inquiry.

Research on Plains Indian women not only requires more breakthroughs in the methods of data collection. It also demands innovation at the level of interpretation as well. Patricia Albers, in her essay on the changing status of Sioux women in post-reservation times, advocates the need for an approach that is more sensitive to identifying incongruities and contradictions in female status. Alan Klein's article which traces shifts in the position of women during the fur trade period, also offers important insights on assessing contradictions and change in female status.

The methodological concerns raised in this book are not exhaustive. Nevertheless, they do identify

11

some of the difficulties researchers encounter in
arriving at a complete and reliable picture of Plains
Indian women over time. More importantly, they offer
insightful directions for overcoming some of these
obstacles.

THEORY

When a new field of inquiry is in the pioneering
stage of its development, the research is often
descriptive in nature. There is an emphasis on
constructing paradigms that reveal the character and
dynamics of the phenomena under investigation. Recent
work in women's studies, including the contributions
in this volume, are no exception. Descriptive
theories in women's studies are usually of two types.

The first has to do with the actual character of
women's experience. For too long, academicians have
taken women's activities for granted. As a consequence, they have not given them the sustained
attention they deserve. Generalizations and preconceptions rather than accurate description dominate
much of this literature on the female experience.

In moving beyond the unsubstantiated assumptions
of many of their predecessors, the contributors to
this book have found that what Plains women did
historically, and what they do today, is much more
complicated and varied than heretofore presumed.
Janet Spector's study of female work in the horticultural villages of the Upper Missouri indicates
that the organization of their labor was highly varied
and dependent on the task at hand. Mary Jane
Schneider's study corroborates this, and it shows that
in the industrial and decorative arts much of women's
work was highly specialized. Beatrice Medicine's
discussion of Blackfeet women indicates that their
role patterns were highly variable, and that some of
their institutionalized role behaviors, notably that
of the warrior, stood in marked contrast to the supposedly passive qualities of feminine personality in
the native Plains. Finally, Raymond DeMallie's work
suggests that the Teton view of femininity and masculinity was very complex and cannot be easily reduced
to simplistic generalizations.

The second type of descriptive theory focuses on

12

the value of women's experience as judged from an insider or outsider's (or emic/etic) point of view. This area, as suggested by both Alan Klein and Patricia Albers, is the most problematic conceptually and the most difficult to deal with empirically. Aside from the problem of discerning whether a given source is making an assessment of status on the basis of a native or European viewpoint, there is also the problem of identifying rampant inconsistencies in the evaluations Euro-American anthropologists make. The inconsistent and contradictory interpretations of female status in the Plains, as elsewhere, reflect a lack of rigor in the criteria anthropologists have customarily used in identifying the relative power and prestige of men vis-à-vis women (Schlegel 1977; Quinn 1977). Lacking rigorous standards for evaluation, existing interpretations of female status in Plains communities are misguided at best and confused at worst. In response to this, Klein and Albers have developed more systematic ways of looking at status in Plains Indian communities.

Developing more refined conceptual descriptions of women's conditions in our own and other societies is not an end in itself. It is a means to formulating more accurate and sophisticated explanations of female role, status, and identity. The current literature reveals two kinds of theoretical direction (Quinn 1977).

In the first, there is an emphasis on the uniformity of female experience cross-culturally (D'Andrade 1966; Rosaldo 1974). It is presumed, often a priori, that women's roles are everywhere mundane and that their status is universally inferior. The idea that women's conditions have been more or less equivalent over a universal time and space leads certain scholars to argue that this equivalency is "caused" by attributes that all women share. Arguments of this kind usually resort to explanations resting on the supposedly demonstrated, but more often presumed, universality of certain physiological and psychological characteristics of women.

In the second approach, the conditions of women are not seen as invariant but rather varied and changing. What women do and how this is evaluated differs from one group to another and over time. As a consequence, it is argued that women's role, status, and identity cannot be explained in terms of some consistent and reductionist set of criteria. Instead, those who advocate the idea that women's experiences are varied take the position that female role and status are subject to the vicissitudes of human society and history (Sacks 1974, 1976; O'Laughlin 1974; Etienne and Leacock 1980). Most of the articles in this book follow this perspective.

The studies of Alan Klein and Patricia Albers, for instance, clearly demonstrate how the power and prestige accorded to Plains Indian women have changed in obvious and subtle ways since the time of European contact. Both essays clearly link this change to transformations occurring in native societies as a consequence of European intrusions. Mary Jane Schneider's work illustrates important dissimilarities among Plains Indian societies in the allocation of their industrial and decorative tasks. Although her study does not account for the variation, it implies that the division of labor cannot be explained away by an appeal to some invariant set of biological or psychological traits. A final illustration is Beatrice Medicine's discussion of variability in the roles of Blackfeet women. From the information she presents, it becomes apparent that even within the same society the existential conditions under which women live are not identical, and as a consequence, the roles females play and the behaviors they exhibit in these roles are not the same. The thrust of her paper, once again, challenges oversimplified and misguided explanations of the female experience.

PRAXIS

A final theme in this book deals with the impact of academic writings on their female subjects. One of the major consequences of the recent wave of feminist literature in this country and abroad has been to create a new awareness among women. Contemporary writings have had a profound impact on changing how women perceive themselves and how they are perceived by men. Changing attitudes in turn, have influenced the ways in which many women and men carry on and organize their day-to-day activities in relationship to each other.

The improved image that women have achieved as a consequence of the efforts of feminist writers has not affected all women equally. Today, American Indian women still live in the shadow of images which grossly misrepresent their conditions to the American public and the world at large (Green 1980). The energy these women have had to expend in challenging distorted stereotypes has been considerable. Although all women in American society have had to justify their abilities and fight for legitimate rights, native women have had to work double-time in their efforts. Like women of other ethnic minorities, Indian women have had to confront the effects of sexism in its most insidious form. They face a peculiar kind of sexism, one that is grounded in the pernicious and ever-present ideologies of racism. Native women are judged not only as females but as Indians. They are oppressed not only by their gender but by their class and ethnic status as well. The stereotypic images from which the larger society draws its picture of Indian women clearly reflect the double-barreled character of their oppression.

It is our hope that the articles in this volume will shed a new light on the conditions of Plains Indian women. Not only do we see these articles as creating a more sound intellectual environment in which to study the role, status, and identity of American Indian women, but we also see them as providing a foundation for bringing about constructive changes in how society as a whole views native women.

Introducing a new awareness about Indian women also expands our understanding of women as a whole. For in coming to terms with the varieties of female experience, there is also the realization that any struggle for women's rights is not advanced by unilateral solutions. It is only when the particular historical experiences of women are exposed, and when the consequences of such experience are understood, that we can meet the challenges for all.

FOOTNOTE

1.   This is just a sampling of some of the
literature devoted to American Indian women.   For a
more complete review see Green (1980).

REFERENCES CITED

Anderson, Robert (1956) The Northern Cheyenne War
    Mothers. Anthropological Quarterly 29:82-90.

Ardener, Shirley, ed. (1975) Perceiving Women. New
    York: John Wiley and Sons.

Barnett, Don and Rick Sterling, eds. (1975) Bobbi
    Lee: Indian Rebel. Richmond, B.C.: LSM Press.

Beck, Lois and Nikki Keddie, eds. (1978) Women in
    the Muslim World. Cambridge, Mass.: Harvard
    University Press.

Berkhofer, Robert F. Jr. (1978) The White Man's
    Indian: Images of the American Indian from
    Columbus to the Present. New York: Knopf.

Bossen, Laurel (1975) Women in Modernizing
    Societies. American Ethnologist 2:587-601.

Bourguignon, Erika (1980) The World of Women.
    New York: Praeger.

Briggs, Jean (1970) Never in Anger. Cambridge,
    Mass.: Harvard University Press.

_____ (1974) Eskimo Women: Makers of Men. In:
    Many Sisters: Women in Cross-Cultural
    Perspective, C.J. Matthiasson, ed. New York:
    Free Press.

Brown, Jennifer S. (1980) Strangers in Blood.
    Vancouver: University of British Columbia Press.

Brown, Judith A. (1970) Economic Organization and
    the Position of Women Among the Iroquois.
    Ethnohistory 17:3-4, 151-167.

_____ (1975) Iroquois Women: An Ethnohistoric
    Note. In: Toward an Anthropology of Women,
    R. Reiter, ed. New York: Monthly Review Press.

Brown, P. and G. Buckbinder, eds. (1976) Men and
    Women in the New Guinea Highlands. Special
    Publication No. 8. Washington: American
    Anthropological Association.

17

Bysiewicz, Shirley and Ruth Van de Mark (1977) The Legal Status of Dakota Indian Women. American Indian Law Review 3:255-312.

Crary, Margaret (1973) Susette La Flesche: Voice of the Omaha Indians. New York: Hawthorn.

Culbertson, Thaddeus A. (1952) Journal of an Expedition to the Mauvaises Terres and the Upper Missouri in 1850, John Francis McDermott, ed. U.S. Bureau of American Ethnology, Bulletin 147. Washington, D.C.

D'Andrade, R.G. (1966) Sex Differences and Cultural Institutions. In: The Development of Sex Differences, E.E. Maccoby, ed. Stanford: Stanford University Press.

Deloria, Ella (1944) Speaking of Indians. New York: The Friendship Press.

Denig, Edwin (1961) Five Indian Tribes of the Upper Missouri. Norman: University of Oklahoma Press.

Etienne, Mona and Eleanor Leacock, eds. (1980) Women and Colonization: Anthropological Perspectives. New York: Praeger.

Ewers, John (1955) The Horse in Blackfoot Indian Culture. Bureau of American Ethnology, Bulletin 159. Washington, D.C.: Smithsonian Institution, United States Government Printing Office.

_____ (1968a) The Emergence of the Plains Indian as the Symbol of the North American Indian. In: Indians on the Upper Missouri, John C. Ewers, ed. Norman: University of Oklahoma Press.

_____ (1968b) Mothers of the Mixed Bloods. In: Indian Life on the Upper Missouri, John C. Ewers, ed. Norman: University of Oklahoma Press.

_____ (1980) Climate, Acculturation, and Costume: A History of Women's Clothing Among the Indians of the Southern Plains. Plains Anthropologist 25:63-82.

Fee, Elizabeth (1974) The Sexual Politics of Victorian Anthropology. In: Clio's Consciousness Raised, M. Hartman and L. Banner, eds. New York: Harper Colophon Books.

_____ (1976) Science and the Women Problem: Historical Perspectives. In: Sex Differences, M. Teitelbaum, ed. New York: Doubleday Anchor Books.

Fernea, Elizabeth and Basima Bezirgan, eds. (1977) Middle Eastern Muslim Women Speak. Austin: University of Texas Press.

Flannery, Regina (1953) The Gros Ventres of Montana, Part I: Social Life. Washington, D.C.: The Catholic University of America Press.

Friar, Ralph and Natasha Friar (1972) The Only Good Indian ... The Hollywood Gospel. New York: Drama Book Specialists.

Friedl, Ernestine (1975) Women and Men: An Anthropologist's View. New York: Holt, Rinehart and Winston.

Greemet, Robert S. (1980) Sunksquaws, Shamans, and Tradeswomen: Middle Atlantic Coastal Algonkian Women During the 17th and 18th Centuries. In: Women and Colonization: Anthropological Perspectives, M. Etienne and E. Leacock, eds., pp. 43-62. New York: Praeger.

Green, Rayna (1975) The Pocahontas Perplex: The Image of Indian Women in American Culture. The Massachusetts Review 16:698-714.

_____ (1980) Native American Women. Signs: Journal of Women in Society and Culture 1980: 248-267.

Grinnell, George Bird (1904) Cheyenne Women's Customs. American Anthropologist, n.s. 4:127-130.

_____ (1923) The Cheyenne Indians. Two Volumes. New Haven: Yale University Press.

Hafkin, Nancy J. and Edna G. Bay, eds. (1976) <u>Women
    in Africa: Studies in Social and Economic
    Change.</u> Palo Alto: Stanford University Press.

Hassrick, Royal B. (1964) <u>The Sioux: Life and
    Customs of a Warrior Society.</u> Norman:
    University of Oklahoma Press.

Hebard, Grace Raymond (1933) <u>Sacajawea: A Guide
    and Interpreter of the Lewis and Clark
    Expedition.</u> Glendale, Cal.: The Arthur Clark
    Company.

Hilger, M. Inez (1952) <u>Arapahoe Child Life and Its
    Cultural Background.</u> Bureau of American
    Ethnology Bulletin 148. Washington, D.C.:
    Smithsonian Institution.

Hungry Wolf, Beverly (1980) <u>The Ways of My Grand-
    mothers.</u> New York: William Morrow.

Jones, David E. (1972) <u>Sanapia: Commanche Medicine
    Woman.</u> New York: Holt, Rinehart and Winston.

Kehoe, Alice B. (1970) The Function of Ceremonial
    Sexual Intercourse Among the Northern Plains
    Indians. <u>Plains Anthropologist</u> 15:99-103.

_____ (1976) Old Woman Had Great Power. <u>Western
    Canadian Journal of Anthropology</u> 6:68-76.

Klein, Laura (1976) "She's One of Us, You Know":
    The Public Life of Tlingit Women: Traditional,
    Historical and Contemporary Perspectives.
    <u>Western Canadian Journal of Anthropology</u> 6:
    164-183.

_____ (1980) Contending with Colonization:
    Tlingit Men and Women in Change. In: <u>Women
    and Colonization: Anthropological Perspectives</u>,
    M. Etienne and E. Leacock, eds., pp. 88-107.
    New York: Praeger.

Lamphere, Louise (1974) Strategies, Cooperation,
    and Conflict Among Women in Domestic Groups.
    In: <u>Woman, Culture, and Society</u>, M.Z. Rosaldo
    and L. Lamphere, eds. Stanford: Stanford
    University Press.

Landes, Ruth (1971) The Ojibway Woman. New York: W.W. Norton and Company.

Latin American Perspectives (1979) Women in Latin America. Latin American Perspectives. Riverside, California.

Leacock, Eleanor (1975) Class, Commodity, and the Status of Women. In: Women Cross-Culturally: Change and Challenge, R.Rohrlich-Leavitt, ed. The Hague: Mouton Publishers.

_____ (1978) Women's Status in Egalitarian Society: Implications of Social Evolution. Current Anthropology 19:247-276.

_____ (1980) Montagnais Women and the Jesuit Program for Colonization. In: Women and Colonization: Anthropological Perspectives, M. Etienne and E. Leacock, eds., pp. 25-43. New York: Praeger.

Leacock, Eleanor and Jacqueline Goodman (1976) Montagnais Marriage and the Jesuits in the 17th Century: Incidents from the Relations of Paul le Jeune. Western Canadian Journal of Anthropology 6:77-105.

Lewis, Oscar (1941) Manly-Hearted Woman Among the North Piegan. American Anthropologist 43(2): 173-187.

Liberty, Margot (1981) Plains Indian Women Through Time: A Preliminary Overview. In: Northwestern Great Plains: Intermontane, and Plateau Ethnography of Ethnohistory: Paper in Honor of J. Verne Dusenberry, L. Davis, ed. Missoula: Big Sky Press, University of Montana.

Linderman, Frank B. (1972) Pretty-Shield: Medicine Woman of the Crows. Lincoln: University of Nebraska Press.

Lowie, Robert (1922) The Crow Woman's Tale. In: American Indian Life, Elsie Clews Parsons, ed. Lincoln: University of Nebraska Press.

Lurie, Nancy (1966) Mountain Wolf Woman: Sister of Crashing Thunder. Ann Arbor: University of Michigan Press.

21

McCormack, Patricia A., ed. (1976) Cross-Sex
    Relations: Native Peoples. The Western Canadian
    Journal of Anthropology 6, No. 3.

McElroy, Ann (1975) Canadian Arctic Modernization
    and Change in Female Inuit Role Identification.
    American Ethnologist 2:662-686.

_____ (1979) The Negotiation of Sex-Role
    Identity in Eastern Arctic Culture Change. In:
    Sex-Roles in Changing Cultures, A. McElroy and
    C. Matthiasson, eds. Occasional Papers in
    Anthropology, Vol. I, pp. 49-60. Buffalo, N.Y.:
    State University of New York at Buffalo.

McElroy, Ann and Carolyn Matthiasson, eds. (1979)
    Sex-Roles in Changing Cultures. Occasional
    Papers in Anthropology, Vol. I. Buffalo, N.Y.:
    State University of New York at Buffalo.

Marriott, Alice and Carol Rachlin (1977) Dance
    Around the Sun: The Life of Mary Little Bear
    in Kanish. New York: Thomas Y. Crowell.

Martin, M. K. and B. Voorhies (1975) Female of the
    Species. New York: Columbia University Press.

Matthiasson, Carolyn, ed. (1974) Many Sisters:
    Women in Cross-Cultural Perspective. New York:
    Free Press.

Maynard, Eileen (1979) Changing Sex-Roles and
    Family Structure Among the Oglala Sioux. In:
    Sex-Roles in Changing Cultures, A. McElroy and
    C. Matthiasson, eds. Occasional Papers in
    Anthropology, Vol. 1, pp. 11-20. Buffalo, N.Y.:
    State University of New York at Buffalo.

Mead, Margaret (1932) The Changing Culture of an
    Indian Tribe. New York: Columbia University
    Press.

Medicine, Beatrice (1975) The Role of Women in
    Native American Societies. The Indian Historian
    8:51-53.

_____ (1978) The Native American Woman: A
    Perspective. Austin, Texas: National
    Educational Laboratory Publishers.

22

Michelson, Truman (1932) The Narrative of a Southern Cheyenne Woman. Smithsonian Miscellaneous Collections 87:3. Washington, D.C.: United States Government Printing Office.

_____ (1933) Narrative of an Arapaho Woman. American Anthropologist 35:595-610.

Nash, June and Helen Safa, eds. (1976) Sex and Class in Latin America. New York: Praeger.

Neill, Edward D. (1872) Dakota Land and Dakota Life (1850-1856). Minnesota Historical Society Collections 1:205-240.

Nelson, Ann (1976) Women in Groups: Women's Ritual Sodalities in Native North America. The Western Canadian Journal of Anthropology 6:29-67.

Niethammer, Carolyn (1977) Daughters of the Earth: The Lives and Legends of American Indian Women. New York: Collier Books.

O'Laughlin, B. (1974) Mediation of Contradiction: Why Mbum Women Do Not Eat Chicken. In: Woman, Culture, and Society, M.Z. Rosaldo and L. Lamphere, eds. Stanford: Stanford University Press.

Paulume, Denise (1963) Women of Tropical Africa. Berkeley: University of California Press.

Pescatello, Ann, ed. (1973) Female and Male in Latin America: Essays. Pittsburgh: University of Pittsburgh Press.

Pond, Samuel W. (1908) The Dakotas or Sioux in Minnesota as they were in 1834. Minnesota Historical Society Collections 12:319-501.

Powers, Marla (1980) Menstruation and Reproduction: An Oglala Case. Signs: Journal of Women in Society and Culture 6:54-65.

Price, John A. (1973) The Stereotyping of North American Indians in Motion Pictures. Ethnohistory 20:153-171.

Quinn, Naomi (1977) Anthropological Studies on Women's Status. In: Annual Review of Anthropology, Bernard J. Siegel, ed. Volume 6, pp. 181-225.

Raphael, Dana, ed. (1975) Being Female: Reproduction, Power, and Change. The Hague: Mouton Publishers.

Reichard, Gladys (1968 [1934]) Spider Women: A Story of Navajo Weavers and Chanters, 2nd ed. Rio Grande.

Reiter, R. R., ed. (1975) Toward an Anthropology of Women. New York: Monthly Review Press.

Rohrlich-Leavitt, Ruby, ed. (1975) Women Cross-Culturally: Change and Challenge. The Hague: Mouton Publishers.

Rosaldo, M. Z. (1974) Women, Culture, and Society: A Theoretical Overview. In: Woman, Culture, and Society, M. Z. Rosaldo and L. Lamphere, eds. Stanford: Stanford University Press.

Rosaldo, M. Z. and L. Lamphere, eds. (1974) Woman, Culture, and Society. Stanford: Stanford University Press.

Rothenberg, Diane (1976) Erosion of Power: An Economic Basis for the Selective Conservatism of Seneca Women in the Nineteenth Century. Western Canadian Journal of Anthropology 6:106-118.

_____ (1980) The Mothers of the Nation: Seneca Resistance to Quaker Intervention. In: Women and Colonization: Anthropological Perspectives, M. Etienne and E. Leacock, eds., pp. 63-87. New York: Praeger.

Sacks, Karen (1974) Engels Revisited: Women, the Organization of Production, and Private Property. In: Woman, Culture and Society, M. Rosaldo and L. Lamphere, eds. pp. 207-222. Stanford: Stanford University Press.

_____ (1976) State Bias and Women's Status. American Anthropologist 78:565-569.

24

Sanday, Peggy R. (1974) Female Status in the Public Domain. In: Woman, Culture and Society, M. Rosaldo and L. Lamphere, eds. Stanford: Stanford University Press.

_____ (1981) Female Power and Male Dominance. Cambridge: Cambridge University Press.

Schlegel, A. (1972) Male Dominance and Female Autonomy: Domestic Authority in Matrilineal Societies. New Haven: Human Relations Area Press.

Schlegel, A., ed. (1977) Sexual Stratification: A Cross-Cultural View. New York: Columbia University Press.

Schneider, Mary Jane (1979) Women's Work: An Examination of Women's Roles in Plains Art and Crafts. Plainswoman 2:8-11.

Shipek, Florence (1970) The Autobiography of Delphina Cuero. Morongo Indian Reservation, Calif.: Malke Museum Press.

Sudarkasa, Niara (1976) Female Employment and Family Organization in West Africa. In: New Research on Women and Sex, D. McGuigan, ed. Ann Arbor: University of Michigan Center for Continuing Education of Women.

Tabeau, Pierre-Antoine (1939) Tabeau's Narrative of Loisel's Expedition to the Upper Missouri, Addnie H. Abel, ed. Norman: University of Oklahoma Press.

Udall, Louise (1969) Me and Mine: The Life Story of Helen Sekaquaptewa as Told to Louise Udall. Tucson: University of Arizona Press.

Underhill, Ruth M. (1979) Papago Woman. New York: Holt, Rinehart and Winston.

Weist, Katherine M. (1980) Plains Indian Women: An Assessment. In: Anthropology on the Great Plains: The State of the Art, W. Raymond Wood and Margot Liberty, eds. Lincoln: University of Nebraska Press.

Weist, Katherine M. ed. (1979) The Narrative of a Northern Cheyenne Woman, Belle Hiwalking. Billings: Montana Council for Indian Education.

Weltfish, Gene (1977 [1965]) The Lost Universe: Pawnee Life and Culture. Lincoln: University of Nebraska Press.

Wilson, Dorothy Clark (1974) Bright Eyes, the Story of Susette La Flesche, an Omaha Indian. New York: McGraw.

Wilson, Gilbert (1971) Waheenee: An Indian Girl's Story Told by Herself to Gilbert L. Wilson. North Dakota History 1 and 2.

PART I

IMAGES OF WOMEN

CHAPTER 2

BEASTS OF BURDEN AND MENIAL SLAVES:
NINETEENTH CENTURY OBSERVATIONS OF
NORTHERN PLAINS INDIAN WOMEN[1]

Katherine M. Weist
University of Montana

INTRODUCTION

Many travelers and traders, journeying up the Missouri River and across the Plains during the eighteenth and nineteenth centuries in search of furs, adventure, and the exotic, described the country through which they traveled--the animals, the rock formations, the waterways, and the native peoples. They were unequivocal about what they saw, expressing opinions about the immensity of the country, the profuseness of the buffalo and antelope herds, the treacherous nature of the rivers, and the "savagery" of the Indians. For them, a major component of what they defined as savage was the position of Indian women, who were frequently referred to as "beasts of burden," "slaves," and "sexually lax." This is not to say that all observers used these characterizations or that all tribes were evaluated as equally "savage," but the overriding emphasis was an explicitly negative estimation of the position of Indian women vis-à-vis that of men.

The descriptions of Indian women as beasts of burden do not appear to alter over time, for both early and late writers employ very similar images. One early trader, Duncan M'Gillivary, after describing the death of a woman in childbirth, commented in 1794 upon what he considered to be "... the miserable conditions of Women in this Country, where they are considered as Slaves of the men and treated accordingly

..." (1929:33). In 1832 George Catlin, a great admirer of Indian culture, depicted the position of Indian women as "... always held in a rank inferior to that of men, in relation to whom in many respects they stand rather in the light of menials and slaves than otherwise ..." (1973:1:118). These evaluations of the lowly state of Indian women continued throughout the century. In 1885, William P. Clark wrote in his The Indian Sign Language:

> In savagery and barbarism women are merely beasts of burden, prized and valued for their skill in fancy or capacity for heavy work, rather than for any beauty of face or figure ... A life of filth, drudgery, and exposure, sustained by the coarsest of food, is not conducive to female perfection of form and feature (1885:407).

Although some, such as Clark, found Indian females unattractive, their physical appearance does not appear to have been a primary or a consistent factor in the negative opinions that early observers held about Plains Indian women. There were many early writings in which Indian women were characterized as "very pretty," "... much fairer than the men; some might be considered handsome anywhere" (Brackenridge 1904:121), and "... these women have in general good features, though hardened by constant exposure to the weather" (Thompson 1916:349).

More influential and enduring than the statements about female physical attributes were the descriptions of women's role and status in Plains Indian society. Some of these were straightforward reports based on what Euro-Americans had actually witnessed and heard. Others were largely moral pronouncements deeply rooted in the observer's own complex attitudes about the proper place of women in human societies. The vast majority, however, combined and congealed ethical judgements with factual observations. Since today's scholars draw upon the writings of early Euro-American observers in reconstructing what Plains Indian life was like in historic times, these sources must be critically evaluated with an eye to distinguishing faithful reporting from moral bias.

The discussion that follows represents both a criticism and an appreciation of the contributions

that early reporters made in assessing the position of
Plains Indian women. Although much of this discussion
concentrates on the nature and origin of biased
accounts, it also examines the kinds of reporting that
most closely approximated the actual conditions under
which Plains Indian women lived in pre-reservation
times.

THE EARLY IMAGES

Early observers, from traders to missionaries,
reached a remarkable consensus in their accounts of
women's status. With few exceptions, Indian women were
purported to occupy a lowly and inferior place in
their society. In drawing this conclusion, most
observers focused on two different but related areas
of female experience: (1) work and (2) marriage.

The character of female labor in Plains Indian
societies was a much discussed subject in early writings. It was one of the easiest areas of female
involvement for male outsiders to observe, and it was
also an area which enabled writers to draw striking
comparisons between the lives of Indian women and
their Euro-American counterparts.

Except for those married to white traders, Indian
women were believed to lead a life of unending, strenuous, and tedious labor which only became more burdensome as they grew older. In some accounts the
so-called "drudgery" of female work was described in
melodramatic tones. The following excerpt from E.D.
Neill's writing on a Dakota woman is a case in point:

> ... From early childhood they lead 'worse
> than a dog's life.' Like the Gibeonites of
> old, they are the hewers of wood and the
> drawers of water for the camp ... Unculti-
> vated and made to do the labor of beasts,
> when they are desperate, they act more like
> infuriated brutes than creatures of reason
> (1872:234-235).

In contrast, other reports simply enumerated the
heavy and backbreaking kinds of labor women had to
perform. Catlin's listing of female occupations among

31

the Mandan is a good example.

> ... procuring wood and water, in cooking,
> dressing robes and other skins, in drying
> meat and wild fruit, and raising corn (maize).
> The Mandans are somewhat of agriculturists,
> as they raise a great deal of corn and some
> pumpkins and squashes. This is all done by
> women, who make their hoes of the shoulder-
> blade of the buffalo or the elk, and dig the
> ground over instead of ploughing it, which
> is consequently done with a vast deal of
> labour (1973:1:121).

Although Catlin argued that women carried out their tasks "... as if from choice or inclination, without a murmur" (Catlin 1973:121), Rudolph Kurz took a more cynical view. He considered women's attempts to escape work as one of their reasons for marrying white men and states that "... an Indian woman loves her white husband only for what he possesses--because she works less hard, eats better food, is allowed to dress and adorn herself in a better way--of real love there is no question" (1937:155).

The underlying criticism in many early accounts was not so much that the women were carrying out manual labor but that the men were either not par-ticipating equally or they were forcing women to do the heavy work. These sentiments are clearly expressed in the following quote from Tabeau's journal:

> This sex is much more unfortunate and debased
> here [Arikara] than the other Savages. It is
> reduced to the most humiliating slavery by
> tyrants, who enjoy all the fruits of its
> labors. Thus, the more women a Ricara has,
> the more opulent is his lodge. Beasts of
> burden of these inhuman monsters, they (the
> women) are loaded with all the work. They
> endure alone all the labor of farming, a
> resource, however, without which the men
> would probably not be able to live, because
> of their sloth and laziness; for it is only
> by its means that the women procure their
> food and the clothes that the men buy from
> strange nations (1939:148).

And Thaddeus A. Culbertson, never one given to thoughtful understandings, remarked about the Dakota:

> Indians despise the female sex; say that woman was made only for doing man's drudgery, and for the gratification of his grossest passion; they say that whites ought not to have women because they don't know how to use them--thank God we do not, in their sense (1952:80).

Finally, Thomas Twiss, in his 1856 report to the Commissioner of Indian Affairs on the conditions in the Upper Platte Agency, commented:

> They [the men] are taught to look upon manual labor as degrading and beneath the rank of the red man, whether he be chief, warrior, or brave. All menial services and labor are performed by women, who are real slaves to the men. The only education of the latter is on the war path, and the only labor the pursuit of game (1856:642).

For some observers, such as Tabeau, Culbertson, and Twiss, the degrading nature of female labor resulted from male idleness, improvidence, and arrogance. Women were beasts of burden, not because of their gender, but because of their relationships with men.

Domestic drudgery was also associated with what was purported to be a "traffic" in women. Duncan M'Gillivary stated that an Indian husband regarded his wife

> ... in the same light as any other part of his property, entirely at his disposal, possessing the Power of life and death over her with no other restrictions, than the resentment of her relations, which if he is a brave Indian gives him little concern (1929:33).

Edwin Denig, bourgeois at Fort Union for many years and married to two Assiniboine women, concluded that "... women among Indians are bought, paid for, and are the property of the purchaser the same as his horses" (1930:506). Due to this, he perceived women to be

33

"... the greatest wealth an Indian possesses next to
his horses. Often they are of primary consideration,
as after war by their labor is the only way he could
acquire horses, the only standard of their wealth"
(1930:506). Catlin estimated the value of the most
beautiful and modest Mandan girl to be equal to "...
two horses, a gun with powder and balls for a year,
five or six pounds of beads, a couple of gallons of
whiskey, and a handful of awls" (1973:1:121).

The observers reasoned that since women were
bought and sold and since they were essential to the
successful maintenance of the lodges, polygyny was a
necessity and further signaled the low position of
women. Catlin considered it essential for

> ... a chief (who must be liberal, keep
> open doors, and entertain, for the support
> of his popularity) to have in his wigwam
> a sufficient number of such handmaids or
> menials to perform the numerous duties and
> drudgeries of so large and expensive an
> establishment (Catlin 1973:1:118).

Denig stated that "inasmuch as women are of great
advantage to the Indians by their labor, a plurality
of wives is required by a good hunter" (1930:504).
Seldom did the observers record the women's attitudes
toward polygyny but according to David Thompson, the
practice was hateful to them because:

> When a fine young woman, proud of herself,
> finds that instead of being given to her
> lover, she is to be the fourth, or fifth
> wife of some Man advanced in years, where
> she is to be the slave of the family, and
> bear all the bondage of a wife, without any
> of it's rights and priviledges, she readily
> consents to quit the camp with her lover
> (1916:353).

One set of behaviors which the travelers and traders had the greatest difficulty in reconciling with
their Euro-American values was what they perceived to
be overt female sexuality outside of marriage.
Typical comments are:

> They were all courtesans; a set of handsome
> tempting women ... The curse of the Mandanes

is an almost total want of chastity
(Thompson 1916:234).

Chastity does not seem to be a virtue (Coues
1897:515).

Prudery is not a virtue of the Indian women
(Maximilian 1906:23:282).

Unfaithful women are now becoming a common-
place--nobody thinks much about such
occurrences. Only old ugly women or those
burdened with children remain with their
husbands; they are exposed to no temptation,
no seduction (Kurz 1937:240).

Many of the journalists attributed the initiation
of sexual relationships not to the women themselves
but to their male relatives. As observed by
Brackenridge in 1811, "... fathers brought their
daughters, husbands their wives, brothers their
sisters, to be offered for sale at this market of
indecency and shame" (1904:130). A number of observers remarked that Indian women were severely punished
if they themselves initiated sexual liaisons, but for
their husbands or fathers to proffer their wives' or
daughters' sexuality was permissible. For example,
Tabeau stated:

> The most peculiar thing is that all goes on
> often in the presence of and even by order
> of a jealous husband. This paradox will be
> no longer a paradox when it is understood
> that a Sioux, as a Ricara, is alive to this
> affront only when his wife, by a secret
> infidelity, departs from his house. There-
> fore, all that which meets with his approval,
> being in order, is not offensive and such a
> man, who would kill or at least turn out
> his wife upon the slightest suspicion,
> prostitutes her himself for a very small
> reward ... (1939:178-179).

In 1833 Maximilian made similar observations about the
Blackfeet:

> Many of the men have six or eight wives, whom
> they are very ready to give up to the Whites;
> even very young little girls are offered.

35

On the other hand, they generally punish
infidelity in their wives very severely,
cutting off their noses in such cases (1976:
105).

The debased status of Indian women was believed
to have had a number of serious consequences. Women
who engaged in unauthorized adulterous activities were
disfigured and cast aside among the Blackfeet; they
ran away from polygynous marriages; they grew old
before their time; they were left to starve when aged;
their children became sickly because they worked too
hard; they sought marriages with white traders so as
to escape their deprived conditions; and in some tribes, especially the Dakota (e.g. Bradbury 1904), they
sought escape through suicide or committed female
infanticide in order to spare their daughters from
living a similar existence.

The idea that Plains Indian women were degraded
by the work they were forced to perform, by the barter
that surrounded their marriages, and by the abuse they
suffered at the hands of their fathers and husbands
was common in early writings, and it was clearly
summed up in a 1868 letter by Lt. George Palmer to the
Chicago Tribune describing the Crow:

The men are indolent and slothful, and look
upon labor as degrading and only fit for
women ... They compel their women to do all
the labor, often reward the overworked
creatures with neglect and cruelty. The
squaw must move the tepees from place to
place, tan all the skins, gather wood,
provide the winter supply of food, and take
care of the ponies, pappooses and dogs;
while her lazy buck rides his horses or
lies on soft robes in pleasant places, and
occasionally pounds her with a club ... The
squaws are sometimes sold to the whites, and
a pretty one may be got for a pony. One of
the chiefs offered me his daughter in exchange for my horse ... Almost all of the
women are filthy, degraded and obscenely
vulgar. It would be difficult to find a
dozen virtuous women in the whole tribe.
They barter their persons in the same way,
unconscious of wrong, as they sell a buffalo
robe, and think a few cups of sugar pays

36

them well for either the one or the other
(Greene 1978:32).

Given the attention devoted to the negative position of Indian women, one would assume that the archi-
tects of Indian policy would have sought to elevate
their status. This, however, does not seem to have
been the case. In the Reports of the Commissioner of
Indian Affairs, little mention is made of women,
leading one to suspect that Indian policies were developed by white males primarily to alter the life styles of Indian males. Those who did take note of women
usually perceived them, because of an inherent feminine nature, as bringing a positive influence to the
"civilization" of savage men. In 1822, Reverend
Jedidiah Morse, commissioned by Congress to survey the
Indian condition and propose future directions,
declared that:

> It is essential to the success of the project
> of the Government, that the female character
> among our native tribes, be raised from its
> present degraded state, to its proper rank
> and influence. This should be a primary
> object with the instructors of Indians. By
> educating female children, they will become
> prepared in turn, to educate their own
> children, to manage their domestic concerns
> with intelligence and propriety, and in this
> way, they will gradually attain their proper
> standing and influence in society (1970:74).

Thomas McKenney, the first Superintendent of the
Bureau of Indian Affairs, and James Hall also spoke
about the advantages of raising Indian women to their
"proper" position. In their History of the Indian
Tribes of North America, they attributed the position
of Indian women to the nature of the hunter's
existence for:

> The savage woman is debarred of the pre-
> rogatives, and deprived from exercising the
> virtues, of her sex, by her wandering life.
> The fireside, the family circle, all the
> comforts, luxuries, and enjoyments which are
> comprised in the word home, are created
> and regulated by female affection, influence,
> and industry--and all these are unknown to
> the savage. He has no home. The softening

and ennobling influences of the domestic
circle are unknown to him; and the woman,
having no field for the exercise of the
virtues peculiar to her sex, never appears
in her true character, nor is invested with
the tender, healthful, the ennobling influences which renders her, in her proper
sphere, the friend and adviser of man. We
would elevate the savage woman to her
legitimate place in the social system, and
make her the unconscious but most efficient,
instrument in the civilization of her race
(1934:3:249).

Obviously for Morse and McKenney and Hall, the
proper roles of women were to provide nurturance,
psychological support, and educational benefits to
husbands and children--all activities considered
appropriate to Euro-American women who were the models
for what Indian women should become. In actuality,
Euro-American women had lost many of the productive
activities they had performed during the seventeenth
and eighteenth centuries. Due to an increase in
industrialization, competition for jobs by large numbers of poor laborers, and the development of a middle
class during the nineteenth century, many women no
longer had their previous economic freedoms and became
more dependent upon men. There arose around women a
"cult of true womanhood" characterized by the virtues
of piety, purity, submissiveness, and domesticity
(Welter 1973:96).

THE SOURCES OF BIAS

In the eyes of the Euro-American observers,
Plains Indian women must have appeared antithetical to
the presumed natural condition of women. Indian women
carried out male labor. They were unsheltered and
frequently sought personal goals. The foundations of
female-male relationships diverged from Euro-American
ones, and Indian attitudes toward sex were distinctly
different from those of Euro-American society, even
though it was the male trader or traveler who frequently sought the attentions of Indian women.

This contradiction between the actual roles of

Indian women and the Euro-Americans' attitudes is examined by Rayna Green in her article, "The Pocahontas Perplex" (1975). In her analysis, she delineates two types of colonial images of Indian women: one was of a pure but distant Pocahontas who was the savior of the righteous white man; the other was of a sexually permissive "Squaw" who sold herself for economic convenience or unrestrained passion. The first image represented the New World mother-figure who, in her nobility, was powerful but unapproachable. Real Indian women, however, as objects of white male sexual desires, were irreconcilable with the Pocahontas image and thus were represented by a negative image--a Squaw living in filth and driven by lust.

Few Plains Indian women attained the level of immortality accorded Four Bears of the Mandan, Broken Arm of the Cree, and Spotted Tail of the Brule for the observers seldom knew them as distinct persons. Those who did become known were women who had acted as go-betweens for the whites and Indians, such as Sacajewea and Medicine-Snake-Woman (Ewers 1968), and thus played a role similar to that of Pocahontas, or epitomized the virtues of womanhood, such as the Crow girl Pine Leaf, whom Beckwourth described as "incapable of fear," "modest," intelligent, and displaying a "becoming demeanor" (1856:202). Certainly none were sexually permissive, and Pine Leaf's attraction for Beckwourth may have been her inaccessibility. Further details on the relationships between the fur traders and Indian women can be found in Walter O'Meara's book, Daughters of the Country (1968).

It may well be that Indian men did consider their wives to be slaves and beasts of burden, and the position of Indian women did decrease during the nineteenth century as Indian involvement in the fur trade increased. In some tribes, such as the Blackfeet, brutality towards women was probably much more common than among other tribes, and some Indian women, such as the one who lamented to Captain Bonneville that her husband treated her as his dog not his wife (Irving 1961:362), fled from unhappy marriages. That Indian women worked hard goes without question. However, the assessments of the position of Indian women by Euro-American men should be viewed with skepticism for a number of reasons.

First, the male observer had to cross over not

only a cultural barrier but a gender one as well. Seldom, if ever, did these observers inquire of native women about their views nor did they have the opportunity, given the nature of Indian society, to talk with the women as they did to the men. One white woman, Fanny Kelly, who lived in Dakota camps as a captive, remarked on the "slavish" existence of the married women who were forced to undertake "unceasing toils." Even so, commented Kelly, "... it is scarcely known in Indian life that a girl has remained unmarried even to middle age" (1973:184), and Indian women, considering "... their life a servitude," "are very rebellious, often displaying ungovernable and violent temper" (1973:196). Passivity was thus not a characteristic of these women. Further ethnohistorical research might demonstrate a relationship between the length of residence in native communities, knowledge of the language and culture, and more positive evaluations about the position of Indian women.

Second, the ethnographic literature, admittedly written at a later date, does not support these nineteenth century views. In fact, early ethnographers, such as George B. Grinnell (1923:1:127) and J.N.B. Hewitt (1910:2:968), explicitly denied that Indian women were slaves. Neither Pretty Shield (Linderman 1972) nor Iron Teeth (Marquis 1978) complained of being overburdened; nor did Plenty Coups (Linderman 1962) and Wooden Leg (Marquis 1962) express the disdain for women that the Euro-American observers attributed to Indian men.

Finally, what might be called the "Beast of Burden" myth was not limited only to Plains societies. Very similar descriptions were applied to Mexican (Trulio 1973), African (Rousseau 1975), and Iroquois women (Rothenberg 1976). In each instance, Euro-American colonial representatives attempted to make comprehensible behaviors in marked contrast to their own and by so doing, assess the changes which these societies must undergo before they could be classed as "civilized." According to Nancy Leis, the effects of colonialism were detrimental to the high status of West African women because the colonial administrators

> ... did not understand the role of women within the family and household or appreciate their social and political impact on the wider society. Their implicit model was

40

the European family where women were partners, but unequal ones, in their contributions to and benefits from the union, and in the status they derived as wives. Any deviation from this model was viewed, at best, as the deleterious effect of social change and the harbinger of moral and family breakdown (1976:123).

ANOTHER VIEW OF PLAINS INDIAN WOMEN

Even though their observations were colored by their own cultural biases, Catlin, Maximilian, Kurz and others witnessed Indian women and men seeking goals, implementing decisions, and in general, acting and reacting within their cultural environment. Not all of what they wrote should be completely dismissed. When their descriptions are placed in a more complete historical and cultural context and when viewed from a different perspective, especially that of contemporary women's studies, their observations indicate a relatively high rather than low status. Although greatly needed, no theoretical evaluation of women's status will be undertaken here; instead I intend only to indicate how the Euro-Amerian observers misunderstood what they saw.

A variety of indicators of women's status has been proposed, including "political participation, economic control, personal autonomy, interpersonal equality, legal adulthood, ideological position" (Quinn 1977:182). The nineteenth century observers considered four criteria to be important: division of labor, polygyny, buying and selling of women, and closely related to this, female control over their sexuality.

The manual labor which Plains Indian women performed was associated with the maintenance of the camps or villages. Many of these tasks did require endurance and strength although possibly not more than white women on New England farms or frontier settlements performed. Cross-cultural studies of women's status indicate that labor by itself need not be associated with a relatively low status, however lack of control over the products of one's labor is (Sanday

41

1973). Friedl hypothesizes that "... the prevalence of male dominance is a consequence of the frequency with which ... men have greater rights than women to distribute goods outside of the domestic group" (1975:9). The classic example of this relationship is the pre-reservation Iroquois in which the women not only grew all the crops but also distributed all foods, even that hunted by men. Women played significant roles in the selection of political leaders and because of their control over food distribution, were able to prevent war expeditions by means of withholding from the men dried corn and meat (Brown 1975).

A somewhat similar configuration is found among the Mandan, Hidatsa, and Arikara horticulturalists of the Upper Missouri. Concentrated in large earth lodge villages, the matrilineal clans and the female and male solidarity groups played essential roles in the functioning of these societies. Matrilineally related women assisted each other with farming activities and traded large quantities of vegetables to visiting nomadic tribes and to the fur and military posts situated nearby during most of the nineteenth century. F.V. Hayden reported in the 1850's that the women traded between 500 and 800 bushels of corn per season to the American Fur Company Fort.

> This trade on the part of the Indians is
> carried on by the women, who bring the corn
> by panfuls and the squash in strings and
> receive in exchange knives, hoes, combs,
> beads, paint etc., also tobacco, ammunition
> and other useful articles for their husbands.
> In this way each family is supplied with all
> the smaller articles needed for a comfortable
> existence; and though the women perform all
> the labor, they are compensated by having
> their full share of the profits (quoted in
> Will and Hyde 1964:196).

Among the nomadic tribes, the amount of control which the women had over the economy is not clear since they were not the ones to supply the major food source--the buffalo. The ethnographic literature, however, indicates that the women were the ones to receive, dry, store, and distribute the meat. Even so, Gros Ventre women were required to distribute meat to visitors according to their husbands' wishes (Flannery 1953:82). Also, extra-societal market acti-

42

vities were primarily under the control of the men who took the buffalo robes tanned by the women to the fur posts to trade. According to the trader Edwin Denig, it took a woman from three to five days to tan one robe, the average being about eighteen to twenty with twenty-five to thirty-five an excellent winter's work (1930:541). What the women got out of their labor is unclear. Flannery reported that "the wives would expect to share in the return thereof which the husband was able to secure from the trader, but this expectation was not always met" (1953:82). Maximilian, however, noted that among the Blackfeet "the women, who know quite well that they profit nothing from their labour since the men barter it for whiskey immediately and bring nothing home, tan the skins only half-way and badly" (1976:107).

Seen in the context of women's labor, polygyny was important to the women for the assistance they gained in the household duties and the pleasure they derived from working with other women. For the men, polygyny was necessary if they were to entertain extensively or trade often at the posts. Oscar Lewis has documented the rapid rise of polygyny among the Blackfeet as they became closely tied to a market economy (1942:38-40). As analyzed by Flannery for the Gros Ventre, one hunter alone could bring in more robes than two women could handle (1953:73). The rise and importance of polygyny may well have been coupled with the imbalance in the sex ratio said by De Smet to have been three women to every two males among the Blackfeet (1905:3:952).

The type of polygyny most prevalent among the Plains tribes was of the sororal variety or the marriage of one man to sisters. Alice Schlegel hypothesizes that sororal polygyny enhances the status of women because sisters can present a united front to their husbands; with nonsororal polygyny, on the other hand, co-wives compete with each other for the attentions of their husband (1972:23). Fanny Kelly found among the Dakota that a man

> ... often marries several sisters if they
> can be had, not because of any particular
> fancy he may have for any but the one who
> first captivated him, but because he thinks
> it more likely to have harmony in the house-
> hold when they are all of one family (1973:

43

184-185).

Kelly, however, would have disagreed with Schlegel for to her "polygamy is inconsistent with the female character, whether in barbarism or civilization" (1973:185).

The Euro-American observers thought that women were bought by their husbands because they noted that men gave horses to the women's fathers or brothers. In actuality, they were probably witnessing only one facet of a set of exchanges between the relatives of the groom or the groom himself and the family of the bride. The mutual exchange of gifts served to cement ties between kin groups and was found among most Northern Plains groups including the Blackfeet (Wissler 1912:9), Arapaho (Elkin 1940:212), and Assiniboine (Rodnick 1938:58). If the bride's family accepted the goods, mainly horses, thus agreeing to the marriage, an equal number of goods, if not more, were returned to the groom's family when the couple started living together. Cross-culturally this type of exchange tends to be associated with an equality between the two kin groups rather than a ranked relationship of giver and receiver (Weist n.d.).

Certain of the transactions observed could have been the buying and selling of captive women. The capturing of Indian women from enemy tribes was a common occurrence throughout the Plains, and although most were adopted into the capturing tribe, many, such as Sacajewea, were given or possibly sold to white traders. Our data on this subject, however, are not complete enough to determine whether the Indians likewise considered the transference of captives to be financial transactions.

Nor are the data detailed enough to answer all questions regarding female sexuality, especially since the attitudes of the women were not recorded. That Indian attitudes toward sex were different from Euro-American ones is clear. Most, if not all tribes, placed great value upon purity, and special rituals were performed among the Dakota (Hassrick 1964:43) and Arikara (Brackenridge 1904:131), honoring chaste girls, and only women who had never committed adultery were permitted to perform certain rites in the Blackfeet (Ewers 1958:175) and Crow (Lowie 1956:312). In all the tribes, female fertility and power were

44

symbolically linked. Among certain tribes, it was
believed that a woman could transfer power from one
man to another by means of sexual intercourse. During
his stay among the Mandan in 1833, Maximilian recorded
being approached by a Mandan woman as part of a ceremony held to ensure a successful buffalo hunt
(1976:182). Alice Kehoe, in her article "The Function
of Ceremonial Sexual Intercourse among the Northern
Plains Indians," notes the widespread distribution of
these rites among the Northern Plains tribes, originating from a Mandan-Hidatsa center. She finds that
among the Mandan

> ... both symbolic and actual intercourse
> between married women and the men from whom
> their husbands wished power were believed to
> reenact intercourse with the life-giving
> bison, ensuring a happy and prosperous life
> for the married pairs (1970:100).

Edward Bruner attributes this belief in the transference of power to be the basis for the white misunderstanding of Indian sexuality (1961:217). If only
because of their technological knowledge and material
goods, the white traders must have appeared as very
powerful individuals to the Indians. But even beyond
this, in some tribes, especially the Crow, women had
freedom in selecting their marriage partners,
divorcing their husbands, and controlling their own
sexuality. That women of their own accord sought
liaisons with white traders and travelers without fear
of punishment speaks of a high rather than low status.

CONCLUSION

No generalizations about the status of Indian
women have been formulated in this paper which only
attempts to make other researchers aware of some of
the difficulties associated with the nineteenth century documents. At least since the publication of The
Savages of America (Pearce 1953), anthropologists and
historians have readily acknowledged that colonial
Euro-American images of American Indians were
distorted due to their cultural biases. Robert
Berkhofer (1978) has recently elaborated upon this
theme, putting forth the proposition that the image of

the "Indian" was a white invention which, although not
a reality, had impact upon literature, art, evolutionary thought, and Indian policy. Neither Pearce or
Berkhofer discussed Indian women as a significant component contributing to these images but, as is evident
from my review of the documents relating to the
Northern Plains, the presumed position and treatment
of Indian women was a major criteria for the designation "savage." As Alfred Miller exclaimed "nothing so
strikingly distinguishes civilized from savage life as
the treatment of women. It is in every particular in
favor of the former" (1968:70). However, these Euro-
American journals, diaries, reports, and letters must
be consulted if any attempt to undertake comparative
and historical analyses of Indian women's roles and
status is to be accomplished. As Valerie Mathers con-
tends "... the historical surface has been barely
scratched on the subject of Indian women" (1975:137).

NOTES

1. I wish to thank John Ewers for his valuable
comments and criticisms.

REFERENCES CITED

Beckwourth, James P. (1856) The Life and Adventures of James P. Beckwourth, Thomas D. Bonner, ed. New York: Harper and Row.

Berkhofer, Robert F., Jr. (1978) The White Man's Indian. New York: Alfred A. Knopf.

Brackenridge, Henry Marie (1904) Journal of a Voyage up the River Missouri; Performed in Eighteen Hundred and Eleven. In: Early Western Travels, Reuben Gold Thwaites, ed., Volume 5. Cleveland, Ohio: Arthur H. Clark Co.

Bradbury, J. (1904) Travels in the Interior of America in the Years 1807, 1810, and 1811. In: Early Western Travels, Reuben Gold Thwaites, ed., Volume 5. Cleveland, Ohio: Arthur H. Clark Co.

Brown, Judith K. (1975) Iroquois Women: An Ethnohistoric Note. In: Toward an Anthropology of Women, Rayna R. Reiter, ed., pp. 235-251. New York: Monthly Review Press.

Bruner, Edward (1961) Mandan. In: Perspectives in American Indian Culture Change, Edward H. Spicer, ed., pp. 187-277. Chicago: University of Chicago Press.

Catlin, George (1973) Letters and Notes on the Manners, Customs, and Conditions of the North American Indians, 2 Volumes. New York: Dover Publishing Inc.

Clark, William P. (1885) The Indian Sign Language. Philadelphia.

Coues, Elliott, ed. (1897) New Light on the Early History of the Greater Northwest: The Manuscript Journals of Alexander Henry and of David Thompson, 1799-1814, 3 Volumes. New York: Francis P. Harper.

Culbertson, Thaddeus A. (1952) Journal of an Expedition to the Mauvaises Terres and the Upper Missouri in 1850, John Francis McDermott, ed. U.S. Bureau of American Ethnology, Bulletin 147. Washington, D.C.

Denig, Edwin T. (1930) Indian Tribes of the Upper Missouri. In: 46th Annual Report of the Bureau of American Ethnology, J.N.B. Hewitt, ed., pp. 375-628. Washington, D.C.

De Smet, Pierre Jean (1905) Life, Letters and Travels of Father Pierre Jean De Smet, 4 Volumes. H.M. Chittenden and A.T. Richardson, eds. New York: Francis P. Harper.

Elkin, Henry (1940) The Northern Arapaho of Wyoming. In: Acculturation in Seven American Indian Tribes, Ralph Linton, ed., pp. 207-258. New York: D. Appleton-Century Co.

Ewers, John C. (1958) The Blackfeet. Norman: University of Oklahoma Press.

_____ (1968) Mothers of the Mixed Bloods. In: Indian Life on the Upper Missouri, John C. Ewers, ed., pp. 57-67. Norman: University of Oklahoma Press.

Flannery, Regina (1953) The Gros Ventre of Montana. I. Social Life. Catholic University of America, Anthropological Series, 15.

Friedl, Ernestine (1975) Women and Men: An Anthropologist's View. New York: Holt, Rinehart and Winston.

Grinnell, George B. (1923) The Cheyenne Indians, 2 Volumes. New Haven, Conn.: Yale University Press.

Green, Rayna (1975) The Pocahontas Perplex: The Image of Indian Women in American Culture. The Massachusetts Review 16:698-714.

Greene, Jerome A., ed. (1978) "We do not know what the Government intends to do ...": Lt. Palmer Writes from the Bozeman Trail, 1867-68. Montana Magazine of Western History 28:16-35.

Hassrick, Royal B. (1964) The Sioux: Life and Customs of a Warrior Society. Norman: University of Oklahoma Press.

Hewitt, James N.B. (1910) Woman. In: The Handbook of North American Indians, F.W. Hodge, ed. Bureau of American Ethnology, Bulletin 30, Vol. 2, pp. 968-973.

Irving, Washington (1961) The Adventures of Captain Bonneville, U.S.A., Edgeley W. Todd, ed. Norman: University of Oklahoma Press.

Kehoe, Alice B. (1970) The Function of Ceremonial Sexual Intercourse among the Northern Plains Indians. Plains Anthropologist 15:99-103.

Kelly, Fanny (1973) My Captivity among the Sioux Indians. Secaucus, N.J.: Citadel Press.

Kurz, Rudolph F. (1937) The Journal of Rudolph Friederick Kurz, J.N.B. Hewitt, ed. U.S. Bureau of American Ethnology, Bulletin 115, Washington, D.C.

Leis, Nancy B. (1976) West African Women and the Colonial Experience. In: Cross-Sex Relations: Native Peoples, Patricia A. McCormack, ed. Western Canadian Journal of Anthropology 6: 123-132.

Lewis, Oscar (1942) The Effects of White Contact upon Blackfoot Culture with the Special Reference to the Role of the Fur Trade. American Ethnological Society, Monograph 6.

Linderman, Frank B. (1962) Plenty-Coups, Chief of the Crows. Lincoln: University of Nebraska Press.

_____ (1972) Pretty-Shield: Medicine-Woman of the Crows. Lincoln: University of Nebraska Press.

Lowie, Robert H. (1956) The Crow Indians. New York: Holt, Rinehart and Winston.

M'Gillivary, Duncan (1929) Journal of Duncan M'Gillivary of the Northwest Company at Fort George on the Saskatchewan, 1794-5, Arthur S. Morton, ed. Toronto.

McKenny, Thomas L., and James Hall (1934) <u>The Indian</u>
<u>Tribes of North America with Biographical</u>
<u>Sketches and Anecdotes of the Principal Chiefs</u>,
3 Volumes.

Mathers, Valerie S. (1975) A New Look at the Role
of Women in Indian Society. <u>American Indian</u>
<u>Quarterly</u> 2:131-139.

Marquis, Thomas B. (1962) <u>Wooden Leg: A Warrior</u>
<u>Who Fought Custer</u>. Lincoln: University of
Nebraska Press.

_____ (1978) <u>The Cheyennes of Montana</u>, Thomas
D. Weist, ed. Algonac, Mich.: Reference
Publications, Inc.

Maximilian, Prince of Wied-Neuwied (1906) Travels in
the Interior of North America. In: <u>Early</u>
<u>Western Travels</u>, Rueben Gold Thwaites, ed.,
Vol. 21-23. Cleveland, Ohio: Arthur H. Clark
Co.

_____ (1976) <u>Peoples of the First Man</u>, Davis
Thomas and Karen Ronnefeldt, eds. New York:
E.P. Dutton & Co. Inc.

Miller, Alfred J. (1968) <u>The West of Alfred Jacob</u>
<u>Miller from the Notes and Water Colors in</u>
<u>the Walters Art Gallery with an Account of</u>
<u>the Artist by Marvin C. Ross</u>. Norman:
University of Oklahoma Press.

Morse, Jedidiah (1970) <u>A Report on the Secretary</u>
<u>of War of the United States on Indian Affairs</u>.
New York: A.M. Kelley.

Neill, E.D. (1872) <u>Dakota Land and Life</u>. Minnesota
Historical Society Collections, Vol. 1,
pp. 205-241.

O'Meara, Walter (1968) <u>Daughters of the Country</u>.
New York: Harcourt, Brace and World, Inc.

Pearce, Roy Harvey (1953) <u>The Savages of America:</u>
<u>A Study of the Indian and the Idea of</u>
<u>Civilization</u>. Baltimore, Maryland: Johns
Hopkins Press.

Quinn, Naomi (1977) Anthropological Studies of Women's Status. Annual Review of Anthropology 6:181-225.

Rodnick, David (1938) The Fort Belknap Assiniboine of Montana. Philadelphia: Ph.D. Dissertation, University of Pennsylvania.

Rothenberg, Diane (1976) Erosion of Power - An Economic Basis for the Selective Conservatism of Seneca Women in the Nineteenth Century. In: Cross-Sexual Relations: Native Peoples, Patricia A. McCormack ed. The Western Canadian Journal of Anthropology 6:106-122.

Rousseau, Ida Faye (1975) African Women: Identity Crisis? Some Observations on Education and the Changing Role of Women in Sierra Leone and Zaire. In: Women Cross-Culturally: Change and Challenge, Ruby Rohrlich-Leavitt, ed., pp. 41-52. The Hague: Mouton Publishers.

Sanday, Peggy R. (1973) Toward a Theory of the Status of Women. American Anthropologist 75:1682-1700.

Schlegel, Alice (1972) Male Dominance and Female Autonomy: Domestic Authority in Matrilineal Societies. HRAF Press.

Tabeau, Pierre-Antoine (1939) Tabeau's Narrative of Loisel's Expedition to the Upper Missouri. Addnie H. Abel, ed. Norman: University of Oklahoma Press.

Thompson, David (1916) David Thompson's Narrative of his Explorations in Western America, 1784-1813. J.B. Tyrell, ed. Publications of the Champlain Society, 12.

Trulio, Beverly (1973) Anglo-American Attitudes toward New Mexican Women. Journal of the West 12:229-239.

Twiss, Thomas (1856) Report to the Commissioner of Indian Affairs. 34th Congress, 3rd Sess., House Doc. 1, Serial 893, pp. 638-645.

Weist, Katherine M. (n.d.) Cross-Cultural Study of the Distribution of Goods at Marriage. Mss. deposited with Department of Anthropology, University of Montana.

Welter, Barbara (1973) The Cult of True Womanhood: 1820-1860. In: Our American Sisters: Women in American Life and Thought, Jean E. Friedman and William G. Shade, eds. Boston: Allyn and Bacon, Inc.

Will, George F., and George E. Hyde (1964) Corn among the Indians of the Upper Missouri. Lincoln: University of Nebraska Press.

Wissler, Clark (1912) The Social Life of the Blackfoot Indians. American Museum of Natural History Anthropological Papers 16:223-270.

CHAPTER 3

THE SHACKLES OF TRADITION

Alice B. Kehoe
Marquette University

Franz Boas declared his work had been motivated by the question, "How can we recognize the shackles that tradition has laid upon us?" (Stocking 1974:124). Anthropologists work within two traditions. Our broad Western European-American cultural tradition encapsulates the tradition of our scholarly discipline: we have been nourished by, at the same time we dialectically argue with, that wider heritage and milieu. The shackles of both our wider, European tradition and our scholarly anthropological tradition are glaringly evident when we attempt to examine the statuses, roles and experiences of Plains Indian women. I shall here discuss the effects of anthropologists' tradition upon our knowledge of Plains Indian societies, and Plains Indian women in particular, drawing upon the Blackfoot, whom I have known for over twenty years, for illustrative example.

We may divide the hindrances upon understanding women's experiences in Plains Indian life into two general categories, practical and intellectual. The practical limited the quantity of data gathered, discouraged replication of data, and severely curtailed work with or by women. Its effects can be relatively easily gauged, if not remedied. The second category of bias is subtle and more pervasive, and thereby more difficult to extricate and contrast with ideal objectivity and completeness. It will be discussed at greater length.

PRACTICAL HINDRANCES

Only one small government agency, the Bureau of American Ethnology, and two independent museums, the American and the Field, made serious prolonged efforts to record Plains Indian cultures in the late nineteenth and early twentieth centuries (the early reservation period). Fearing that the native cultures would be lost when the adults of the pre-reservation generation died, these three organizations attempted to send ethnographers to the reservations to salvage as many data as possible. With funds and personnel limited, the best strategy was thought to be the assignment of one ethnographer per tribe. He was to record texts from the elders of that tribe, and then move on to another tribe when the memories of the few most highly regarded elder tribesmen seemed reasonably well registered. Women were not encouraged to be ethnographers, although a few, notably Alice Fletcher, braved convention. To judge from our experience with Samuel Barrett in 1963, who forbade me to accompany my husband when in 1963 Barrett was organizing ethnographic film projects, even wives of ethnographers were not permitted to aid their husbands in the field. Standard practice was one male ethnographer interviewing, with the assistance of an interpreter from the community, one or a few middle-aged or elderly men of the reservation. The interview took place in the ethnographer's tent or hotel room, or in the home of the interpreter or informant. Information was recorded as texts and then organized for publication under etic headings such as "religion," "marriage," or "warfare."

To work with women informants was difficult for the typical classic ethnographer. Indian women were accustomed to being put down by Euro-American men and tended to be uncomfortable in their presence, anticipating disrespect. Women often were (and are) hesitant to explain women's roles and concerns through male interpreters to male ethnographers, in many instances because they believe(d) it dangerous to discourse on matters touching upon spiritual power before persons who have not been properly instructed to handle such knowledge. Ethnographers also faced a problem with publication of descriptions of sexual behavior or female physiological functions: editors of monographs insisted that these data could appear only in bowdlerized phrases or in Latin (Kehoe 1970).

Information on Plains Indian women was usually given by the older tribesmen who provided the bulk of the ethnographic data. Many aspects of women's behavior were considered improper for publication, and often closed to men's observation by the Indian women themselves, or by the scruples of the male ethnographers regarding the propriety of women's physiological functions. The traditional Plains Indian ethnographies are not participant observation of ongoing behavior of the period, but scheduled interviews of a few men, by a man, sometimes cursorily supplemented with interviews of one or a few older women. The early ethnographers worked remarkably hard, but there were too few of them, they were too narrowly chosen (by gender), and too poorly funded to produce the range of data that would be ideal for us. Ongoing Indian behavior of the period was assumed to represent attenuated, emasculated traditional culture undergoing acculturation to Euro-American patterns. A full generation would pass before anthropologists, finding no survivors from pre-reservation adulthood, would study acculturation per se. Contemporary behavior might be mentioned in field notebooks and might eventually be published in pseudo-fictional sketches (Wissler 1938), but it was an indulgence, not an obligation, of the ethnographer to record it. The life of Indian women on the early reservations must be ferreted out of asides and informal memoirs, and what is gleaned cannot be taken as even approaching completeness or depth.

Limitations on the quantity of data, lack of data replication, of contemporary observations, of work by or with women, are hindrances to analysis that can be quickly noted, if not remedied. The second major source of bias is more challenging to wrestle with: the implicit premises from which data were sought, arranged, and named. The covert biases stem from the ethnographer's own culture and disciplinary training. In effect, the Plains ethnographer was translating Plains Indian life into a totally foreign language, late-Victorian American English. The classic Plains ethnographies must be read as the results of naive translators, shackled by the grammar and semantics of their own native language, struggling with information produced out of a quite different semiotic.

INTELLECTUAL LIMITS

The clearest conflict between unexamined premises and alien cultural patterns can be seen in the classic ethnographers' evaluation of women's statuses and roles. Reared during the Victorian era, these ethnographers accepted a society in which the Industrial Revolution had divorced households from places of employment and thereby forced women to choose between compensated employment and motherhood. Concomitantly, capitalism emphasized the division between the moneyed and the proletariat. A leisured wife and mother was in a very real sense an ornament to her husband, a conspicuous symbol of his power exercised through wealth. Working women, whether laboring without pay in their homes or employed outside the home, were associated with less wealth, less power, assigned to a lower social status. Leisured women were strongly enjoined from physical activity and encouraged to appear frail and weak; husbands tried to spare these ladies the force of bestial masculine passion by copulating as quickly as possible, thus rendering it unlikely their wives would reach orgasm and reinforcing the stereotype of the passive, passionless lady. The upper-class lady was contrasted antithetically with the physically strong, more aggressive and possibly lusty lower-class working woman. Women in other societies who were physically strong, independent, perhaps lusty were perceived as innately inferior to the Victorian lady, and the societies with such "degraded" women predominating were characterized as primitive and little evolved.

Underlying the Victorian notion of ladies' frailty was an ancient conceptualization of the female that entered European scholastic tradition with the Greeks. Aristotle considered women to be, not alternative or complementary types of adult human, but imperfect, immature. Across the Mediterranean, Jewish philosophers cited Genesis to conclude that, Eve having been created from Adam's rib, women were secondary to, and an inconsequential portion of, men. These ideas had not always been dominant in the eastern Mediterranean. Pre-Indo-European Eastern European Neolithic peoples seem to have seen male and female as aspects of an androgynous unity, exemplified in their clay figurines which viewed from one angle are large-breasted, long-necked curtailed women, but viewed at a right angle to the preceding appear as the male genitals (Gimbutas 1974). This pre-Indo-European conceptualization of the two sexes as aspects of a single life force, was replaced by the historic dichotomy, which received the stamp of Christian orthodoxy when Thomas Aquinas accepted the Aristotelian position. The Enlightenment failed to dislodge the tradition, Hegel arguing that "man ... is the active principle while woman is the passive principle because she remains undeveloped" (quoted in de Beauvoir 1952: 6). Victorians were taught that both science and religion agreed on the natural inferiority and subordination of women to men.

The ethnographer of the early reservation period saw Indian women through the lenses of European elitist scholars who denigrated women and also manual work. Although in the sixteenth century Bartolome de las Casas had praised Aztec ladies because they prepared their husbands' food and clothing with their own hands, not leaving those tasks to servants (Sinclair 1977:26), the Victorians saw in such labor not love or humility, but evidence of a race impaled in a lower stage of evolution. If all women in a society performed necessary work, then, Victorians believed, either the race was incapable of refinement, or its primitive technology and social organization brutalized its members. The idea that a woman might glory in her physical strength and achievements as does a young man was inconceivable to an educated Victorian.

Their vocabulary betrays the class-bound criteria brought by the ethnographers to the Indian reservations: "The Indian division of occupations, between men and women, always made the men the providers and defenders against the enemy, and imposed upon the women a wide range of drudgery and manual labor ... Of necessity women took the place of servants in the capacity of wives ... Although it was customary for Indian women to perform the menial work, while men filled the more exalted vocation of providing and defending ..." (McClintock 1910:188-189, 235). The Indian evaluation of these occupational spheres is only indirectly and belatedly mentioned: "The superiority of women in all household arts ... was a marked feature of their social life. The same idea is suggested in a very primitive and curious Blackfeet legend, which ... describes the clothes and lodges of the men as poor compared with those used by the women, and alludes to the great benefits resulting to the men, after the women chose them as mates" (McClintock 1910:236-237).

Not all the ethnographers so readily perpetuated their class's prejudices. Clark Wissler carefully chose objective statements, eschewing impressionistic adjectives and cliches: "The women dress the skins, make their own clothes, ... They make most of their own utensils ... It is a disgrace both to himself and his women, for a man to carry wood or water, to put up a tipi, to use a travois, to cook food when at home and above all to own food or provisions ... this applies especially to married men" (Wissler 1911:27). Near the end of his life, Wissler disclosed the depth of the sincere respect he had come to feel toward the Indians he considered teachers and colleagues, not mere informants:

> In the same measure that Wolf Chief was one
> of the greatest Indians I ever met, so also
> was his wife the finest of women. Her
> countenance was feminine, but with the stamp
> of leadership. Her carriage was graceful
> but always expressing dignity. It was an
> inspiration to see her ... In time I learned
> to know this woman and held many interesting
> conversations with her ... Mother-of-all
> [Wolf Chief's wife], like her husband, was
> apt to surprise one with bursts of folk-
> wisdom and though always dignified and high-
> minded had a sense of humor. She encouraged
> me to describe the lives of white women,
> especially in the great towns. One day I
> told her of women who had nothing to do but
> lead a dog around by a string. This seemed
> to her such an absurdity that she indulged
> in peals of laughter, supported by a chorus
> of other women present ... nothing she had
> ever heard was so silly ... I wish a
> translation could carry the fine style of
> narration employed by this old lady
> (Wissler 1938:331-333).

Recounting how "white people were hopelessly incon-sistent," a medicine man states:

> 'If I should have a quarrel with my old
> woman and ... give her a good beating ...
> the agent, he would have me arrested ...

> If again the old woman and I should
> quarrel ... she might ... knock me down
> with a stick of firewood ... But [the
> agent] laughs at me ... says he is glad
> I got it once ... What kind of thing is
> white man's justice!'
>
> Can the reader adequately explain this
> situation! If he can, he is far on the
> road to an understanding of the Indian
> problem. As One-spot talked, I saw in
> imagination, the shadowy forms of knights
> and ladies, the flower of Chivalry, an
> historical vista, giving shape to customs
> and ideals, none of them truly rational,
> but still very real to us. I tried to
> explain all this to One-spot but in the
> end he again shook his head saying, 'that
> it did not make sense' (Wissler 1938:
> 307-308).

Wissler's apprehension of the effects of his own
enculturation, and his commitment to the primacy of
observation over received knowledge, color his textbook on anthropology: "As a rule, primitive women do
not actively participate in government or in rituals.
Everywhere war and hunting are restricted to men and
while this is generally true of other functions, it is
observable, however, that women may be rulers, may
develop cults, and may serve as priests. In all of
these, however, they usually achieve prominence after
the child-bearing stage" (Wissler 1929:193-194).

More typical, more congruent with the prevailing
paradigm, is Goldenweiser's statement in his textbook
paralleling Wissler's:

> The warrior, as noted before, is of course
> a man, a fact of double connotation,
> occupational and social. The fact that
> the warrior or fighter, who is skilled in
> the wielding of weapons, is always a man,
> inevitably stands for a certain social pre-
> eminence. It is in fact likely, though
> difficult to prove, that one of the earliest
> incentives for the socio-political dis-
> franchisement of woman [note the singular]
> came in consequence of her helplessness ...
> The leader--chief, king, priest, ceremonial

official, judge--is pre-eminently a man.
We know, of course, of women in each and all
of these positions, but these are individual
instances--the opposite is the rule, which
gives a peculiar slant to primitive
society ... As to power, openly and
officially exercised, this has always
been a man-made world. Nor should we
misunderstand certain facts, in particular
places, which seem to point the other way:
for example, the political rights of
Iroquois women or the presence of queens
in Africa ... 'pine tree' chieftainship
[bestowed by the Iroquois on 'some women']
was a strictly personal distinction which
vanished, as a social factor, with its
bearer: meanwhile things political pursued,
undisturbed, their androcentric course ...
Next to the political sphere, that of
religion is heavily weighted against woman.
There are, we know, medicine-women as well
as men, also female shamans ... But there
is another side to all this. An African
medium is, after all, not the priest; the
latter is a man, always; quite as in North
America, where medicine-women and
sorceresses occur, but the priests,
whether Omaha or Zuni, are men. Similarly,
with religious societies: those of men
are always more numerous, and they set the
style; the women's societies are patterned
after them ... Woman is handicapped in
matters sacred by the fact that she herself is not merely a human but also a woman
--a peculiar creature with a distracting
and at times repulsive periodicity in her
life cycle, a peculiar and only partly
understood relationship to the fact of
birth, and a fascinating but often excessive and always disturbing influence
on man _via_ sex (Goldenweiser 1937:140-142).

Goldenweiser continues in this vein for three more
pages, disparaging Margaret Mead, "the genial anthropologist whose fate it is to upset established
notions" (1937:143), and impugning her description of
the respect and power enjoyed by Tchambuli women in
New Guinea. The shackles of tradition are blatantly
advertised not only in Goldenweiser's own tortured

arguments against allowing instances of women's power to subvert his patriarchal dogma, but--unhappily--in the popularity of his textbook, which by 1946 had gone through six printings.

THE PARADIGM OF CLASSICAL ANTHROPOLOGY

Goldenweiser's dogma on women is part of a broader set of dogmas drawn from European folk conceptualizations, classical learning, and structured argumentation based on oppositional dualism. This set of dogmas was the paradigm of anthropology during its first century as a discipline. Every ethnographer had to fit his data into the paradigm, directly, or by contending differences point by point: the dogmas were implicitly accepted, or had to be explicitly rejected. Rejection in toto would have been revolution, and probably would have met supercilious denunciation. The best of the classic ethnographers, such as Wissler, Lowie, and Mooney, felt the falsity of the body of dogma, but could only undermine it by inserting demurrers and concentrating on presenting carefully worded, full observations. Astute readers could then draw their own conclusions on the incompatibility of the data with the erroneous generalizations of the traditional paradigm; editors, meanwhile, would pass the material as conforming to criteria of scholarship. An unpublished scientist is, after all, ineffective, and thoroughgoing revolutionaries have never been well received in the United States.

Classical, or traditional, anthropology developed on the model of comparative anatomy, the glamor science of the late eighteenth and early nineteenth centuries (Ackerknecht 1954). Comparative anatomy had been established as a theoretical science by Georges Cuvier in his series of Leçons, 1800–1805. Observations from anatomy, physiology, zoology, botany, and paleontology were to be organized and classified, and from the classified data, principles or "laws" were to be induced. Eventually, the set of discovered laws would constitute the mechanics of the natural world. Principles should be tested against new observational data. The world is a laboratory of natural experiments analogous to the laboratory where physical scientists test their hypotheses. The "comparative method" entailed the collection of data, the dissection of the body of data into recognizable traits or attributes, the classification of natural objects on the basis of shared attributes, and the construction of generalizations (principles or laws) congruent with the classifications.

The comparative method, properly pursued, is exemplified in Franz Boas' work and exhortations (Boas 1896) to his colleagues. The method has become associated, notwithstanding, with the nineteenth-century evolutionists excoriated by Boas. These thinkers claimed to base their research on the comparative method, but perverted it by making it deductive, not inductive: they compared data after they had formulated principles. Paul Radin remarked (1932:7), "One gets the impression that the actual facts are being used as mere illustrative material for a psychological and philosophical position arrived at independently of them." The cart was placed before the horse, and no matter how energetically the horse was whipped, the cart budged not an inch from its ancient ruts.

The comparative evolutionists were predecessors of, or contemporary with, Darwin. Their work was not influenced by his theory, but by Greek and medieval scholastic cosmogenies. Comparative anatomy did not itself involve evolution. The Aristotelian concept of the Great Chain of Being, a logical series from simple to complex with no implication of organic processes of change, had been popular with eighteenth-century biologists, and Cuvier himself believed in the fixity of species (Lovejoy 1959). Most nineteenth-century anthropologists accepted a pre-Darwinian notion of evolution, a modification of the Great Chain of Being, postulating that the complex grew out of the simple germs of early creation--the metaphor of a plant unfolding from a seed was popular. Growth could be arrested in an early stage by a faulty genetic endowment or by an unfavorable environment. Where we cannot observe the millennia of the growth of a species, we can use these small stunted varieties as clues to the earlier stages of the species' history. Pre-Darwinian evolution was thus compatible with the notion of fixity of species. Indeed, many thinkers accepted the fixity of species as the sine qua non of comparative anatomy, for who can compare unstable phenomena? Fixity of species and the postulation of

Platonic ideal types were two aspects of a strongly normative position in nineteenth-century anthropology. As late as 1952, Radin affirmed:

> One of the fundamental traits of these major civilizations [Egyptian, Sumerian-Babylonian, Hebrew, India, Christianity and Mohammedanism] was their essential instability, the frequent social-economic crises through which they passed and the amazing vitality of ... fictions ... that there had never been any instability or change and ... that stability existed eternally, but in the afterworld not in this ...
>
> Contrasted with these major civilizations, there have always existed other civilizations, those of aboriginal peoples, where societies were fundamentally stable, where no basic internal social-economic crises occurred ... Here we have an amazing antithesis which it is of fundamental importance to remember if we wish to understand the civilizations of aboriginal peoples and to see them in their proper perspective (Radin 1952:7-8).

Today, such a position appears ludicrous. Fifty years ago, Lowie (e.g., 1924:ix-x) and Wissler (1929: 36-38) gave caveats against it. It would seem to clearly contradict the principle of uniformitarianism, which is the basis of the historical sciences. Nevertheless, the whole paradigm of classical anthropology took shape around that "amazing antithesis," "the assumption that primitive peoples are to be equated with the illiterate and backward peoples among ourselves" (Radin 1932:6). The task of anthropology was to fit the little folk societies, stunted by racial imperfections or poor environment, into the Great Chain of Being crowned by the nearly fully evolved English-speaking Caucasoid educated class.

Boas realized that "to apply our classification to alien cultures ... may lead to a misunderstanding of the essential problems involved" (quoted in Smith 1959:50). Ideally, classification derives from the attributes of the subjects; in practice in nineteenth-century anthropology, it was most often an exercise in remarkably arbitrary assignments stemming from postulates embedded in the European intellectual tradition. Lewis Henry Morgan, for example, erected a ladder of evolutionary development in which the invention of writing followed the mastery of the smelting of iron. There was no classification for a society that had writing but not iron technology. Therefore, all the native peoples and nations of the Americas, including the fully literate Mexican nations of A.D. 1500, could not be classed as civilized because their lack of smelted iron relegated them to barbarian status, or lower. Familiar though he was with the mnemonic symbols of Iroquois ritual leaders, Morgan could not recognize their symbols as hieroglyphs because the Iroquois were not metallurgists. The rigidity of the classifications fostered dichotomization of societies into opposing categories, particularly civilized versus primitive, a tendency strongly advanced by the Judaeo-Christian penchant for structuring argument through oppositional dualism (Kehoe 1981:504).

The fatal flaw in the comparative methodology of the nineteenth century was, as Radin pointed out (1932:10), the failure to place organisms, or societies, in their contexts. As the anatomists virtually ignored ecology, so the anthropologists glossed over political realities. Peasantries, lower classes, and the marginal tribal peoples of Europe such as Albanian mountain groups, were seen as encapsulated survivals, not as part-societies in national or imperial polities. Travellers' tales, administrators' reports, and missionaries' epistles were mined for evidence of the low state of the conquered peoples of the colonies, with no acknowledgment, or perhaps even realization, of the chauvinism of these agents of imperialism. Races and societies were pushed into Procrustean beds of logical classifications speciously supported by these biased or naive observations. The dominance of the equation illiterate=primitive ("old-fashioned, simple, rude"--Concise Oxford Dictionary) made assignment to classifications easy. Did Plains chiefs' wives scrape hides, sew, and pitch tipis with their own hands? then Plains tribes were low on the ladder of societal evolution, like the peasants whose women's hands were callused by hard labor. No poetry or philosophy would be found in the dungheaps of drudgery, and none should be looked for. Any apparent complexity in the culture of a "primitive" society was either a misapprehension that would be resolved when the fieldworker's data were more fully analyzed (a self-fulfilling prophecy), or possibly an aberration from type.

The classic ethnographers went into the field primed with the body of knowledge accumulated in a half century of the science of comparative ethnology. Collections of data had been dissected, organized, classified, and generalizations drawn. Goldenweiser sums up this body of knowledge (1937:407-410):

> The characteristics of primitive culture?
> ... The primary local unit of cultural life
> is numerically small ... also isolated
> geographically ... Primitive culture['s]
> patterns are set in a rigid frame. Primitive
> culture is stiff-jointed and the number and
> kinds of movements it can make at short
> notice are limited ... The material equip-
> ment of a group persists by its own inertia
> ... each growing generation simply finds
> these objects there to be picked up where
> they were left by their fathers ... Primitive
> tradition ... is shallow, and the historical
> inquisitiveness of the primitive is slight
> ... [and] equally limited geographically.
> ... Everywhere in primitive society the
> elders are in the saddle. It is the fathers'
> generation that rules ... They stand for
> established routine, a fearful avoidance
> of the new, a sagacious management and
> occasional exploitation of the young ...
> Division of labour and specialization are
> ... not unknown in primitive life. Even
> so, the group is in the main strikingly
> homogeneous ... The individual here is
> but a miniature reproduction of the group
> culture ... Contrary to what is found
> under modern conditions, the primitive group
> lives in close communion with nature ...
> Every breath of cultural life is dominated
> by natural things and events ... Owing to
> deficient familiarity with other cultures
> and the consequent lack of comparative
> cultural material, no conscious idea of
> progress can develop. Under such conditions
> the economic adjustment is taken almost as
> a fact of nature. It may be sorely inade-
> quate, but it works after a fashion and is

65

accepted as final.

This set of dogmas derived from the a priori antithesis of the classes "civilized" and "primitive," was the paradigm of anthropology during its first century as a discipline.

A paradigm shift is certainly occurring in our generation. The iceberg of frozen beliefs, of which the patriarchal dogma is the tip, that impeded the observations and theory-building of the classic ethnographers is drifting out of the channel of anthropological voyaging. Whether this is simply drift as the weight of data comes to fall outside the conventional framework, or the result of the decline in classical learning that formerly enculturated educated men in the traditional model, received terminology is increasingly critically examined (e.g., Fried 1975). Revisionist studies demonstrate that Northern Plains people did not live out their lives in small, bounded, stable ethnic units (e.g., Sharrock 1974), and suggest that, far from being tied to a simple subsistence economy, they were engaged in an interethnic, industrializing commercial economy of hide and pemmican production (T. Kehoe 1973:195, Fig. 12; 1976). The nineteenth-century dichotomy between civilized and primitive has been repudiated, and without it the whole house of cards collapses. In the following section I shall examine the status of Blackfoot women from the position that the legend mentioned by McClintock is not "primitive" or "curious," but the legitimate expression of the Blackfoot evaluation of women.

THE STATUS OF BLACKFOOT WOMEN

To the Blackfoot, woman:man::culture:nature, pace Lévi-Strauss. The myth referred to by McClintock describes a primeval world in which women and men occupied separate camps. The women's "lodges all were fine inside. And their things were just as fine," but the men "were very poor ... They had no lodges. They wore raw-hides ... They did not know too, how they should cut dried meat" (Uhlenbeck 1912:167). The men were eager to cohabit with the women--one gets the impression as much for civilized comforts as for sex--

66

and the women magnaminously each chose a husband to join her in her lodge. Napi (Old Man) spurned the chief of the women because she dressed plainly. His punishment was to be outcast, transformed into a pine tree teetering on the edge of a cut bank. The man who rejects a decent woman's offer of a home will be outcast, paralyzed, and threatened with imminent oblivion.

The primeval Blackfoot women, in the myth, were self-sufficient. They obtained their food and hides by impounding bison (according to Blood legend, the drive and pound site near Cayley, Alberta, excavated by Forbis was the one anciently used by these women [Forbis 1962:61]). Mistresses of the arts needed for the good life, they were proud, and passed on both arts and pride to their daughters:

> In pre-reservation days a woman was judged
> by the number and quality of skins she had
> dressed, the baskets she had woven, or the
> pottery moulded; and her renown for such
> accomplishments might travel far. When by
> chance you met a woman who had distinguished
> herself, it was proper to address her in a
> manner to reveal your knowledge of her
> reputation, as: "Grandmother, we are happy
> to look upon one whose hands were always
> busy curing fine skins" (Wissler 1938:290).

Myths also recount the role of women as critical intermediaries between men and Powers. The four most important Blackfoot ceremonies were obtained through women. The Natoas (Sun Dance) medicine bundle is said to have originated in the contention of two bull elk over an elk woman. The elk's husband bought off his rival by giving him the headdress and clothing now in the Natoas bundle. This elk subsequently passed on the bundle to an owner of a beaver bundle, whose wife wore the costume; much later, the Natoas was separated from the beaver bundle. Beaver bundles themselves came to men through a Blackfoot woman who went under water to a beaver's lodge. On her return, she was visited by the beaver, who graciously taught the bundle ritual and contents to the woman's husband. The Thunder or medicine pipe was a gift to the Blackfoot from Thunder, whom a Blackfoot woman married and bore two sons. Another woman is said to have married Morning Star, son of the Sun and Moon, and to

67

have brought the holy digging stick in the Natoas bundle with her when she returned to earth from her husband's abode. Finally, iniskim (bison fetishes, usually fossil ammonites) which call bison herds into pounds were first revealed to a woman during a famine. The magic songs taught by the holy rock to the worthy woman were then given by her to the people. (These legends are in Wissler and Duvall 1908:74-90; Wissler 1912:209-215, 242-244).

Women as intermediaries between men and Power are recognized in the major Blackfoot rituals. The contents of medicine bundles must be unwrapped by women, who then hand the holy objects to the men leading the prayers. Women also have the responsibility of the daily care of medicine bundles. The Sun Dance depends upon the willingness of a woman to serve as Holy Woman, custodian of the Natoas bundle and focus of the rituals. If no woman feels compelled to undergo the burdensome sacrifices entailed in the role, as has happened in recent years, no Sun Dance can be held. The so-called men's societies (in Blackfoot, "all comrades") regularly initiated a wife or, for a bachelor, another female relative with each male member. The women members joined in the songs and dances of the societies' formal meetings, although their role seems to have been secondary in that the primary function of the societies seems to have been the organization of a cooperating group of hunters and warriors (Wissler 1913:384-385). The most prestigious and feared of the societies, the Bloods' Horns, initiated male members through sequent intercourse between the sponsoring member, the initiate's wife, and the initiate, the power passing physically through the two copulations. Ceremonial transfer of spiritual power through sexual intercourse was a Mandan and Hidatsa trait contrary to Blackfoot mores, and it seems likely the Horn ritual was borrowed from these eastern peoples (Kehoe 1970), but position of women as intermediary fits Blackfoot practice.

Women independently act as shamans, doctoring the sick and invoking spiritual power on behalf of the young or unfortunate. Wissler (1912:263), McClintock (1910:142, 244-250), and Ewers (1955:245) each testify to the many instances of women achieving recognition in this role. The Bloods had a women's lodge, the Ma'toki, which relegated its few male participants to auxiliary roles, but the function of this society is

not clear. Goldfrank implies (1945:41-42) that in the
late 1930s, Blood women neglected the Ma'toki in favor
of the Horns. The initiation ritual and participation
of women in the Horns suggest they were considered
true members of this society, and it may be that under
the official discouragement of societies on the reserves, Blood women considered it better strategy to support one society than to attempt to maintain competing
organizations.

Camp was the domain of the women (Wissler 1938:
286-287). The tipi, its furnishings, the food in it,
clothing and other manufactures belonged to the woman,
hers to give as she pleased. The marriage ceremony
consisted of the woman inviting her intended to par-
take of food she had prepared (Wissler 1912:86).
Women ridiculed men who attempted to perform suste-
nance activities (McClintock 1910:236; Wissler 1938:
286). On the other hand, all secular activities normally pursued by men were open also to women, should
they wish to join. Women occasionally hunted, and it
was not unusual in the nineteenth century for women to
ride with war parties, stealing horses and engaging in
mounted combat along with their male comrades (Ewers
1955:190). Women were less likely to seek the glory
road than were men, who had little other opportunity
to earn respect, and the fact that they less often
risked their lives in war probably accounts for the
lesser frequency with which women sought visions
(Wissler 1912:91-92; cf. Lowie 1924:206 for a similar
statement on the Crow). It would seem that Blackfoot
women had more options than men, and more easily
achieved esteem. Their families and tipis were
constant mute witness to women's capabilities, whereas
men had to recount again and again their ephemeral
deeds in war lest they be forgotten. On formal occasions, nevertheless, women stood forward and "counted
coup" on their deeds of repute (Wissler 1911:30; see
also A. Kehoe 1976:70, 73), from repulsing seducers to
producing fine robes. Blackfoot society was
accustomed to publicly honor women who fulfilled the
ideal of self-sufficiency, skill, and generosity
expressed in the myth of the primeval women.

CONCLUSION

The traditional picture of the Plains Indian woman is really that of an Irish housemaid of the late Victorian era clothed in a buckskin dress. Superficial similarities between the physically strong, hardworking, illiterate Indian woman and the Victorian menial allowed ethnocentric Euro-American observers to allocate to the Indian the demeaning status of the lower-class Euro-American woman. This easy denigration of the Indian woman was fostered by the dominant paradigm of classical anthropology, in which an emphasis on classification derived from comparative anatomy set up a fundamental dichotomy between "civilized" and "primitive," with the latter class including all illiterates. The attributes assigned to the two classes were antithetical and drawn from European myth and philosophical speculation.

A moment's reflection will suggest that the patriarchal dogma of the universal subjection of the weaker sex cannot possibly be appropriate to hunting, warring societies such as the historic Plains Indians. During the many days in which the men of a band were absent on hunts or war parties, the women of the camp were responsible for the welfare of the families. Women were accustomed to making decisions, often during crises. They had to be capable of providing food and other necessities if the men did not return promptly. Only a highly complex capitalist society—the Victorian—could carry even a minority of women who were frail and dependent. Anthropologists must free themselves of the tradition rooted in nineteenth-century ideology and begin anew.

REFERENCES CITED

Ackerknecht, Erwin H. (1954) On the Comparative
Method in Anthropology. In: Method and Perspective in Anthropology, Robert F. Spencer,
ed., pp. 117-125. Minneapolis: University of
Minnesota Press.

Boas, Franz (1896) The Limitations of the
Comparative Method in Anthropology. Reprinted
in: High Points in Anthropology, Paul Bohannan
and Mark Glazer, eds. (1973), pp. 84-92.
New York: Alfred A. Knopf.

_____ (1974) An Anthropologist's Credo. Re-
printed in: A Franz Boas Reader, George W.
Stocking, Jr. ed., p. 124. New York: Basic
Books.

De Beauvoir, Simone (1952) The Second Sex. H.M.
Parshley, trans. New York: Bantam Books.

Ewers, John C. (1955) The Horse in Blackfoot Indian
Culture. Smithsonian Institution, Bureau of
American Ethnology Bulletin 159. Washington:
Government Printing Office.

Forbis, Richard G. (1962) The Old Women's Buffalo
Jump, Alberta. National Museum of Canada
Bulletin 180, pp. 57-123. Ottawa: Queen's
Printer.

Fried, Morton H. (1975) The Notion of Tribe. Menlo
Park: Cummings Publishing Company.

Gimbutas, Marija (1974) The Gods and Goddesses of
Old Europe, 7000 to 3500 B.C. Berkeley: University of California Press.

Goldenweiser, Alexander (1937) Anthropology. New
York: F.S. Crofts and Co.

Goldfrank, Esther S. (1945) Changing Configurations
in the Social Organization of a Blackfoot Tribe
During the Reserve Period. American Ethnological Society Monographs 8. New York: J.J.
Augustin.

Kehoe, Alice B. (1970) The Function of Ceremonial Sexual Intercourse Among the Northern Plains Indians. <u>Plains Anthropologist</u> 15:99-103.

_____ (1976) Old Woman Had Great Power. <u>Western Canadian Journal of Anthropology</u> 6:68-76.

_____ (1981) Revisionist Anthropology: Aboriginal North America. <u>Current Anthropology</u> 22:503-517.

Kehoe, Thomas F. (1973) <u>The Gull Lake Site.</u> Milwaukee Public Museum Publications in Anthropology and History 1. Milwaukee: Milwaukee Public Museum.

_____ (1976) New Interpretation of Prehistoric Plains Economy. Paper read at the American Anthropological Association Annual Meeting, Washington, D.C.

Lovejoy, Arthur O. (1959) Buffon and the Problem of Species. In: <u>Forerunners of Darwin: 1745-1859</u>, Bentley Glass, Oswei Temkin, William L. Straus, Jr., eds., pp. 84-113. Baltimore: The Johns Hopkins Press.

Lowie, Robert H. (1924) <u>Primitive Religion.</u> New York: Grosset and Dunlap.

McClintock, Walter (1910) <u>The Old North Trail.</u> London: Macmillan.

Radin, Paul (1932) <u>Social Anthropology.</u> New York: McGraw-Hill Book Company, Inc.

_____ (1952) <u>The World of Primitive Man.</u> London: Abelard-Schuman.

Sharrock, Susan R. (1974) Crees, Cree-Assiniboines, and Assiniboines: Interethnic Social Organization on the Far Northern Plains. <u>Ethnohistory</u> 21:95-122.

Sinclair, Andrew (1977) <u>The Savage.</u> London: Weidenfeld and Nicolson.

Smith, Marian W. (1959) Boas' "Natural History"
Approach to Field Method. In: The Anthropology
of Franz Boas, Walter Goldschmidt, ed., pp.
46-60. American Anthropological Association
Memoir 89.

Stocking, George W. Jr., ed. (1974) A Franz Boas
Reader. New York: Basic Books.

Uhlenbeck, C. C. (1912) A New Series of Blackfoot
Texts. Verhandelingen der Koninklijke Akademie
van Wetenschappen te Amsterdam, Afdeeling
Letterkunde n. r. 13 (1). Amsterdam: Johannes
Muller.

Wissler, Clark (1911) The Social Life of the
Blackfoot Indians. American Museum of Natural
History Anthropological Papers 7, Pt 1, pp. 1-64.
New York: American Museum of Natural History.

_____ (1912) Ceremonial Bundles of the Blackfoot
Indians. American Museum of Natural History
Anthropological Papers 7, Pt. 2, pp. 65-289.
New York: American Museum of Natural History.

_____ (1913) Societies and Dance Associations of
the Blackfoot Indians. American Museum of
Natural History Anthropological Papers 11, Pt. 4,
pp. 359-460. New York: American Museum of
Natural History.

_____ (1929) An Introduction to Social Anthropology. New York: Henry Holt and Company.

_____ (1938) Indian Cavalcade. New York:
Sheridan House.

Wissler, Clark and D. C. Duvall (1908) Mythology
of the Blackfoot Indians. American Museum of
Natural History Anthropological Papers 2, Pt. 1,
pp. 1-163. New York: American Museum of
Natural History.

PART II

WOMEN'S WORK

CHAPTER 4

MALE/FEMALE TASK DIFFERENTIATION AMONG THE HIDATSA:
TOWARD THE DEVELOPMENT OF AN ARCHEOLOGICAL
APPROACH TO THE STUDY OF GENDER

Janet D. Spector
University of Minnesota

The rise of feminist anthropology raises a series
of challenging questions for archeologists. The significance of gender in social life has been well documented in numerous recent publications (see Rosaldo
and Lamphere 1974; Reiter 1975 for collections of
articles on the anthropological study of gender), but
to date, the study of gender behavior has not been the
focus of archeological research. The present investigation was stimulated by two essentially archeological
questions about gender and society. First, how might
our views of patterns of adaptation, change and stability in prehistory or early historic periods be
altered by the consideration of gender? In other
words, what role did gender behavior play in shaping
the responses of populations to changes in their
social or natural environments? This kind of question
immediately raises the issue of archeological methods,
a second concern stimulating this study: to what
extent is it possible to retrieve information about
gender from archeological sites and assemblages? The
desire to bring together perspectives of contemporary
archeology and feminist anthropology has stimulated
the development of a new analytical framework, male/
female task differentiation, introduced and
illustrated in this paper using data on the historically known Hidatsa Indians of the Great Plains.

INTRODUCTION

The approach taken in this study is similar to
the work of a number of other "ethnoarcheologists"
interested in social organizational or behavioral
questions (see David 1971; Binford 1975; Schiffer
1976:5-6; Yellen 1977 for examples of ethno-
archeology). In this kind of approach the archeologist initially examines the relationships between
material and non-material dimensions of specified
behavior in contemporary or ethnographically known
cultural settings so that "... understandings of the
relationships between material and non-material
derived from maximum information well controlled can
then be fed back into the traditional archeological
contexts for more precise inference" (Deetz 1972:115).
Lewis Binford, for example, studied the butchering
practices of contemporary Eskimo hunters and the animal remains left behind at their butchering sites, to
better understand the distributional patterns of
various animal bones at archeological sites (Binford
1975:11-30). Similarly, William Longacre is examining
the transmission of knowledge about ceramic manufacturing techniques in a group which still produces pottery for domestic use to more reliably interpret the
spatial distribution and variability of ceramic
remains in archeological contexts (Longacre, personal
communication). The long range goal of these and
other ethnoarcheological investigations is to enhance
our ability to describe and explain cultural processes
operant in the past by increasing our capacity to
interpret archeological assemblages.

The attempt to design and employ an ethnoarcheological research approach to the study of gender
began with the development of an analytical framework
suitable for the reanalysis of selected ethnographic
data--that is, a framework which highlights information of particular interest to the archeologist. At
the core of the proposed framework is the analysis of
activities, an orientation similar to that suggested
by Michael Schiffer (1976:49-53, 1977:3). More specifically, the task differentiation framework focuses on
the organization of males and females in the execution
of tasks and the spatial, temporal and material dimensions of those tasks. This focus on activities
reflects the primary concerns of the research: first,
to explore the feasibility of studying gender in
archeological contexts and second, to better

understand the relationships between gender and patterns of adaptation, change and stability.

In the first case, it seems logical to assume that the structure of archeological sites--the frequency, variability and distribution of material remains and the spatial arrangements and physical characteristics of structures and facilities--is related to the kinds of activities engaged in by a given population within a particular environmental setting. In discussing the structure of archeological sites, archeologists have often focussed on the cultural and natural factors operating after site abandonment and the way factors like erosion, decay or conditions of abandonment alter or distort the archeological record (Schiffer 1976:27-43). In the present study, the approach taken first examines the possible relationships between the activity patterns of males and females and their activity settings in ethnographically known contexts. When relationships between gender and activity settings can be demonstrated in on-going cultural systems, we can then consider the factors which might act to distort these relationships in archeological sites, hopefully setting the stage for the eventual examination of gender utilizing the archeological record.

The activity orientation of the task differentiation framework is also relevant to the study of gender behavior and adaptation, change and stability through time. It seems reasonable to suggest that men and women in a given population might respond differentially to changes in their social or natural environments depending on the kinds of tasks they engage in; the geographical spaces they utilize in the performance of tasks; the scheduling of their tasks; and the materials (artifacts, structures, facilities) they use and/or produce as a part of their task assignments. The framework proposed here illuminates similarities and differences in the activity patterns of males and females by permitting the analytical separation of the sexes prior to generalization about the group as a whole. As important, the framework reduces the likelihood of androcentrism (male centered biases) which has too often characterized anthropological research and discourse (see Reiter 1975; Rosaldo and Lamphere 1974; Noble 1978; Leacock 1978 for discussion of androcentric bias in anthropology).

This paper presents the results of preliminary research on the task differentiation approach. Much work remains to be done before the framework might be adapted for the study of gender in archeological contexts. The purpose of this paper is to introduce the framework and to illustrate some of the implications of the framework through the case of the 19th century Hidatsa Indians. In an effort to refine and test the utility of the approach, data presented on the Hidatsa by Bowers (1965) and Wilson (1917, 1934, 1971) were re-analyzed. Not unexpectedly, the analysis was handicapped by certain problems in the ethnographic accounts. Both Bowers and Wilson studied the Hidatsa during the early decades of the 20th century, working with elderly informants to reconstruct traditional Hidatsa culture. In many cases their descriptions lack chronological control, making it difficult to get a sense of the group at any one point in time. Second, these ethnographers, like many of their contemporary counterparts, were not interested in specific details of material culture, so important to archeologists. Finally, neither Wilson nor Bowers was particularly concerned with the sexual division of labor. The Bowers account of Hidatsa social and ceremonial organization suffers from a pervasive androcentrism, peripheralizing the roles and experiences of Hidatsa females by emphasizing the lives of men and boys. Wilson, in contrast, focused his attention almost exclusively on women, but his work is limited to a narrow range of activities. In spite of these limitations, combining information provided by Bowers and Wilson within the task differentiation framework, did permit the refinement of the approach and suggested implications of the framework for future research on gender.

GENERAL BACKGROUND ON THE 19th CENTURY HIDATSA

The Hidatsa are commonly described as one of the earth lodge village groups of the Great Plains. These groups were basically sedentary hoe agriculturalists whose subsistence depended primarily on horticultural products and secondarily on bison and other animal resources prior to the disruptions and cultural changes triggered by events of the contact period (Spencer and Jennings 1965:339). Linguistically, the

Siouan speaking Hidatsa were closely related to the Crow, but their cultural patterns during the 19th century resembled those of their neighbors, the Mandan.

During the early years of the 19th century, the Hidatsa reportedly consisted of three, independent village groups, distinct both culturally and historically, living in close proximity along the Knife River in North Dakota. By 1837, following small pox epidemics which greatly reduced their numbers, these three groups coalesced and along with members of the Mandan tribe, they moved to a new village on the Knife, known as "Like-a-Fishhook." By 1862, they were joined at that village by the Caddoan speaking Arikara. These three groups continued to live together on the Knife River, until 1885 when they were forced to move to the Fort Berthold Reservation (Bowers 1965:10-35).

In describing the Hidatsa during the mid-19th century, both Bowers and Wilson relied on the recollections of elderly informants interviewed in the early decades of the 20th century. According to Bowers, traditionally the basic economic unit of the Hidatsa was the household, or "extended matrilinear family," based on matrilocal residence (Bowers 1965:159). Typically, he reports, a household consisted of older parents, daughters with their husband or husbands, unmarried daughters and sons, and usually a few orphans belonging to the clan of the females (Bowers 1965). According to Wilson's major informant, Buffalo Bird Woman, there were about 70 earth lodges housing these family units, in Like-a-Fishhook village during the 1840's (Wilson 1971:44). Though this village was the permanent home base of the Hidatsa, groups of households often left the village at different times of the year to hunt buffalo and other animals, setting up temporary camps along the route to the animals. The people also moved to temporary winter camps, close to fuel (wood) supplies, but for the most part Hidatsa household units lived together in the permanent village, with each extended family residing in their own earth lodge.

HIDATSA TASK DIFFERENTIATION

The attempt to reanalyze the ethnographic data on the Hidatsa presented by Bowers and Wilson in terms of gender behavior, started with the identification of tasks performed by males and females. Operationally, a task has been defined here as a segment of activity which has discrete parameters in terms of the social unit of task performance, that is, the segment of the population engaged in the task; the season, frequency and duration of the task; the location of task performance; and the material--artifacts, structures and facilities--associated with the execution of the task. The following table illustrates how information was organized within the framework for the analysis of activities involved in the procurement and processing of horticultural products (cultigens).

Unfortunately, given the limitations of the Bowers and Wilson reports, it was not possible to establish a complete task inventory for the mid-19th century Hidatsa. Some activities--the procurement and processing of cultigens, lodge construction, buffalo procurement and processing--are described in considerable detail. Other activities, including small game hunting, warfare, ceremonies, childrearing, trading, to name but a few, are activities alluded to in the ethnographies but poorly described for purposes of this research. Even when particular tasks involved in activities could be defined, details on task organization, timing, locations and materials were not specific enough to permit full employment of the task differentiation framework. Nonetheless the focus on male and female activity patterns did offer new perspectives on the Hidatsa obscured in the reports of Bowers and Wilson.

The most striking feature of Hidatsa task differentiation is the contrast between the activity patterns of the men and women. With the exception of actually killing animals, Hidatsa women procured and processed all food resources. From what can be abstracted from the ethnographic accounts, the women also collected and processed other natural resources utilized by the group--wood, water, wild plants, herbs, bark and reeds. Female work groups similarly performed the tasks associated with processing buffalo and other animal skins, and constructing and maintaining structures (e.g. earth lodges, temporary

82

TASKS ASSOCIATED WITH THE PROCUREMENT AND PROCESSING OF CULTIGENS

Task	Social Unit	Task Setting	Task Time	Task Materials
Garden Clearing	Women of lodge; occasionally assisted by elderly men	Gardens (3/4 mile from summer village)	Spring-Fall	hoes, rakes, digging sticks
Planting	Women of lodge; assistance from related women from other lodges	Gardens (3/4 mile from summer village)	mornings; Spring-early summer	hoes, rakes, wooden bowls
Weeding	Women of lodge; occasionally assisted by elderly men	Gardens (3/4 mile from summer village)	Early summer	hoes, rakes
Crop Protection	Young girls of lodge, usually two	Gardens (3/4 mile from summer village)	daily/all day; late summer - harvest in fall	scarecrows, watching stage, ladder, associated cook hut and cooking equipment

Task	Social Unit	Task Setting	Task Time	Task Materials
Corn Harvesting	Women of lodge; young men assist in transport of crop to village	Gardens (3/4 mile from summer village)	August – September	Baskets, horses and gear for transportation
Corn Husking	2-3 women of lodge with assistance of young men	Gardens (3/4 mile from summer village)	September	?
Corn Shelling	Women of lodge	Threshing booth- lodge exterior	September	Threshing booth, flail stick, mussel shells
Corn cob burning	1 or 2 women of the lodge	Periphery of village	daily; after day's threshing; September	baskets; skin wrappers
Corn Storage	Women of lodge; often mother daughter	lodge interior/ lodge exterior	September – November	cache pit, skins
Corn Grinding	1-2 women of the lodge	lodge interior	daily; year round	corn mortar

Task	Social Unit	Task Setting	Task Timing	Task Materials
Corn Cooking	1-2 women of the lodge	lodge interior	daily; year round	clay pot, wooden stirring spoons, paddles, wooden bowls, horn spoons, sticks, corn mortar, hearth
Bean Harvesting		NO INFORMATION		
Bean Threshing	1-2 women of the lodge	garden	Fall	tent cover (skin), stick, basket or wooden bowl
Bean Storage	1-2 women of the lodge	lodge exterior	Fall	cache pit, skin bag
Bean Cooking	1-2 women of the lodge	lodge interior	daily; year round	central hearth and cooking equipment (see corn cooking)
Squash Harvesting	1-2 women of the lodge	garden	Fall	baskets

Task	Social Unit	Task Setting	Task Timing	Task Material
Squash Drying (includes picking, slicing, stringing, drying)	Women of lodge and "hired" old women of village assisted by young males	lodge interior/ lodge exterior	one month; fall	baskets, squash knife, spits, skin robes, wooden needle, drying stage (lodge exterior), squash rack (lodge exterior) drying stage (lodge interior)
Squash Storage	1-2 women of the lodge	lodge interior/ lodge exterior	Fall	Old tent cover or skin; cache pits (with corn)
Squash Cooking	1-2 women of the lodge	lodge interior	daily; year round	clay pots, wooden paddles, wooden bowl, hearth
Sunflower Harvesting	Probably women of the lodge	garden	?Fall	?
Sunflower Threshing	1-2 women of the lodge	lodge roof/ lodge exterior	late fall	baskets, knife, skins, stick

86

Task	Social Unit	Task Setting	Task Timing	Task Materials
Sunflower Parching	1-2 women of the lodge	lodge interior	late fall	clay pot, stick horn spoon, wooden bowl
Sunflower Storage	1-2 women of the lodge	lodge interior	late fall	skin bags
Sunflower Grinding	1 woman of the lodge	lodge interior	late fall	corn mortar
Sunflower Cooking	1-2 women of the lodge	lodge interior	daily; year round	clay pot, wooden paddle, wooden bowl, central hearth
Processing Gourds		NO INFORMATION		
Clear Tobacco Gardens	older males	tobacco garden	early spring	hoe, rake and/or buffalo rib
Tobacco Planting	1-2 men	tobacco garden	spring	buffalo rib

Task	Social Unit	Task Setting	Task Timing	Task Materials
Weeding Tobacco Garden	1-2 men	tobacco garden	May – June	buffalo rib
Harvesting Tobacco	1-2 men; girls of lodge might assist old men	tobacco garden	June-August: blossoms; Sept.-Nov.: plants	bark and scrotum (buffalo) baskets
Tobacco Drying	1 man	blossoms: lodge interior (near lodge shrine); plants: lodge interior near cache pits	June-August: blossoms; Sept.-Nov.: plants	hides, plank, spit
Tobacco Storage	1 man	lodge interior	September-November	cache pit or skin package

dwellings, specialized activity structures) facilities (e.g. drying racks, storage racks, cache pits) and household furnishings. The only male participation reported for resource procurement and processing or in the construction and maintenance of structures and facilities was some occasional assistance in the gardens of elderly men; some male assistance in transporting harvested crops from gardens to the village; the killing and butchering of meat; the procurement and processing of tobacco; and the erection of the four main poles in earth lodges. The men appear to have been engaged for the most part preparing for hunts and raids, preparations which involved long hours of discussion, days of fasting, vision quests and self-torture.

In addition to distinctions in the kinds of tasks performed consideration of parameters of task differentiation highlights other differences between the sexes. Women of individual households--sisters, mothers and daughters--constituted the major unit of female labor, with most tasks performed by one to three women of an earth lodge. Male activities, in contrast, do not appear to have followed this household pattern. Male task groups tended to be larger than female groups and involved members of several households with labor commonly divided by age. On summer buffalo hunts, for example, younger men performed tasks concerned with scouting for buffalo and tending horses. Older men participated in planning and ritual acts associated with the hunt. The men of other age groups engaged in activities like policing the hunting camps or actually killing and butchering the animals.

Task settings, like task organization, were significantly different for Hidatsa men and women. Women's activities took place primarily in gardens, located within a mile of the permanent village, lodge interiors and the areas immediately adjacent to their lodges. Though men spent some time inside the lodges visiting with other men or planning hunts and raids, many more of their activities took them outside the boundaries of the villages or temporary camps. This pattern can again be illustrated in the example of the summer hunt. Both males and females of various households travelled great distances from the permanent village in search of buffalo herds. Once they located the animals the men generally stayed outside of the camps killing and butchering buffalo, while the women remained at the camps processing meat and hides inside or near the lodges or tipis.

The temporal dimensions of men's and women's lives also differed. Though the details of timing in terms of task frequency and duration are poorly documented in the ethnographies, it appears that men had few activities scheduled on a daily basis. Groups of men are reported to have spent days at a time away from the villages on raiding expeditions, stopping along the way to hunt and perform rituals with few indications of time constraints. In contrast, Hidatsa women had a number of tasks at any time of the year scheduled on a daily basis. Garden work, resource processing like cooking or manufacturing implements, all seem to have been rather tightly scheduled each day. Women's activities also appear to have been more closely tied to seasonality than men's in part a function of the time defining characteristics of horticultural work.

The material dimension of Hidatsa task differentiation, like temporal features, was difficult to abstract from the accounts of Bowers and Wilson. Wood and animal skins were the primary raw materials used in the manufacture of structures, facilities, clothing and artifacts. Responsibility for collecting wood and processing hides was with the women. Given the greater number and variety of tasks performed by the women, it seems likely that they utilized more materials and a wider range of materials than the men did. They do appear to have been engaged in the production of more material goods than men.

IMPLICATIONS OF THE TASK DIFFERENTIATION APPROACH

There is certainly much more to know about Hidatsa task differentiation than was possible working with the published reports of Wilson and Bowers. The value of the reanalysis of their data in terms of the framework was that it permitted a clearer understanding of the implications of the approach for future research on gender.

The potential of the approach is perhaps best illustrated by describing how the framework might be used to structure research in the field where a group could be observed directly. A primary value of reanalyzing the Hidatsa data was that it helped to specify the kinds of information crucial to the full employment of the framework. The initial step in such a study would be to determine the full range of tasks engaged in by the population and the organizational, spatial, temporal and material characteristics of each task. Once these basic descriptive data are collected, the analysis could move to a higher level of abstraction emphasizing the sets of relationships between tasks and the dimensions of task differentiation. This step of the research can be envisioned as the construction of a series of activity maps wherein the investigator would essentially map out or graphically represent the types of tasks taking place at any given time.

One series of activity maps should focus on task organization, highlighting the spatial and temporal relationships between task actors. We know that among the Hidatsa, small groups of women from each household performed a series of horticultural tasks on a daily basis. In mapping these tasks it would be important to determine how each work unit was related to other work units. One picture might be that each female task unit worked in their gardens at the same time as other housheold units, implying some kind of temporal coordination of women through scheduling. If the gardens were located in close proximity, the actors would also be connected in a spatial sense. If the task actors are spatially and temporally linked in this way, they have the potential of interactions precluded in a system where the task units are separated either spatially or temporally. For any one task identified for a community, there are various time and space relationships possible between the work units. The units may be working independent of other units performing the same task; they may be linked through scheduling but separated spatially; or they may be performing their tasks at the same time and in locations close enough to permit social interaction. Each variant of the time/space organization of task actors suggests different kinds of relationships between members of the community.

A second kind of activity mapping should highlight the temporal dimension of task organization. By plotting out the range of tasks engaged in by a popu-

91

lation at any given time period (time of the day,
week, season etc.) we would have another means of
studying the relationships between particular tasks
and task actors. When Hidatsa women were in their
gardens, for example, it would be important to see
what tasks were being performed by other women and men
near the gardens or in settings distant from the gardens. A series of time specific maps would illustrate
the scheduling system for the group as a whole; the
distribution of the population geographically at
various times; and indicate some of the equipment
demands of the task system. If many tasks are scheduled concurrently and take place in settings
separated by considerable distances, a higher demand
for equipment would exist for the group as a whole
than would be the case if tasks were scheduled sequen-
tially or if they were performed in close proximity
permitting the sharing of equipment and facilities.

A third type of activity mapping could focus
directly on the spatial dimensions of task differentiation. In addition to identifying the locations of
each task performed, it would be useful to distinguish
those spaces used for many tasks, i.e. multi-purpose
settings, from those locations which are more task
specialized. The interiors of earth lodges among the
Hidatsa were dense with activity as many different
female tasks took place in that setting. We might
expect that lodge size and the arrangement of artifacts and facilities in the lodges would be different
if they were used for a smaller number or another set
of activities. The spatial maps would also allow the
graphic representation of proximic relations between
men and women performing different tasks at the same
time, permitting the detection of regularities in such
relationships. Finally the focus on the spatial
dimension of task differentiation might draw attention
to possible distinguishing characteristics of spaces
used primarily by women compared to spaces used primarily by men. Among the Hidatsa, the only hint of
such gender distinctions is the fact that the settings
utilized primarily by females tend to be characterized
by a greater number of stationary facilities--drying
racks, storage racks and pits, wooden mortars and so
on--than the spaces used primarily by men.

A final set of activity maps constructed to
define relationships between task differentiation
parameters could focus on the material dimensions of

92

tasks. In the study of the Hidatsa it was sometimes possible to define the material unit of different tasks--those artifacts, facilities and structures associated with the tasks--but the material linkages between task actors could not be determined. In graphically representing these relationships the emphasis would be on the way materials were used during task performance, that is, whether actors shared the materials necessary for executing the task or if each actor was essentially materially autonomous, possessing their own set of necessary equipment. The sharing of equipment suggests very different kinds of spatial and temporal relationships between actors than the kind of time and space flexibility permitted if each individual has his or her own set of equipment.

The notion of activity mapping has been used to illustrate some of the possible relationships between task parameters of particular interest to the ethnoarcheologist interested in the study of gender. The manner in which actors use materials, combined with the organizational, scheduling and locational aspects of task performance all presumably structure the material demands and characteristics of the task system. These equipment demands in turn affect the frequency and duration of resource procurement tasks necessary to supply raw materials for the manufacture of that equipment. It is doubtful that the specific regularities in these kinds of relationships can be systematically examined through analysis of existing ethnographic information. It may well be necessary to conduct ethnographic field studies, like Binford, Longacre and other ethnoarcheologists, before the task differentiation framework can be adapted for application to archeological assemblages. We still need to know much more about the specific relationships between gender behavior as seen through task differentiation patterns and activity settings.

Though the archeological application of the framework must await further research, the reanalysis of Hidatsa data did demonstrate the potential of the approach for purposes of studying possible relationships between gender and culture change. In spite of limitations of the ethnographies, it can be established that the lives of Hidatsa men and women during the mid-19th century were impressively separate and distinct. The males and females participated in different, often unrelated tasks; they utilized different geographical spaces; the tempo of their lives was different; and the volume and kinds of materials produced and used by each sex was different. This kind of sexual segregation or gender autonomy was not indicated by either Bowers or Wilson, yet it seems a crucially important aspect of Hidatsa life.

First, the distinctiveness of male and female activity patterns among the Hidatsa (and other sexually segregated groups) suggests that generalizations about the "culture" of the group must be made with great caution. The importance of households, clans, age grades or other conventionally used ethnographic constructs may differ significantly in reference to men and women in groups with this type of task differentiation system. Among the Hidatsa the household does seem to be an important social unit if the analysis centers on the lives and activities of women. It seems less appropriate for describing men's activities which are typically organized in a manner cross-cutting household units. Even generalizations about seasonal patterns or life cycle in a system like the Hidatsa must be made separately for the men and women prior to generalizations about the group as a whole.

The task differentiation framework also exposed some of the dangers involved in the assessment of relative status between men and women, a subject of considerable interest in recent years to a number of anthropologists (see Rosaldo and Lamphere 1974). Many researchers have pointed out the problems of androcentrism in studying status differences where the assumption is made that what men do is of greater importance than what women do. Bowers is certainly guilty of this kind of bias. In describing the social organization of the Hidatsa, for example, Bowers emphasizes the importance of councils and leadership, cultural domains dominated by the men. It appears that the women did not participate in planning hunts or in raiding, activities centrally important to the men and routinely discussed in council meetings of older, prominent men. It was in the context of hunts and warfare that male leadership among the Hidatsa is most conspicuously important. However, in working with Wilson's data it becomes equally apparent that the men were excluded from participation in female activities, particularly resource procurement and processing, or the construction of structures, facilities, and material goods all centrally important to the lives of the women and to the survival of the group.

In a sexually segregated task system like the Hidatsa, both males and females have access to information, knowledge and materials unavailable to the opposite sex. Though the data are not altogether clear, it appears that decision-making was also sexually segregated among the Hidatsa with women in control of their spheres of activity and men involved in decision-making about male activities. It becomes problematic to determine the relative status of men and women in this type of system without arbitrarily attaching more importance to the experience and activities of males, as Bowers did, or females. A more fruitful and interesting focus of analysis may well be the examination of the specific bonds between males and females when they seem most systematically linked to members of their own sex.

In addition to demonstrating the dangers of generalizing about groups as a whole and illustrating the potential of a framework which permits the analytical separation of the sexes for a better understanding of gender behavior, the task differentiation approach also offers new perspectives on the subjects of adaptation, change and stability patterns through time--one of the central concerns inspiring the research. In reanalyzing the ethnographic data in terms of this framework it became clear that the introduction of new items of technology, contact with new groups, population fluctuations and other changes in the social or natural environment are all factors which would have differentially affected Hidatsa men and women. Though it was not possible to fully employ the framework, with more precise information about a group, it should be possible to trace the specific impacts of any single change factor throughout the task differentiation system and eventually to compare the impact of the same kind of change factor on groups with different task systems. One might suggest that changes which draw off male or female labor in a sexually segregated task system like the Hidatsa would affect the group quite differently than in a system where men and women work together in performing tasks. Similarly, changes which affect task scheduling, materials or settings will all have varying effects on a group and on the male and female actors within the group depending on the task system operating.

CONCLUSIONS

This study was stimulated by the desire to bring together the concerns and perspectives of feminist anthropology and contemporary archeology, potentially adding an important time dimension to the study of gender and society. Research began by examining some of the possible relationships between the material and non-material aspects of gender behavior in an ethnographically documented cultural setting, a basic step toward enhancing our abilities to interpret archeological assemblages more reliably. For purposes of reanalyzing selected ethnographic data on the Hidatsa Indians a new framework, male/female task differentiation, was developed. This framework highlights distinctive features of male and female activity patterns, focusing particularly on tasks and their organizational, temporal, spatial, and material dimensions, all aspects of behavior theoretically observable in the archeological record.

The research on task differentiation is still in its preliminary stages. The analysis of the Hidatsa, handicapped in some ways by limitations of the ethnograpic reports, did permit refinement of the approach and illustrated the potential of the framework for archeology and ethnography. For the Hidatsa specifically, implementation of the framework exposed a number of important contrasts in the lives of men and women. Though a complete description of Hidatsa task differentiation was not possible, the analysis demonstrates that generalizations about Hidatsa culture must be made with great caution, clearly distinguishing the lives and experiences of men and women. The analysis further suggests that Hidatsa men and women undoubtedly responded differently to conditions of change brought about by contact with Euro-Americans during the latter part of the 19th century.

The next steps toward testing the utility and promise of the approach are to increase the sample of groups analyzed, particularly through implementation of the framework in a field setting where collection

96

of data can be carefully controlled. Through expansion of the ethnographic sample we can begin to define regularities and variability in task differentiation patterns. Equipped with better understanding of this aspect of gender behavior, we can eventually transform the framework for archeological purposes, adding new dimensions to the study of fundamental cultural processes of adaptation, change and stability.

REFERENCES CITED

Binford, Lewis   (1975)   Historical Archeology: Is it
     Historical or Archeological? <u>Popular</u>
     <u>Archaeology</u>, Volume 4, Number 3-4, pp. 11-30.

Bowers, Alfred   (1965)   Hidatsa Social and Ceremonial
     Organization. Smithsonian Institution. <u>Bureau</u>
     <u>of American Ethnology Bulletin</u>, 194.

David, Nicholas   (1971)   The Fulani Compound and the
     Archaeologist. <u>World Archaeology</u> 3:111-131.

Deetz, James   (1972)   Archaeology as a Social Science.
     In: <u>Contemporary Archeology: A Guide to Theory</u>
     <u>and Contributions</u>, Mark P. Leone, ed., pp.
     108-117.

Leacock, Eleanor   (1978)   Women's Status in Egali-
     tarian Society: Implications for Social
     Evolution. <u>Current Anthropology</u>, Volume 19,
     Number 2, pp. 247-275.

Longacre, William (1977)   Personal communication.

Noble, Barbara   (1978)   <u>Sexual Politics and</u>
     <u>Theorizing: An Example from Anthropology</u>.
     Mimeographed, Department of Anthropology,
     University of Minnesota.

Reiter, Rayna, ed.   (1975)   <u>Toward an Anthropology</u>
     <u>of Women</u>. Monthly Review Press.

Rosaldo, Michelle, and Louise Lamphere, eds.   (1974)
     <u>Woman, Culture and Society</u>. Stanford University
     Press.

Schiffer, Michael   (1976)   <u>Behavioral Archeology</u>.
     Academic Press.

_____   (1977)   A Preliminary Consideration of
     Behavioral Change. To appear in: <u>Trans-</u>
     <u>formations: Mathematical Approaches to Culture</u>
     <u>Change</u>, Colin Renfrew and Kenneth Cooke, eds.
     Academic Press.

Spencer, Robert F., and Jesse D. Jennings (1965)
The Native Americans: Prehistory and Ethnology
of the North American Indians. New York:
Harper and Row.

Wilson, Gilbert   (1917)   Agriculture of the Hidatsa
Indians: An Indian Interpretation. Studies in
the Social Sciences, No. 9. University of
Minnesota.

_____   (1934)   The Hidatsa Earthlodge.   Anthropological Papers, Vol. XXXIII, Part V.   The Museum
of Natural History.

_____   (1971)   Waheenee: An Indian Girl's Story
Told by Herself to Gilbert L. Wilson.   Reprinted
in: North Dakota History, Vol. 38, Nos. 1 and 2.

Yellen, John   (1977)   Archaeological Approaches to the
Present.   Academic Press.

CHAPTER 5

WOMEN'S WORK: AN EXAMINATION OF WOMEN'S ROLES IN PLAINS INDIAN ARTS AND CRAFTS

Mary Jane Schneider
University of North Dakota

INTRODUCTION

The excellence of Plains Indian arts and crafts has long been recognized. Artists such as Bodmer, Catlin and Miller were entranced by the beautifully tanned robes decorated with painted designs or quillwork, and the elaborately decorated shirts worn by leading men of the villages they visited. These early explorers commented on the fine quillwork and collected examples to be exhibited in cities of the eastern United States and Europe. Despite this interest in, and early recognition of, Plains arts and crafts, there has been a general lack of interest in the role of the artist and artisan (Schneider 1976) in Plains Indian society. This is especially true about the role of women as artists.

There is a considerable amount of information concerning processes used in making and decorating items, but the details are often lacking. For many tribes, details will be given for one manufacturing process, such as tanning, and the production of other items such as bowls, spoons, and rawhide containers will be mentioned only in passing or not at all. In addition to the lack of information regarding the arts and crafts of a specific group, the data that are given frequently are presented in such a way that it is impossible to determine whether the items were made or used by men or women. The effect of this lack of detailed information has been to create a picture of the role of women in Plains Indian art that is not all together accurate.

101

Two common ideas about Plains Indian women are
(1) that the women were drudges, no better than slaves,
who worked night and day to provide for their family's
needs and (2) that women produced secular and mundane
objects while men made and decorated items of social
and ritual importance.

The idea that Indian women were drudges has been
around a long time. In his description of Mandan
culture, Maximilian (Wied-Neuwied 1906:281) noted that
"The women have nothing to indemnify them for their
incessant and laborious work, not even good clothing,
for this right of the fair sex in Europe, is claimed
among the Indians by the men. It is singular that
these women, who are condemned constantly to work like
slaves, refuse to do any work whatever if they marry a
white man." This paper will show that there was
something to be gained from hard work, specifically
wealth and prestige.

The second idea is not entirely distinct from the
first, but naturally develops out of the idea of women
as drudges. If women are cast in the role of slaves,
then they cannot possibly have anything to do with the
important social and religious aspects of tribal life.
This view has been most recently expressed by Ted
Brasser (1972:57) in a paper describing Plains Indian
art.

> As with most tribal peoples, there was a
> definite division of craftwork by sex.
> Women prepared skins and made clothing,
> tipi-covers, and rawhide containers. They
> carried out all quillwork and beadwork,
> silk embroidery and conventional geometric
> painting. Men, on the other hand, produced
> equipment for the hunt, war and ceremonial
> activities. They carved wooden bowls, horn
> spoons and stone pipes, they painted
> realistic and symbolic pictures on tipi
> covers, tipi-linings, robes and shields.

It is the contention of this paper that this view
is not only an over-simplification, but that it represents a Euro-American view of women's work which is
contradicted by the facts.

The Euro-American idea that art is produced by a
uniquely gifted individual, almost always male and

102

almost always after "suffering," has thoroughly biased the collection and presentation of information regarding the production of arts and crafts by Native Americans. We have failed to recognize that art objects may be started by one person and finished by another, that objects may be made and decorated by one person for the use of another, or that several people working together may make an item. In addition, the early anthropologists often neglected to find out who made certain items and assumed that they were the work of one sex on the basis of their knowledge of which sex would have done the work in Anglo culture. For example wood carving is, among Euro-Americans, a male-oriented craft. The assumption, then, is made and repeated, as in the citation above, that wooden bowls were made by Native American men. This may be true for some Native American societies, but was not true for all. Among the Pawnee (Weltfish 1965:464-465), wooden bowls were carved by women who were specialists in the art. Blackfeet women (Ewers 1958:121), Assiniboine women (Lowie 1909:12), Cheyenne women (Grinnell 1972:212), and Hidatsa women (Wilson 1909:155) also made bowls, as did men in these societies. Of the Plains tribes for which this information is available, only among the Omaha (Fletcher and LaFlesche 1972:338) was wood carving a specifically male craft.

Another example will suffice to demonstrate that this is not a single instance, but part of a recurring pattern in the description of Plains arts and crafts. The making of horn spoons and ladles has been cited as a man's craft. Yet Cheyenne (Grinnell 1972:212) and Pawnee (Weltfish 1965:465) women made the horn spoons for their people, while both men and women (Wissler 1910:30; Ewers 1958:121) made them for the Blackfeet.

The remainder of this paper will examine the division of labor in detail and then demonstrate how the work of women was valued and how it contributed to the wealth and prestige of the woman and her family. The information used in the paper is drawn from the standard ethnographies of the Plains Indians, but extreme care has been taken to include only those instances where the information clearly and precisely indicates the sex of the maker and/or user of the item. This caution has excluded many of the classic descriptions because they are too ambiguous.

DIVISION OF LABOR

The tasks assigned to men and women by the society in which they live seem to fall into two different kinds. There are those differentiations that arise because of basic differences in biology, for example, since women are child-bearers they most often are also child rearers, and differentiations which seem to develop without reason. These tasks are the ones which may be done by men in one society and by women in another, because either sex could do them equally well. It should be obvious that there is a danger in assuming that because a job is done by women in one society, that it is the work of women in all societies. There is also a danger in assuming that because a task is normally done by women, that it is always done by women or vice versa. The division of labor in Plains Indians societies was not hard and fast, but depended upon a number of variables. In all the crafts performed by Plains Indians we find a number of different variables operating to blur the division of labor.

Industrial Arts

Hides of buffalo, deer, elk and other animals were the mainstay of Plains Indian arts and crafts. They formed the base for clothing, tipis, containers, ropes and many other objects. Immediately after butchering, the hide was scraped down to remove the flesh and fat. If rawhide was needed the subsequent treatment depended upon the item to be made. Women made parfleches and containers for sacred objects from rawhide, while men used rawhide to make drums, shields and other items. Rawhide rope was another necessity for Plains peoples. Women and men both made rawhide rope among the Blackfeet (Ewers 1955:73) although most often it was made by the women. Mandelbaum notes (1940:22) that among the Plains Cree "women prepared the thongs, but men did the plaiting." Men made rawhide rope among Oglala (Standing Bear 1928:78).

Tanning hides was also done by both men and women, with the deciding factor being the animal from which the hide was taken and the degree of skill required to tan the skin. Women were always responsible for tanning white buffalo hides, bear, beaver, wolf and coyote hides. Some of these restrictions

104

could be removed by special ceremonies, while it was necessary for men or captive women to do the work in other situations. Among the Pawnee (Weltfish 1965: 456) bear, beaver and fox skins were prepared by men for their own use. A similar situation seems to have existed among the Assiniboine for Denig (1930:541) notes "Wolf, bear, fox, rabbit, beaver, hare, ermine, lynx, otter, rat, mink, etc. are not dressed for market and all these are skinned, stretched and dried by the men and boys." Cheyenne women (Grinnell 1972: 198) "Believed that if they should dress a bearskin the soles of their feet would crack, and hair would grow over their faces." And Assiniboine women (Lowie 1909:56) "refused to dress a wolf skin at any price."

Special importance and ceremonies were attached to the tanning of a white buffalo hide. Among the Assiniboine (Lowie 1909:52) the tanning was done by the wives of chiefs. Elaborate ceremonies were held by the Cheyenne (Grinnell 1972:200-204) and Dakota (Fletcher 1884:260-275) in which the white buffalo hide was tanned and consecrated. Among the Cheyenne, the woman called upon to tan the hide was a middle-aged or old woman who had spiritual power and was known to be a good tanner. This woman had to be prayed over and absolved from the taboos before she could dress the hide (Grinnell 1972:273). Among the Dakota, the tanner had to be a virgin.

In addition to the special circumstances surrounding certain animal hides, there is also a difference between tanning buffalo and tanning elk, deer and antelope hides. The latter hides are thinner than buffalo and require different tools and techniques. Grinnell (1972:217) says

> The Cheyenne women were good tanners of
> buffalo skins, and many of them tanned
> deerskin well. When tanning the skins of
> deer or antelope, or of mountain sheep,
> the most skillful were careful not to break
> into the epidermis when they removed the
> hair. In this way their deerskins had a
> smooth, even surface. A deerskin that was
> very thick might be thinned down, and so
> made rough, on both sides. Such a skin
> would be used for the uppers of a moccasin,
> but not for leggings, shirts, or tobacco
> pouches.

Wissler (1910:69) gives details for this process among the Blackfeet, pointing out that different tools were used to tan deerskins, and implies that the work was done by women. Weltfish's sources (1965:451, 452), however, claimed that Pawnee men did all the tanning of deer and elkskins.

Even the making of clothing was not solely the responsibility of women. When men were away from camp on a long trip they took the necessary materials and tools to make and repair their own moccasins. Among the Pawnee (Weltfish 1965:455-456), shirts were worn by only a few of the highest ranking men. These shirts were made by a limited number of men who received a pony for their work. The materials were supplied by the man (courtesy of his wife?) who was purchasing the shirt. The quillwork down the front was done by the wife of the shirt-maker. A similar situation existed among the Oglala (Wissler 1912:39) where shirts were made by old men. Also among the Oglala, whenever quillwork was needed on ritual regalia, four virgins were called to do the work. The materials to make the regalia were collected from women of the camp before the beginning of the dance in which the items were to be used.

Women also were involved in making ritual regalia. Among the Crow, preparations for the Sun Dance involved both men and women in the making of ritual paraphernalia (Lowie 1915:19-22). When the possessor of a Sun Dance Doll had agreed to participate in the ceremony on behalf of the vower or "whistler," he asked his wife to procure a tanned deerskin. This hide was taken to a virtuous woman who carried it to the doll owner's lodge where it was blessed and cut up. The virtuous woman then sewed a kilt for the vower from the hide. The doll owner's wife likewise produced a buffalo robe that had never been worn and moccasins were made for the vower by the wife of a man who had killed and scalped an enemy.

Although there is more information regarding hide working than there is for other industries, there are some other crafts for which information concerning variability in the division of labor is available. The making of wooden bowls has been discussed above. Wooden mortars and pestles show a similar difference in production. Among the Pawnee, women made all the wood objects they used, including mortars, whereas the manufacture of wooden objects was done by the men among the Omaha. A little more information is available about saddle-making. Blackfeet women were saddle-makers (Ewers 1955:81), as were Kiowa women (Mishkin 1940:45). In both instances there was a certain amount of specialization involved. Pawnee men made the saddles used by their people, while among the Cheyenne (Grinnell 1972:206) saddle-making was a cooperative process in which the horn foundations were made by the men and the coverings put on by the women.

Although pottery making, basketry and weaving were almost exclusively women's crafts, often involving specialization, there were some variations to this pattern. Lowie (1909:12) notes that Assiniboine men claimed to have made and used pottery. Mat weaving was done by both men and women among the Mandan-Hidatsa (Wilson 1910:133) and, according to Bowers (1965:165), men helped make pottery among the Hidatsa. Pawnee men made their own saddle bags from old buffalo hides which they got from the women (Weltfish 1965:452).

Unlike the production of arts and crafts in contemporary American society, women often cooperated in the production of household items. This cooperation eased the work-load of the individual woman and provided a social atmosphere as well.

A group of women were seated on the ground, sewing a large tipi covering which was spread out before them. They seemed to be thoroughly enjoying themselves, gossiping, smoking, and eating while at their work, much after the fashion of the neighborly quilting bees of our grandmothers (McClintock 1910:232).

Decorative Arts

In addition to the productive work of women, they were also concerned with decorative work, especially quillworking and painting. It is hard to maintain that men made items used in ceremonial activities, when women did the hide tanning and decorating. Decorating, in fact, often turns out to be a cooperative task, with men and women doing different processes. Several Arapaho women (Kroeber 1902-07:122) might paint a parfleche at the same time so that the hide would not have to be turned and the work would be done before the hide became too dry. Luther Standing Bear (1928:16) tells us that among his people men painted the designs on the rawhide containers made by women to hold sacred objects. Similarly the Pawnee used rawhide bags for transporting buffalo meat. These bags were decorated with cosmic designs which could only be painted by a person with the necessary religious qualifications. Unfortunately, Weltfish (1965:260) doesn't tell us whether this person was male or female or whether it mattered. Even the painting of designs on tipi-covers was a cooperative effort. For example, among the Omaha (Fletcher and LaFlesche 1972:353-354)

> Men outlined designs on their tent covers.
> These represented symbolically their visions
> and so were more than a mere decoration, as
> they implied an invocation in behalf of the
> household. In the putting on of the color
> a man's wife or children might assist.

And McClintock (1936:21) makes a similar comment about Blackfeet tipi designs.

> The wife was skilled in the making of tipis
> and was known also as a good decorator. She
> painted pictures of both war and hunting on
> the tipi-cover illustrating adventures in
> the life of her husband; figures of men and
> animals and Indian camps, in red, yellow,
> and blue; pictures of fights with hostile
> Indians, marking the camps and places where
> they took place.

Mandelbaum (1940:211, 286) notes that "since the women of the household owned the tipi cover, her approval of the design had to be secured before it could be painted."

Even the classic distinction between design types --women use geometric and men use representational-- has its variations.

Gilbert L. Wilson (1909:133) collected a dress made by White Bear Woman and decorated by her husband Red White Buffalo with pictures and symbols representing his war honors and Kroeber (1908:196) collected a pair of moccasins from the Gros Ventre which had been beaded and decorated by a woman, but were designed by an old man and symbolized his war exploits. Howard (1965:80) says:

> Representative artwork was usually done by
> men. Realistic designs of horses, bison,
> and dancing men were painted on tipi covers,
> shields and robes. If, as often happened,
> a woman wished to use a representative
> design in her beadwork, she would ask a
> male relative to sketch it for her, then
> follow his sketch in her beading.

These examples should suffice to indicate that the division of labor between men and women was neither so definite nor so hard and fast as we have been led to believe. To be sure, men and women did different things, all of which were vital to their survival, but to generalize from one society to another is not safe. Women made items which we have been accustomed to believe were made by men. Women were involved in the production of sacred and ritual objects, while men were able to perform every day tasks frequently considered to be women's work.

STATUS AND PRESTIGE

The second point made by this paper is that the contributions of women were recognized by the Plains peoples, even though they have not been so recognized by anthropologists and art historians. Excellence in craftwork brought prestige and wealth to the woman and to her family.

There was no way a girl could grow up without knowing what was expected of her in the way of craftsmanship. An old Omaha man (Fletcher and LaFlesche 1972:333) recounted how old men would talk to young girls and point out their duties to them.

> If you are a thrifty woman, your husband
> will struggle hard to bring you the best
> of materials for your tent and clothing and
> the best of tools. If you have a good tent,

men and women will desire to enter it. They will be glad to talk with you and your husband.

If you are willing to remain in ignorance and not learn how to do the things a woman should know how to do, you will ask other women to cut your moccasins and fit them for you. You will go from bad to worse; you will leave your people, go into a strange tribe, fall into trouble, and die there friendless.

The ideal woman was one who "was virtuous, expert at feminine tasks, and physically attractive (Lowie 1956: 59). "Girls began early to learn the skills necessary to becoming a good wife and virtuous woman. Girls who could quill and bead, who knew how to prepare hides, and who were good cooks were recognized as potentially good wives ... Such a girl would attract fine young men of the best families, who would bring many gifts and horses as her bride-price; she would bestow honor on her family" (Hassrick 1964:42). Virtue was not unconnected to skills. "My mother would always tell me that the main purpose of her teaching me, as well as the object of my owning my own bed, was to keep me at home, and to keep me from being away to spend my nights with my girl chum. This was done so that there would be no chance for gossip by other people" (Michelson 1932:2). The girl who tended to her quilling was too busy to get into trouble with men and would make a good marriage.

Among the Plains Cree (Mandelbaum 1940:244) and Teton (Hassrick 1964:41-42) when a girl had her first menses she was secluded in a tent away from the camp. During this time she was required to spend four days practicing quilling and hide tanning. This would insure that she would be an industrious woman.

When a girl reached marriage age and had demon-strated that she had the necessary skills and virtues to make a good wife, her hand would be sought by the parents or relatives of some man. Marriage was by bride-price or gift exchange between families. These gifts not only indicated the ability of the man to support the woman, but reflected the esteem in which the girl was held. Weltfish (1965:22) notes that one of her informants remarked with pride that six horses had been given for her.

Although each woman was expected to be familiar and expert in the industrial arts such as tanning hides, etc., many of the arts were done by specialists. Specialization occurred in a number of different ways. Women who were especially talented in some decorative art would be asked to make things by women who were not so talented. This transaction would be accompanied by an exchange of gifts or produce. Most Plains Indian groups had some sort of specialized arts that were known only to a few. These varied from group to group. Tipi-making was universally a specialty. Among the Pawnee, buffalo hair rope making, mortar and pestle making, wooden bowl making and gambling basket making were all specialized crafts. Among the Omaha only a few women knew how to braid buffalo hair lariats. Basketry and pottery were specialized crafts among the Mandan and Hidatsa, while mat making could be done by anyone but was, in fact, limited to a few individuals because of the difficulty of the process.

Specialization was maintained in two ways: through the regulation on the part of the teachers who were selective in the number of people they taught (Weltfish 1965:443-444) and through rituals which were required to do the work without peril. A woman not only had to indicate a deep desire to learn one of the specialized crafts, but the teacher had to be persuaded that she was deserving of being taught. A woman who was poor might ask to be taught a craft in order to increase her ability to earn and so raise the family's status.

> Such a woman was the wife of Chief's-Road. Giving the old lady a gift she said, "I want you to take pity on me and teach me to make a buffalo hair belt. You know that I am poor and we can't seem to work out anything. What I want is for you to take pity on me so that it may earn something for us. My husband can't make much and my sister can't do anything (Weltfish 1965:443).

If the teacher judged that there was sufficient need in the village to provide work for another person, she would agree to demonstrate the techniques to the learner. After the teacher was certain that the novice was sufficiently skilled in the craft she would send customers to her and the novice would be in business on her own. Teachers were always paid for teaching their knowledge.

Secrecy was also maintained in order to protect the knowledge of the crafts. This secrecy might involve the techniques or it might involve rituals which were necessary to do the work correctly and safely. Thus a woman who did quillwork without the proper rituals might go blind or suffer in some other way (Dempsey 1963:53). Ornamenting a tipi was done after the camp had moved to a new spot so that only those "in the know" would be around. Basket-makers and potters worked in areas hidden away from the rest of the people so that their techniques would not be observed (Wilson 1977:104).

Among a number of Plains societies, for example Sioux, Cheyenne, Arapaho, excellence in quillwork was maintained by a guild. One of the clearest descriptions of the guild comes from Kroeber's work on the Arapaho (Kroeber 1902-07) in which he describes how a woman became a member of the quillworking society and how the society functions. There were seven sacred bags which contained incense, paint, and implements for marking and sewing. Possession of one of these bags included the rights and ceremonies necessary to put quills on buffalo robes, cradle-covers, and to sew ornaments on tents. When a woman wished to make something decorated with quills, she summoned a member of the quilling society and asked her assistance. When the society had assembled to watch the person quill her object, a feast was given for the society. During the feast a horse was given to some poor person in the camp. The older members of the society began the ceremony by telling of the robes they had ornamented. This recital was equivalent to counting coup and the statement had to be verified by a witness or by swearing on the arrow or the pipe. After the ritual, the women were given food and sent home. Later, the novice asked an old woman to draw the pattern on the robe she intended to decorate. This person also received a gift. In quilling the robe, women met in a selected tipi from which men were excluded.

Societies similar to the quill-working society were those for tipi-makers of the Oglala and tipi decorators of the Cheyenne.

The first decorated tipi I made was after I
had had my fourth child. Of course when I
was a girl my mother permitted me to look on
when she made decorated tipis. There is a
rather long ceremony in connection with the
making of tipis. I became a member of the
"tipi decorators" which is composed of women
only. I was very carefully instructed never
to disclose the ceremony in the presence of
men (Michelson 1932:8-9).

The woman who excelled in crafts not only had a chance
to become a member of a select group, but she could
also increase her family's status and wealth by
working for others and by teaching her craft. Fees
received for teaching have been discussed above in
connection with a poor woman desiring to learn a craft
in order to raise her family's income. Additional
examples abound in the literature, although the Mandan
and Hidatsa must be considered the most outspoken
about the advantages to be gained from maintaining a
monopoly in crafts. Buffalo Bird Woman (Wilson 1977:
104) commented "Basket-makers would not let others see
how they worked, because if another wanted to learn
how to make baskets she should pay a good price for
being taught." Bowers (1973:91) notes for the Mandan:

Payment for training was so highly developed
in Mandan society that a young woman assisting
her mother in the making of clay pots would
prepare a simple feast to which the females
of the household were invited in order to
receive the right to assist in the making of
pots and to make vessels of her own after her
mother died. Within the family group the
payments were usually insignificant so far
as the value of the goods was concerned. It
was felt that the small payment in goods
expressed the young woman's respect for her
mother. The Mandan also believed that payments expressed societal values.

And Michelson's informant noted that even as a child
she was well paid by the parents of her friends when
she made moccasins for them.

In other situations, too, women were paid for
their work. The girl who tanned the white buffalo

hide in the Oglala ceremony (Fletcher 1884:261) received a dress, belt, leggings, moccasins and a horse from the owner of the hide. She was given a similar outfit on the second day of work.

The ability to design tipi-covers was a specialty that brought wealth to the possessor. When a new tipi-cover was needed, the owner prepared the necessary hides, sometimes with the aid of friends, and then called a designer to assist in laying out the hides and directing the sewing. Among the Crow (Lowie 1922:223), the lodge designer received four different articles for her work. Weltfish (1965:460) reports that a gift to a Pawnee woman for designing a tipi amounted to $9.25 worth of merchandise, including flour, sugar, coffee and calico. In addition, the tipi designer was fed for the four days that she worked on the tipi. Among the Cheyenne (Grinnell 1972:229) the lodge-maker received a pair of moccasins, a robe, a blanket, a wooden bowl or some other item for her work. Assiniboine (Lowie 1909:14) and Plains Cree (Mandelbaum 1940:211) women also hired a tent cover cutter to direct the sewing of a new tipi. This woman, and all those who came to help, were given a feast and other compensation. Wilson (1909:108) notes that a man paid a robe and a big bowl of food to have a tent made.

Making robes also led to wealth. Although a woman had to buy her way into the Arapaho quilling society, whenever she made a robe and gave it away she received a horse for it (Kroeber 1902-07:29). Wilson (1909:129) noted a similar occurrence among the Mandan-Hidatsa. A steer robe ornamented with quills by Owl Woman was given to Black Chest who would give her a pony in return.

The Blackfeet, too, recognized the need to pay well for special items.

> According to the informants, only three women
> in her grandmother's camp had the right to
> do quillwork. If persons wanted something
> quilled, such as a suit, moccasins or a
> ceremonial object, they would give gifts
> to one or all of these women (Dempsey 1963:53).

An industrious and talented woman could increase her husband's fortunes through payment received for

114

her work. Since the man's position depended upon his ability to give away large amounts of goods, the woman's contribution was vital to his status and prestige. In addition, she often received recognition for her work similar to that received by a man for war honors. Wilson (1912:52) collected information from Mahidiweash about honor marks given to women for their work.

An honor mark goes to one who shows great industry--one who is a great worker and finishes hundreds of hides for robes and tents. Mahidiweash had such a mark given her by her "aunt" Sage. This honor mark was a woman's belt, a ma-ipsu-haashe--and it could only be acquired by gift, as a reward to a great worker.

Wissler (1910:65, 70) makes a similar point about women's work among the Blackfeet. "It was not only woman's work, but her worth and virtue were estimated by her output." And "women took pride in the number and quality of robes they dressed, often keeping records and referring to them when about to perform a ceremony." Hassrick (1964:42) says "accomplishments were recorded by means of dots incised along the handles of the polished elkhorn scraping tools. The dots on one side were black, on the other red. Each black dot represented a tanned robe; each red dot represented ten hides or one tipi. When a woman had completed one hundred robes or ten tipis she was privileged to place an incised circle at the base of the handle of her scraper." In addition, a quilling count was kept which recorded a woman's work and "just as a man displayed his war honors in the Red Council Lodge, so a woman displayed her abilities" (Hassrick 1964: 43). The Sioux (Hassrick 1964:42-43) also had a quilling contest in which output was measured and the four top women were publicly honored. The Kiowa associated high status with craftsmanship. When asked to name the most famous women, Mishkin's (1940:55) informants gave twelve who were famous for their craft work, including tipi-making, saddle-making and bead-work.

In some instances, sacred power was associated with craft production. Dreams often indicated supernatural sanction to participate in craft-work. The Sioux believed in Double-Woman or Deer Woman, who

gives people a chance to choose between skill in
crafts and less worthy occupations. Wissler (1912:
93) describes the dream:

> As the woman comes up to the door and looks
> in she beholds the two deerwomen sitting at
> the rear. By them she is directed to choose
> which side she shall enter. Along the wall
> of one side is a row of skin dressing tools,
> on the other, a row of parfleche headdress
> bags. If the former is chosen, they will
> say, "You have chosen wrong, but you will
> become very rich." If she chooses the other
> side, they will say, "You are on the right
> track, all you shall have shall be an empty
> bag." This means that she will be a
> prostitute and otherwise an evil woman.

This dream indicates very clearly the relationship
between virtue, crafts, wealth and good social
standing. Wissler goes on to note that women who have
this dream are especially wakan or powerful in a religious sense. Not only do they become skilled in
decorative arts, but they may also go into a trance
(vision?) and obtain power to make shields and other
war medicines. Women who had dreamed this dream
formed a society and performed a mysterious dance in
which they located buried objects and flashed mirrors
about. These women also painted the spider design on
their robes (Wissler 1907:50).

The correlation between skill in craftwork,
dreaming and sexuality is further indicated by the
effect of the dream upon men. When men dreamed of
Double-Woman they either became insane with longing
for the creature or they became a berdache, a male
transvestite. Berdaches were considered not only to
have unusual power, but also to excel in crafts
usually practiced by women (Wissler 1912:92; Hassrick
1964:121-123; Bowers 1965:165; Howard 1965:142).

The manner in which a woman could obtain wealth
and status through her craftwork, is analogous to the
manner in which a man obtained wealth and status
through brave exploits. The individual, male or
female, who most closely approximated the ideals, was
assumed to have received supernatural assistance.
Women counted robes and tipi covers in much the same
way that men counted coups. It is likely that women,

too, had a certain amount of political power. The kind of power being considered here is the kind described by Elizabeth Colson (1977:375-386) as "remunerative" rather than "coercive" power. In summarizing the papers in The Anthropology of Power she notes:

> Implicitly, at least, they defined power as a relationship between people with different resources. They found sources of power in control over such specific resources as land, money, strategic position in a communication network, and sometimes in the ability to convince others that they had supernatural support.

In this model, the person who has control over some resource desired or needed by others, offers access to that resource in exchange for something else. Alternatively, a person who desires a resource offers something to the person who controls it. This negotiation process places the controller of the resource in a position to make demands of the seeker. It also requires that the seeker act in a manner that will guarantee access to the resource. Thus, when a man needed quillwork to put on some ritual regalia he was forced to go to a woman to get it, either to his wife or some other member of the quilling society. He would have to act in an appropriate manner in order to have this request fulfilled. In effect, this would enable women to control his behavior in some way suitable to them. This would give women a form of covert political power which has not heretofore been acknowledged.

This idea is confirmed by Grinnell (1972:I, 156-157),

> Among the Cheyennes, as already said, the women have great influence. They discuss matters freely with their husbands, argue over points, persuade, cajole, and usually have their own way about tribal matters. They are, in fact, the final authority in the camp. There are traditions of women chiefs, and of women who have possessed remarkable mysterious powers or have shown great wisdom in council. If in later days the women did not take part in councils,

they nevertheless exercised on the men of
their families an influence that can hardly
be overestimated, and in the councils so
frequently held, where only men spoke, this
influence of the women was always felt.

Lowie (1956:61) comments that even a woman who
failed to live up to the Crow ideal of womanhood was
not shunned. Women were given freedom and independence and were active participants in ceremonies. He
also notes that a man would not even attempt to
influence a woman in the disposition of her property.
Weltfish (1965:53-63) implies that Pawnee women also
had a certain amount of say over the men. One woman
who had fought the Ponca when the men had been afraid
never let the men forget her deeds and never permitted
the men to tell her what to do.

SUMMARY

This paper has presented evidence to indicate
that the long held view of Plains Indian women as
drudges is erroneous. The division of labor between
men and women was not only not exclusive, but the
kinds of duties which were considered appropriate for
men and women varied from group to group. It is not
possible to assume that because a task was done by
women in one group that it was done by women in all
groups. Neither can we assume that we know the sex of
the maker of an item simply on the basis of who would
have made the item in Euro-American culture.

Unlike the role of Euro-Americans in craftwork,
Plains Indian women received recognition, often
public, for their work. In addition it brought them
and their families wealth and prestige.

REFERENCES CITED

Bowers, Alfred   (1965)   Hidatsa Social and Ceremonial
    Organization. Bureau of American Ethnology
    Bulletin 194. Washington.

_____ (1973)   Mandan Social and Ceremonial
    Organization. University of Chicago, Midway
    Reprints.

Brasser, Ted   (1972)   Plains Indian Art. In:
    American Indian Art: Form and Tradition.
    New York: E.P. Dutton and Co.

Colson, Elizabeth   (1977)   Power at Large: Meditation
    on "The Symposium on Power." In: The Anthro-
    pology of Power, Raymond Fogelson and Richard
    N. Adams, eds. New York: Academic Press.

Dempsey, Hugh   (1963)   Religious Significance of
    Blackfoot Quillwork. Plains Anthropologist
    No. 8-19, pp. 52-53.

Denig, Edwin T.   (1930)   Indian Tribes of the Upper
    Missouri: The Assiniboin. Bureau of American
    Ethnology Forty-Sixth Annual Report. Washington.

Ewers, John   (1955)   The Horse in Blackfoot Indian
    Culture. Bureau of American Ethnology Bulletin
    159. Washington.

_____ (1958)   The Blackfeet. Norman: University
    of Oklahoma Press.

Fletcher, Alice   (1884)   The White Buffalo Festival
    of the Uncpapas. Sixteenth and Seventeenth
    Annual Reports of the Peabody Museum of American
    Archaeology and Ethnology, pp. 260-275.

Fletcher, Alice and Francis LaFlesche   (1972)   The
    Omaha. Lincoln: University of Nebraska Press.
    Bison Books.

Grinnell, George Bird   (1972)   The Cheyenne Indians.
    Lincoln: University of Nebraska Press. Bison
    Books.

Hassrick, Royal   (1964)   The Sioux. Norman:
    University of Oklahoma Press.

Howard, James (1965) The Ponca Tribe. Bureau of
American Ethnology Bulletin 195. Washington.

Kroeber, Alfred (1902-07) The Arapaho. American
Museum of Natural History Bulletin 18.

_____ (1908) Ethnology of the Gros Ventre.
Anthropological Papers of the American Museum
of Natural History, Vol. 1.

Lowie, Robert (1909) The Assiniboine. Anthropological Papers of the American Museum of
Natural History, Vol. 4, Pt. 1.

_____ (1915) The Sun Dance of the Crow.
Anthropological Papers of the American Museum
Natural History, Vol. 16.

_____ (1922) Material Culture of the Crow
Indians. Anthropological Papers of the American
Museum of Natural History, Vol. 21.

_____ (1956) The Crow Indians. New York: Holt,
Rinehart and Winston.

McClintock, Walter (1910) The Old North Trail.
London.

_____ (1936) Painted Tipis and Picture Writing
of the Blackfoot Indians. Master Key, Vol. 10.

Mandelbaum, David (1940) The Plains Cree.
Anthropological Papers of the American Museum
of Natural History, Vol. 37, Pt. 1.

Michelson, T. (1932) Narrative of a Southern
Cheyenne Woman. Smithsonian Miscellaneous
Collections, Vol. 87, pp. 1-13.

Mishkin, Bernard (1940) Rank and Warfare among
the Plains Indians. Monographs of the American
Ethnological Society. Seattle: University of
Washington Press.

Schneider, Mary Jane (1976) Plains Indian Art.
Paper presented at the Thirty-Fourth Plains
Conference, Minneapolis, Minnesota.

Standing Bear, Luther (1928) My People, the Sioux.
New York: Houghton Mifflin Co.

Weltfish, Gene (1965) The Lost Universe. New York:
Ballantine Books, Inc.

Wied-Neuwied, Maximilian, Prince of (1906) Travels
in the Interior of North America. In: Early
Western Travels, Vol. 23.

Wilson, Gilbert (1909) Field Notes.

_____ (1910) Field Notes.

_____ (1912) Field Notes.

_____ (1916) Field Notes.

_____ (1977) Mandan and Hidatsa Pottery Making.
Plains Anthropologist 22:97-105.

Wissler, Clark (1907) Some Protective Designs of the
Dakota. Anthropological Papers of the American
Museum of Natural History, Vol. 1.

_____ (1910) Material Culture of the Blackfoot
Indians. Anthropological Papers of the American
Museum of Natural History, Vol. 5.

_____ (1912) Societies and Ceremonial Associations
of the Oglala Division of the Teton-Dakota.
Anthropological Papers of the American Museum
of Natural History, Vol. 11.

CHAPTER 6

THE ROLE OF SIOUX WOMEN IN THE PRODUCTION OF CEREMONIAL OBJECTS: THE CASE OF THE STAR QUILT[1]

Patricia Albers
University of Utah

Beatrice Medicine
University of California - Northridge

INTRODUCTION

A view widely held in the anthropological literature on sex roles and art is that women confine their artistry to objects made for domestic use and appreciation. This view is expressed aptly in the following quote:

> If the tribal artist is usually anonymous, then women as artists are doubly anonymous. Their artistry is expressed within the private sphere of domestic life on objects to be used in the household rather than to be publicly displayed ... In general, the pots, baskets, or blankets that women make and use are admired as skillful and attractive handicrafts, but they do not receive the respectful attention paid to display pieces such as totem poles or masks made by men (Hammond and Jablow 1976:88-89).

The above statement, although valid in many societal contexts, is not universally applicable. When examined against the ethnographic evidence on Plains Indian populations, it does not hold true. Among the Sioux, Pawnee, Arapaho, and Mandan, to name a few of the many native groups on the Plains, women made important contributions to the social and ceremonial art of their communities (Schneider 1979).

In historic times, Plains Indian women applied
their industrial and decorative skills to a wide
variety of ceremonial objects. Among other things,
they constructed and designed tipis used on sacred
occasions, they made and decorated the hide robes
given as well as displayed at honorific ceremonies,
and they fabricated and embellished many of the containers carrying ritual paraphernalia (Wissler 1904,
1912; Kroeber 1907; Lowie 1922; Hassrick 1964;
Weltfish 1965; Schneider 1979).

The important role that Plains Indian women
played historically in the production of art objects
for ritual use continues today. Among the Sioux, this
tradition is most evident in the making of star
quilts. In post-reservation times, the star quilt has
become an object of considerable social and ceremonial
importance. It ranks as one of the most prestigious
items given and displayed at honoring ceremonies, and
it figures importantly in other rituals as well,
including Yuwipi. But despite the fact that it occupies a significant place among the modern Sioux,
neither the star quilt nor its makers have received
much attention in anthropological writings.

Our general purpose in this paper is to examine
the historical provenience and contemporary role of
the star quilt. In doing this, we give special consideration to the continuing importance of female artwork in the ceremonial life of the Sioux. It is our
contention that star quilts are descended from ceremonial hide robes bearing the morning star design, and
that Sioux women have been influential in adapting
this new art form to an old tradition.

HISTORICAL PROVENIENCE

In the late nineteenth century, when the Sioux
were first settled on reservations, many changes were
taking place in the industrial work and decorative art
of women. As hides grew scarce, women increasingly
applied their skills to textiles imported from
Euro-American traders. Through their own ingenuity,
women learned to transform new materials into traditional forms and uses. Textile clothing was tailored
in the fashion of the buckskin dress, and cloth

leggings were decorated with ribbon applique in a manner reminiscent of linear quillwork designs. Many of the early adaptations that Sioux women made to textiles did not involve a dramatic change in technique. Except for the fact that cotton thread and steel needles replaced sinew and bone awls, sewing skills remained essentially the same.

Another ingenious adaptation is described by Ella Deloria, who writes:

> ... Out of G.I. muslin they made very large wall-coverings, a carryover from the dew curtains of a tipi and called by the same term, ozan. On these they painted beautiful designs and made lively black and white drawings of historical scenes of hunting or battles or peace-making between tribes, and courtship scenes, games, and suchlike activities of the past. People went visiting just to see one another's pictographs and to hear the stories they preserved. I barely remember one such wall-covering which had been given to be sold, the proceeds to be used for missionary work. My father brought it home, and my mother had it hung to cover most of two sides of our fourteen-by-fifteen foot dining room in the rectory. This interesting mode of decoration passed out quite suddenly when it became the fashion, perhaps about 1908, to build frame houses (1944:93).

Apart from their decorative value, dew curtains had a functional use. In the tipi, these curtains were a means of insulation. By creating an air vacuum against the tipi's inner wall, they prevented frost from forming in the seating area. The modified curtains that Ella Deloria described served a similar function in the early log houses and an additional one as well, namely, to keep dust from falling out of the chinks between the logs.

When painted dew curtains passed out of fashion, a new form of decoration, the quilt,[2] rapidly took their place. Aside from its function as a bed-covering, the quilt served as a wall-hanging in early reservation homes. Even as late as the nineteen-sixties, quilts were still a familiar sight in the houses of many elderly Sioux, hanging against walls, over windows, and in door frames.

The art of quiltmaking has been practiced by Sioux women for nearly a century. It was introduced to them through government and church agencies. As part of an overall effort to educate the Sioux in the ways of White people, women were taught a wide variety of "civilized" domestic skills. Quilting, along with such techniques as breadbaking, tatting, and crocheting were learned in women's church societies, they were taught by government "field matrons,"[3] and they were featured in the domestic science curriculum of federal and parochial boarding schools.

Of all the new techniques that Sioux women learned, quilting was one of their favorites. Within a short period after its introduction, quilting became a dominant handicraft on Sioux reservations. It was a popular activity in the meetings of women's church guilds, in the auxiliaries to such military associations as the American Legion, and in informal household gatherings as well. At annual fall and summer fairs, quilts became a major item displayed and entered in domestic art competitions. Today, quilting ranks second only to beadwork as the most widely practiced decorative art among Sioux women.

There are many reasons for the widespread adoption of quilting among the Sioux. One reason that it gained such popularity was the social nature of its production. More than any other "civilized" domestic skill, quilting lent itself to cooperative work patterns. In quilting, as in the preparation and decoration of hides, Sioux women divided their labor. Some specialized in cutting fabric pieces, others devoted themselves to piecing the quilt top, and still more concentrated on quilting or tying the quilt top to its lining and filling. Aside from the comradeship that it offered, such cooperation afforded a more efficient use of labor. Greater efficiency was achieved not merely because there were more workers but also because labor tasks were divided according to skill and expertise.

Another reason for quilting's wide acceptance was that it produced an object with obvious functional utility, and it did so inexpensively. In the cold and stormy winters of the Northern Plains, warm covering has been essential. Although store-bought blankets have always been available to the Sioux, they tend to be costly. Quilts, in contrast, can be made easily from whatever materials are on hand. Used clothing from "mission boxes,"[4] flour sacks, and even Bull Durham tobacco bags are ripped apart, and their fabrics used for quilt top pieces, backs, and fillings. Today, as in the past, most quilts made for home consumption are fabricated out of secondhand muslin, cotton, or woolen goods. Household quilts, known to the Sioux as "winter quilts," usually entail simple patchwork patterns. The most common variety consists of square fabrics sewn together and "tacked" with yarns to hold the quilt batting in place.

New fabric, whenever it is available, is reserved for quilts given and displayed on ritual occasions. Star quilts are sometimes used in Sioux homes as bed-coverings and wall-hangings, but they are most often seen in ceremonial settings. Star quilt fabrics are either purchased or acquired as gifts in give-aways, and they are quilted rather than tacked.

The most compelling reason, in our estimation, for the widespread adoption of quilting is that its design principles correspond to the Sioux's own decorative tradition. The art of making pieced quilts involves a technique whereby simple geometric shapes, including squares, rectangles, triangles, and diamonds, are combined into more complex patterns. Such a design technique was followed by Sioux women in their traditional painting, beadwork, and quillwork (Wissler 1904; Lyford 1979).

Over the years, Sioux women have worked out many different geometric designs in their quilts. The star, however, is the most prevalent. The vast majority of quilts using this motif are dominated by a single star, but multiple and broken star patterns are not uncommon. The single star quilt is made up of small diamond-shaped patches pieced together in eight sections. When joined, these sections, also diamond in shape, form an eight-sided star.

The geometric layout of the star pattern is fairly standardized in Sioux quilts, although there is a great deal of diversity and ingenuity in the use of color. For the diamond-shaped pieces that form the star, Sioux women employ many different colors. The

127

most popular colors, however, are traditional ones, including red, yellow, blue, white, and black. For the quilt's background, white is the most favored color, but light hues of blue and yellow are common. Even more variable is the arrangement of color. Some quilts contain only a few colors which are repeated in specified sequences to produce a flat, shaded, or bold (that is, three-dimensional) effect, and others consist of multiple colors with little or no repetition.

Variation in star quilts is also produced by using different textures of fabric and by combining solid colored materials with printed ones. In recent years, there has been considerable innovation in the use of variegated fabrics. For a short time during the early seventies, silks and satins were becoming fashionable materials for star quilts in some reservation communities. Even so, the vast majority are made from cottons in solid colors.

The design principles and color arrangements of Sioux star quilts are remarkably similar to the geometric paintings on some nineteenth century hide robes. There is a group of painted robes in which the central design is formed by arranging diamonds in progressively larger circles. This group is represented by, among others, the "War Bonnet" and "Morning Star" patterns. The morning star design bears the closest resemblance to the star motif on Sioux quilts. Although the diamonds of the morning star are laid out in a different fashion, the overall effect of this pattern is nearly the same as that found on star quilts.

The star pattern used by Sioux quiltmakers, however, is not unique. It is virtually identical in geometric composition to the "Star of Bethlehem" or "Lone Star" design found in Anglo-American quilting. This design, which dates back to the eighteenth century, was favored by quiltmakers on both sides of the Atlantic, being especially popular in England and the northeastern United States.

Because the Sioux star quilt shares an affinity with both an indigenous and Anglo-American design tradition, there has been some debate over its origin. One position is that Sioux women independently invented the star pattern on their quilts from the traditional morning star design. In effect, they modified this design to fit the requirements of a new technique, namely, quilting. Such an origin is possible, but not likely. It is more probable that Sioux women borrowed the star quilt pattern from the Anglo-Americans who taught them to quilt, and that in the process of doing so, they transposed the symbolism of the morning star from an old medium to a new one. Identifying the "Star of Bethlehem" with the "Morning Star" pattern would have been easy for them to do, especially since there is such a striking resemblance in design.

SYMBOLISM AND CEREMONIAL USE

Today, the Sioux clearly attribute the star quilt's design to decorative and symbolic traditions surrounding the morning star. The morning star, which appears in the East in early April, has always been an important symbol in their myth and ceremony. It represents the direction from which spirits of the dead travel to earth, and by extension, it signifies a continuing link between the living and the dead. More generally, the morning star symbolizes immortality (Wallis 1923:44-45).

The star quilt and its morning star symbolism figure importantly in the Yuwipi ceremony. Here religious practitioners, known also as Yuwipi, summon the spirits of the dead to assist them in curing, prophecy, and the finding of lost objects (Kemnitzer 1976). In their rites, the Yuwipi are wrapped and tied in the same manner as the dead. Star quilts, which now replace the red-painted buffalo hide of former times, are the most prevalent wrapping. Lame Deer explains this:

> In the old days, we used buffalo hide for this, but now we make do with a large star blanket, a quilt with many colored pieces of cloth forming the design of the morning star. The background is usually white. These blankets are beautiful. Some people are buried in them. They are big enough to cover the whole man, including his head (1972:193).

When appearing as a dead person, the Yuwipi beckons

the spirits who will release and assist him in performing rites necessary to the purpose of the ceremony. Since the morning star guides the spirits of
the dead to earth, its appearance on quilts is helpful
in bringing these spirits to the aid of the Yuwipi as
well as the recently deceased.

At contemporary funerals and wakes, star quilts
are draped over caskets and/or hung in back of them.
Before burial, one of the quilts laid before the
deceased is used in wrapping the corpse, although some
christianized Sioux prefer to have the quilts laid at
the corpse's side. Both customs are recognized and
respected by funeral homes throughout the Northern
Plains.

Star quilts used in Sioux mortuary practice have
a double meaning. Aside from their purely eschatolo-
gical symbolism, these quilts are quintessential symbols of family honor and respect. This symbolism is
associated with the Sioux's honorific traditions, and
the ceremonial contexts in which it appears are ubiquitous.

Since early reservation times, star quilts have
been one of the most highly prized contributions that
parents make to setting up their son or daughter's
household at marriage. Among traditional families,
who still make "collections" for the newly married,
the star quilt is considered an essential gift. When
given, it bestows recognition and respect on a
couple's marriage. Today, one often hears elderly
Sioux complain that "she didn't even have a star quilt
to her name." When this is said, it implies that a
girl's marriage has not been honored in the customary
way.

Next to beaded moccasins, the star quilt is now
the major gift that a sister makes for her brother's
first child. In recent times, however, this traditional practice has become more generalized. In some
Sioux communities, it is not uncommon for grand-
parents to give these quilts to their newborn
grandchildren, irrespective of their birth order, nor
is it unusual for a woman's sister to give her infant
niece or nephew a quilt. But whoever gives the quilt,
esteem and respect are being paid to the child.

When Sioux return home from military service or

college and when they make some notable accomplishment within or outside their community, their families, but more often outsiders, will present them with a star quilt as a sign of respect and honor. Generally speaking, whenever achievements are recognized and honored, the star quilt is present.

Star quilts are not only presented to people being honored, but they are also given to others on behalf of the honored. Today, star quilts are one of the most prestigious items in the Sioux give-away system. They are given at memorial feasts, naming ceremonies, homecoming celebrations for veterans, and in the "donations" of powwow officials. When given away for honorific purposes, star quilts bestow respect on both the giver and receiver.

The generous giving of star quilts can be interpreted in either of two ways. Traditionally, it was a sign of the esteem that a family had for its honored member. As the Sioux might put it, "They thought so much of that child they gave lots of star quilts away." While such an interpretation still holds in some situations, there is an increasing tendency to view the ostentatious giving of star quilts as a way for a family to gain prestige and influence.

In recent years, star quilts and other give-away items have been caught in the inflationary spiral that surrounds the modern give-away system. Fifteen years ago, it was customary for families to donate only a few star quilts in their give-aways. Now, it is common for them to give away as many as ten. In fact, we have witnessed a number of give-aways where over twenty-five quilts were donated. Although inflation in star quilt giving is not of the same magnitude as that experienced in Northwest Coast potlatching a century ago, many of its causes and consequences are the same.

Since World War II, Sioux give-aways have been injected with a sense of quid pro quo that was not present in early reservation times. In contrast to the past, when honorific giving involved no expectation of return, reciprocity is now expected. Many families who give away valued objects like star quilts presume that their generosity will be returned at some future date, either in the form of material goods or support. Tribal politicians often stage elaborate

131

give-aways to retain and increase their influence among a particular constituency. But most Sioux make donations to maintain and expand their friendship networks within and outside their home community (Albers 1974). In order to cover the growing number of reciprocal obligations they incur in the course of their travels at powwows and family feasts, many Sioux find it necessary each year to increase the amount and value of the gifts they donate at their own give-aways.

For people of limited means, gaining prestige and influence through the give-away system can be costly. Star quits, for example, sell from thirty-five to two-hundred dollars in Sioux reservation communities. In families, where the women know how to quilt, honor and prestige can be gained with little monetary investment, although the labor-time expended can be considerable. Families, however, which lack accomplished quiltmakers must purchase quilts for honorific purposes. Only the very wealthy in Sioux communities can afford to buy large numbers of quilts for these purposes, and as a consequence, they are the ones that tend to derive the most prestige, or at least become the most well-known, in today's powwow circles.

Families give star quilts to those they hold in highest regard. In the past, prestigious items were given either to people who held a special affinity with the honored or who were aged, widowed, and orphaned. Giving valuable gifts to people not in a position to make a return is considered the most honorable form of generosity, and traditional families who continue to give in this manner are revered in their communities. Today, however, it is more common for recipients of star quilts to be friends or accomplished persons in a family's own community and neighboring ones.

At powwows, for instance, quilts are often given to popular singers and dancers, who have befriended a family or whose talents are simply admired by that family. In either case, the recipient receives recognition and prestige. In fact, some singers and dancers now drape star quilts over the back of their folding chairs. Such an act, of course, is a way to publicize their popularity.

In the last decade, the star quilt has taken on

even wider symbolism. Today, it is an important
marker of Sioux ethnicity, in general, and of traditional Sioux ways, in particular. In this role, the
star quilt has become an important display item, functioning like a banner or flag at important family and
community gatherings. Some families now keep a special star quilt to display at their own honoring ceremonies, and a few use them as backdrops on which
graduation and family pictures are hung. Star quilts
bedeck cars and floats in annual powwow parades, and
they often decorate the walls of auditoriums and gym-
nasia where special competitive events and pageants
are held. Star quilts also cover the entrance to a
sweat lodge, they are hung at the door of tipis used
for secular or sacred purposes, and they are draped
around the sides of Sun Dance enclosures.

Star quilts are even worn as shawls in dancing.
Not infrequently, male dancers without costumes will
carry a star quilt over their shoulders in a fashion
reminiscent of the hide robe. Some women are now
taking star quilt tops and making them into ladies'
shawls. At the 1976 Rosebud Fair, such a quilt was
embellished with feathers, hair pipes, and beads.

Since their appearance in early reservation
times, star quilts have taken the place of the
decorated hide robes which once commemorated honor,
respect, and achievement in the lives of those who
wore, gave, or displayed them. But unlike the hide
robes of the past, where designs were varied and
linked to specific kinds of honor, star quilts embody
a single design motif with multiple meanings.
Beginning as a symbol of immortality and associated
with mortuary practice, the star quilt has come to
represent the preservation of family and community
honor. Finally, it has achieved the status of an ethnic banner, upholding all of those meanings and symbols that signify Sioux traditionalism.

The varied symbolism associated with the star
quilt is not without precedent in Sioux decorative
art. Clark Wissler (1904:272-274) describes many
Sioux designs with varying, and often contradictory,
interpretations. The diamond-shape widely used in
traditional artwork, and now an elementary component
of star quilts, simultaneously represents a female
symbol of fertility, the turtle, and a male symbol of
war, the feather. Even more complex motifs, as

reported by Wissler, carry diverse meanings depending
on the context in which they are used. The star
quilt's varied symbolism and functions certainly conform to this pattern.

WOMEN AS CEREMONIAL ARTISTS

The star quilt's rise to eminence in Sioux ceremonial life is a fascinating example of syncretization
in design, symbolism and function. Even more
interesting is the fact that an object of such public
reverence and esteem is made by women.

Ever since the end of the eighteenth century, and
perhaps before that time, the Sioux have supported and
advanced the artistry of women in many institutional
contexts. In the pre-reservation era, secret
societies were formed to promote as well as protect
specialized skills in areas such as quilling (Wissler
1912:98; Hassrick 1964:191). Ceremonial feasts and
contests were held to publicize artistic accomplishments (Hassrick 1964:42-45). Supernatural powers that
fostered skill and inspired design were sought in
visions as well as dreams (Wissler 1904:93). Finally,
an essential feature of a young girl's menstrual
seclusion, isnati, and her socialization more
generally, was to encourage proficiency and creativity
in the decorative arts (Hassrick 1964:41-42).

In the past, artistic talents brought honor to a
woman and her family when she was young, it insured a
respectable marriage match, and it opened many avenues
to wealth and prestige in later life. Whether applied
to secular or sacred objects, the artistic talents of
women were highly esteemed and sought after. The work
of a talented artisan, when not made on behalf of a
family member, was commissioned and demanded by people
from near and far. Women were paid highly for their
artistic creations. A skillfully decorated robe, for
example, brought one horse in return (Hassrick
1964:41-45).

Today, Sioux women sill draw prestige for their
excellence in decorative arts such as beadwork and
quilting. But, in contrast to the past, they do not
realize much in the way of wealth. While talented

artisans are able to make earnings from their work, the sums they receive are insignificant when one considers the labor involved. With the help of other women, a good quiltmaker can put together a star quilt in a few days, but working alone, it often takes a week of steady work at long hours. When the costs of materials are taken into account, an average quiltmaker's earnings amount to about sixty cents an hour. Importantly, women are drawn to quilting not for wealth, but for the admiration and respect it brings.

Those who excel at quiltmaking take great pride in their work. They spend considerable time in selecting fabrics, in arranging their patterns, and in choosing particular color combinations. They are able to identify unique features of their own star patterns and to discern subtle differences in the designs of others. Although Sioux women do not hold proprietary rights over their designs, as they once did in the secret quilling societies of the past, they frown upon and rebuke those who copy the work of others.

Quiltmakers also keep careful records, albeit in their memory, of the number and kinds of quilts they have completed. This is reminiscent of the quilling counts that Sioux women kept in former times. Such counts were displayed on the dew cloths hanging in household tipis as well as in the Red Council Lodge, and they were placed alongside those marking the war honors of men (Hassrick 1964:43).

Many of the designs Sioux women use in their star quilts conform to traditional patterns, others involve creative insight, and some are derived from visions as well as dreams. Especially proficient and creative quiltmakers are said to have supernatural powers, which they derive from figures like "Double-Woman." Wissler describes the meaning of one such figure:

> As the woman comes up to the door and looks in she beholds two deer women sitting at the rear. By them she is directed to choose which side she shall enter. Along the wall of one side is a row of skin dressing tools, on the other, a row of parfleche headdress bags. If the former is chosen, they will say, "You have chosen wrong, but you will become very rich." If she chooses the other

side, they will say, "You are on the right
track, all you shall have shall be an empty
bag." This means that she will be a
prostitute and otherwise an evil woman
(1912:93).

The symbolism of the two deer women is still found in
the visions of female artists among the Sioux, but the
options are not always expressed in moral terms.
Instead, as one quiltmaker told us, the deer women
gave her a choice between traditionalism and
assimilation.

When Sioux women work on quilts, they do so with
great concentration and devotion. As one quiltmaker
put it, "I get so involved in this quilting, I even
forget to eat and sleep." Neighbors and family of
this same woman often joke that they never visit her
when she is quilting because she gets so preoccupied
that she forgets to feed them. Under normal circumstances, such a lapse in etiquette would be considered an insult to a visitor, but it is tolerated,
indeed even expected, when artists are at work.

In some reservation communities, like Rosebud,
accomplished quiltmakers draw public recognition
through the exhibition of their work at the annual
summer fair. Elsewhere, prestige is gained more
informally. It comes from the ever present display of
star quilts on ceremonial occasions and their more
recent appearance as sale items in reservation craft
outlets. Quilts with stunning designs are admired and
discussed by everyone, but women are especially fond
of drawing attention to the work of accomplished
quiltmakers.

Since quiltmakers attempt to develop unique star
designs, it is fairly easy to distinguish the work of
one woman from another. The creations of a talented
quilt designer are sought after by people not only in
her own community but in others as well. Many of the
best quiltmakers can hardly keep up with the demand
for their work, and some now hire other women to
assist them in the technical aspects of their production. Not uncommonly, acclaimed quiltmakers devote
themselves to designing and piecing together quilt
tops but parcel out the actual quilting process to
women known for their excellence and speed in this
task.

A question that remains to be asked is why have the Sioux maintained a tradition where women make important contributions to the ceremonial art of their comunity? One possible answer is that, unlike Western societies, there has never been a clear-cut separation between public and domestic spheres. In the Sioux scheme of things, family and community are one and the same thing. By extension, then, domestic art is _ipso facto_ public, and vice versa. In all Sioux ceremonies, at least those practiced today, the line between familial and community involvement is thin. The two are so intertwined, in Sioux praxis and belief, that most ceremonial objects associated with each are interchangeable. When there is no dramatic distinction between domestic and public ceremonies and when such separation is not sex-linked, it logically follows that women and men can make art objects to be used in either or both settings.

CONCLUSION

In conclusion, this paper has argued that Sioux women continue to make important contributions to the ceremonial life of their communities through their quilt work. Quilts with a star motif, although introduced to the Sioux through Anglo-American influences, have come to be associated with traditional meanings and functions. Today, these quilts are ubiquitous in their ceremonial use, and they play a prominent role in the preservation of Sioux traditions.

NOTES

1. This paper originally appeared as "Star Quilts," *Native Arts West*, June 1980. *Native Arts West* is no longer being published.

2. In both Lakota and Dakota dialects, the word for quilt is *owi^{n}ja*. This noun is derived from the verb, *owi^{n}sya*, which means "to spread on the ground" as in a tipi or now "to spread on the bed." *Ozan*, the term for dew curtains, is also translated as "bed curtain." Its verb form, *oyuzan*, means "to spread (hang) on a wall." More specifically, it means to spread out on a wall next to a bed, *oyunke*.

3. A field matron was a federal employee, who functioned like a county agent. Aside from quilting, the field matrons taught canning, baking, crocheting, and sewing to Indian women.

4. Throughout the Northern Plains, it has been customary for Christian missions to acquire second-hand clothing from patron churches in the East. This clothing is distributed in boxes which are either given away or sold at a nominal fee.

REFERENCES CITED

Albers, Patricia   (1974)   The Regional System of the Devil's Lake Sioux.   Ph.D. Dissertation, University of Wisconsin-Madison.

Deloria, Ella   (1944)   Speaking of Indians.   New York: Friendship Press.

Hammond, Dorothy, and Alta Jablow   (1976)   Women in Cultures of the World.   Menlo Park, California: Cummings Publishing Co.

Hassrick, Royal B.   (1964)   The Sioux: Life and Customs of a Warrior Scoiety.   Norman: University of Oklahoma Press.

Kemnitzer, Louis   (1976)   Structure, Content, and Cultural Meaning of Yuwipi: A Modern Lakota Ritual.   American Ethnologist 3:261-280.

Kroeber, Alfred   (1907)   The Arapaho.   American Museum of Natural History, Bulletin 18:1-229, 279-454.

Lame Deer, John, and Richard Erdoes   (1972)   Lame Deer: Seeker of Visions.   New York: Simon and Schuster.

Lowie, Robert   (1922)   Crow Indian Art.   American Museum of Natural History, Anthropological Papers 21:271-322.

Lyford, Carrie   (1979)   Quill and Beadwork of the Western Sioux.   Boulder, Colorado: Johnson Publishing Company.

Schneider, Mary Jane   (1979)   Women's Work: An Examination of Women's Roles in Plains Art and Crafts.   Plainswoman 2:8-11.

Wallis, Wilson   (1923)   Beliefs and Tales of the Canadian Dakota.   Journal of American Folklore 36:36-101.

Weltfish, Gene   (1965)   The Lost Universe.   New York: Basic Books.

Wissler, Clark   (1904)   Decorative Art of the Sioux
    Indians. American Museum of Natural History,
    Anthropological Papers, Bulletin 18:231-275.

_____   (1912)   Societies and Ceremonial Associations
    in the Oglala Division of the Teton Dakota.
    Amerian Museum of Natural History, Anthropo-
    logical Papers 11:1-97.

PART III

THE STATUS OF WOMEN

CHAPTER 7

THE POLITICAL-ECONOMY OF GENDER:
A 19TH CENTURY PLAINS INDIAN CASE STUDY

Alan M. Klein
Northeastern University

INTRODUCTION

That trade with Europeans and Americans dramatically affected Plains Indian society is a truism after
more than a century of expert testimony. Traders such
as Edwin Denig (1930), and J.W. Schultz (1935)
detailed the deleterious impact of "civilization" on
the groups they came to know. Missionaries and military men, despite their biases, spoke of this as well
(e.g. DeSmet 1969; Dodge 1970). Even white captives
took time out from their invectives concerning their
captors to note the generally debasing influences of
Western society on Indians (e.g. Kelly 1973).

Most of these 19th century accounts focused on
the ill effects of alcohol on Plains Indians, with a
generous sprinkling of disgust for the vulgar traits
borrowed from whites (e.g. cursing in English, sloth-
fulness, orgies, and dependence on whites). The
descriptions, with few exceptions, dealt with
intangibles such as "morality" and "character."

Serious anthropological study of changes in 19th
century Plains society began in earnest during the
1940's with a series of monographs by Mishkin (1940);
Lewis (1942); Goldfrank (1943); and Richardson and
Hanks (1945). This was followed in the 1950's by
Jablow (1950); Secoy (1953); and Ewers (1955). These
studies outlined the impact of the horse, gun, and fur
trade in a careful way, isolating their effects on
social, economic, political, and religious institutions (Klein 1980). Other works followed, looking at

143

the Plains historically, but as a region rather than on a tribe by tribe basis (Oliver 1962; Holder 1970; Ray 1974).

While material in the area is voluminous and detailed there has been little attempted in the area of changes on the nomadic mode of production (in particular, the relations of production).[1] It is sometimes felt that the traditional designation of "division of labor" accounts for the Marxist notion of relations of production. It does so only insofar as it discusses how production tasks are assigned to one group or another (e.g. on the basis of sex or age). However, the Marxist concept of relations of production takes into account an articulation between task organization, property rights, method of distribution, political considerations, and ideological rationale. In short, it fuses material from a number of institutions as it pertains to the totality of production, and it does so processually.

My study of four Northern Plains groups (Teton Dakota, Assiniboines, Gros Ventre, and Blackfoot) indicates a severe rupture of the traditional 18th century relations of production in the wake of increased use of/and dependence upon the horse and hide trade. Specifically, these changes apply to the relations between women and men in the political economy. The loss of women's position in egalitarian societies is often treated as a single issue (Reiter 1976; McElroy and Mathiason 1979 contain articles in which this is very evident). At times such analysis even hints at male complicity. This study reveals that the loss of women's position is masked by other issues: an era of unprecedented prosperity; crises in provisioning the society; the rise of male dominated institutions; and incursions by whites. Merging with, and to some degree obscuring the changes in gender in the political economy is the relationship between individual and collective economic tendencies. It is the inter-relationship between these two issues that is examined in this study.

Marxist analysis has experienced something of a renaissance in the post 1970's (Meillassoux 1974; Terray 1972; Bloch 1975; Godelier 1977; Murphy 1970). Only three studies however have been attempted for the entire Plains area. Albers (1982a, 1982b), Moore (1974, 1980), and Klein (1977, 1980) have attempted,

144

using Marx's analytical mode, to answer questions still plaguing us, and to reinterpret old data. Albers' work focuses on the reservation period and particularly the Devil's Lake Sioux, and while important, lies outside the reaches of this study. Moore's work on the 19th century Cheyenne is germane to this study however. He examines Cheyenne political history as a struggle between an emerging emphasis on male-dominated institutions and declining female presence. These changes were fostered by the Cheyenne move onto the plains, a move which wrought qualitative changes in their economic system. Many of the contradictory data on Cheyenne social structure begin to make sense when viewed from Moore's perspective. His focus is not directly on the relations of production--centering instead on socio-political variables--but his work is pregnant with possibilities for an economic analysis.

While changes in economic patterns are widespread, nowhere are they more profound than along the male/female axis. And while I intend to examine various aspects of the impact of both horse and hide trade it is to the gender axis that much of my attention is turned. There are two reasons for this: (a) the sexual division of labor was so fundamental to Plains economics via the domestic mode of production; and (b) it has never been systematically examined from a critical perspective.

The impact of colonialism (in the guise of trade) upon women has been subject to study. Leacock (1954, 1978) has given us a quarter century of analysis, and co-edited at least one anthology on the subject (Etienne and Leacock 1980). As a result of her, and other feminists who worked more generally, anthropologists have come to terms with a new and more substantial understanding of women in society (Rosaldo and Lamphere 1974; Reiter 1976). In keeping with this topic, a symposium on women in the Plains was convened in 1977 at the annual Plains Conference. Here were found many attempts to write women back into history and ethnography. Yet for all the effort, a fundamental error had been committed. Nineteenth century Plains women were not analyzed in relation to the far reaching changes of the hide trade and the horse.[2]

The changes affecting women were total, though stemming from core institutions, and need to be viewed diachronically in order to glimpse their totality. In order to make such a comprehensive analysis manageable I will focus on two axes which seem to encapsulate most of the changes: male/female and individual/ group.

Previous studies have generally argued whether or not the changes which came to Plains societies were positive or negative, but did so unilaterally (Mishkin 1940; Holder 1970; Ray 1974). What they did not see was that one segment of society may have benefited at the expense of others. However, scholars such as Lewis (1942), Ewers (1955), and Richardson and Hanks (1945) have built a critical basis on which further examination can take place. In order to assess the accuracy of any statements on the nature of changes in the 19th century one must compare it to the preceding period.

TIME PERSPECTIVE AND VARIABLES

Any detailed analysis of pristine Plains politi- cal economy is out of the question. As with most cultures, we are dealing with historical accounts, hence a degree of contact is assumed. Nevertheless, valid comparisons can be made. The period under study covers roughly one hundred and thirty years (1750 to 1880); a period which for the societies in question constitutes their emergence and existence as classic Plains societies. This period is subdivided into two social formations: the earlier (roughly 1750 to 1800) during which the traits needed to make the transition to full fledged Plains status were being formed; and the later (1800 to 1880) in which the Plains complex had reached classic proportions.

The traits that I rely on are but two of a constellation of traits. They are the horse and hide trade (but could include the Sun Dance, guns, military complex, etc.). It is important to remember that it is not one or another of these two traits that makes for changes of the sort that we discuss, but both of them as they relate not only to Plains society but to each other.

The horse arrived in the northwestern Plains approximately around 1720, and the Blackfoot were the first of the four groups to come into contact with

146

them (Roe 1951; Ewers 1955). Shortly thereafter the Gros Ventre, close allies of the Blackfoot, received them. The Teton, on the other hand, came into contact with horses later, around the 1760 to 1765 period (Ewers 1955:5). The Assiniboines--always poor in horses--came into contact with them sometime during the third quarter of the 18th century. A period of time elapsed between the first mention of horses in a group and their presence in large enough numbers to effect any real change. Thus for the Blackfoot and Gros Ventre, perhaps 1740 to 1750 is a possible watershed, while for the Teton Dakota and Assiniboines something closer to 1770 or 1780 is more appropriate.

If the Blackfoot and Gros Ventre were the first to get horses, they were the last to be traded with by Europeans and Americans. Cocking, in 1772, and Hendry before him (1754) were the first sent out for the purpose of instituting trade with them (employees of the Hudson Bay Company). They commented on the reluctance of these people to engage them in trade. The Teton Dakota and particularly the Assiniboines had lengthy trade contacts with fur traders, but not in the classic Plains sense. Their relations with the English and French trade was part of an older fur trade which revolved around small pelts (e.g. beaver).

By the 19th century both the horse and the buffalo hide trade had become sufficiently established to affect the mode of production of most northern Plains societies. Thus, comparisons between the 18th century formative period and the 19th century classic period are made with an eye to examining key features of the economy.

THE 18th CENTURY MODE OF PRODUCTION

Before the horse and hide trade, Plains life was closer to the margins. Life on foot mitigated against long overland travel, hence extensive contact of any means. Subsistence, while sufficient, was precarious. Buffalo hunting was frought with difficulties, failing almost as much as it succeeded. The economy was one geared for use (i.e. consumption).

While the Blackfoot and Gros Ventre had the use of the horse and gun by the second half of the 18th century they were essentially unfamiliar with foreign trade. Both Hendry (1907), and Cocking (1908) point out that these tribes were well supplied with horses and capable of living exclusively off the buffalo herds by the time of their visits. So closely bound up are trade and horse that the presence of only one does not result in qualitative alteration of society. Despite their familiarity with them there is no evidence that the presence of horses qualitatively altered Blackfoot and Gros Ventre modes of production. It appears that the horse was used to augment the traditional "pound method" of hunting (Ewers 1955:31; DeSmet 1969:1031). The Teton Dakota and Assiniboines also used such methods as the pound and cliff drive (Denig 1930:504; Boller 1972:35).

The subsistence mode was generally of a classic hunting and gathering variety, supplemented by secondary strategies of raiding and trading. While hunting of buffalo was the keystone of the economy it bore little resemblance to the 19th century form. A closer look at the methods and subsistence strategies of the 18th century reveals the nature of the political economy and production relations.

Buffalo hunting was the mainstay from prehistoric times. Frison (1978:340) points out that Plains hunters developed increasingly more efficient methods of taking game throughout the late prehistoric period. Hunting methods ranged from stalking (Catlin 1973:V.1:274); firing the prairies (Roe 1951:158); trapping (Ewers 1937:37), and stoning (Parkman 1911:289); to cliff drives and pounds (Henry the Younger 1898:V.2:520; DeSmet 1969:V.2:658). The organization for these hunting styles ranged from individuals, to small groups, to large groups (Cocking 1908:109; Wissler 1910:40; Strong 1941; DeSmet 1969:V.3:1029). Despite the diversity, however, it was the large scale hunting projects such as the pound or cliff drive which were most important (Wissler 1910:40; Roe 1951:637; Wedel 1961:59; Frison 1978:345). Not only did this method assure the most success and largest number of animals taken, but it included the use of large numbers of people as well. These undertakings had the effect of building the importance of the concept of band and tribe calling to mind Emile Durkheim's notion of mechanical solidarity.

Despite the social flexibility demanded by the

Plains adaptation (including an array of subsistence strategies) it was the large scale hunt which imprinted the economic and political system. Hence, collective hunting methods dominated, while individual methods remained distinctly secondary.

Gathering

There is virtually nothing given us on this subject by early explorers. Wedel (1961:283) notes that the archaeological record points to the increased use of implements for grinding vegetables and fruits in the period after 2500 BC; all of which indicates that gathering was coming to be more relied upon. From studies of similar hunter and gatherers we are now in a position to claim an overall increased importance of gathering in the total economy (Lee 1968, 1980).

Nineteenth century sources also document the importance of gathering to the total caloric intake of the society, and moreover, that it was a woman's task (Maximilian 1906:V.23:109; McClintock 1910:238; Wissler 1910:20; Denig 1930:582). The precariousness of the hunt underscored this interpretation. Despite the efficiency of the pound and cliff drive, it often failed (Henry the Younger 1898:V.2:620; Cocking 1908:113; M'Gillivray 1929:65). Even in the 19th century there were periods during which the buffalo were not to be found and in which survival of the group depended almost entirely on the efforts of women (Denig 1930:504, 582).

Raiding and Trading

As subsistence strategies these were fairly unimportant during the 18th century. With the exception of the Assiniboine who had long been dependent on inter-tribal and European trade, the others either shunned it altogether or traded only to supplement their economy. Inter-tribal trade between horticultural villages and nomadic hunters did, however, take place regularly. Both Ewers (1968) and Holder (1970) described this trade as the exchange of surpluses between groups. While regularized, this trade formed only a small part of the overall production considerations of nomadic hunters. Neither based their modes of production on this trade.

European trade during the second half of the 18th
century was primarily that of hunters supplying the
trade posts with provisions (Cocking 1908:118; Fidler
1967:283; Ray 1974:129-133). The Hudson Bay Company
had no real interest in buffalo hides during this
time, and tried in vain to get Plains nomads to trap
small furs. The Teton Dakota, as well as
Assiniboines, did trap beaver to some extent while the
Gros Ventre and Blackfoot refused. Sources also mention slaves being traded to the northern posts
(Cocking 1908:110; Umfreville 1954:91). However, as
the groups in question moved closer to the best buffalo country near the Missouri River, and as they
increasingly adapted the classic Plains pattern, they
left off trading in these goods.

Raiding, present during this century, likewise
represented a secondary institution. M'Gillivray
(1929:65), Henry the Elder (1966:299), Chardon
(1932:9), all mention raiding, most of which was for
horses but other goods were taken as well. What is
important, was that goods taken in raiding were individually owned; and since horses were taken in this
manner they too were privately held. Additionally,
this institution was male centered. Thus, horses came
into nomadic society as private property of men.

18th Century Relations of Production

The efficacy of large scale hunting and the
requirements it made on social organization resulted
in the "pound method" as a determining agent in Plains
society. The most important feature of this method
was its collective form. Virtually every facet of its
undertaking required significant amounts of labor;
labor requirements which were clearly beyond the capabilities of small encampments, and individuals. An
intensification of the band-level of organization
resulted, and one which found expression at the tribal
level as well, since both were amenable to this style
of hunting. Construction of the pound, with its
attendant requirements of gathering the materials, and
the construction of the pound itself required every
able-bodied person (Grinnell 1892:234; Henry the
Younger 1898:V.2:518; Roe 1951:637; Flannery 1953:56).
This fed other organizational and ideological institu-

tions such as the Sun Dance and tribal gatherings.

The division of labor surrounding the actual use of the pound represented the most elaborate that existed on the Plains. Five basic tasks, all synchronized, were required to assure the success of the pound: decoys, scouts, flanks, hunters, and spiritual guarantor (Klein 1977:184-189).

Every act of production implies a mode of distribution of the product. Property rights were likewise inherent in the pound as well as in other subsistence practices. Individualized hunting of buffalo fostered individual rights over the product, and collective ownership is found in the collective forms of the hunt (Grinnell 1892:234; Henry the Younger 1898:V.2:510; Ewers 1968:8; DeSmet 1969:V.3:1031). Since the collective forms represent the most important productive sphere in Plains society, the property rights inherent in them take on an added significance.

It was through the collective nature of Plains hunting and distribution that the egalitarian structure of society was institutionalized. While land and resources were held in common, much else was individually held (especially manufactured goods such as lodges, tools, weapons). The collective properties of the pound and cliff drive, given their all-important standing in the economy, intensified tribal egalitarianism: between individuals, and between men and women. Studies of other band level foragers indicate that where women play a significant role in primary production spheres, and especially where their presence in collective hunting is required, their position is roughly comparable to men (Turnbull 1966; Friedl 1975). Statements by early travelers and traders point up the slave-like status of women, but as regards their position in political economy their presence in key sectors assures them a place of significance.

The essentially equal distribution of the product of the hunt among families made dependency between them less likely. Each was assured an equal share of meat and hides from which most other manufactures resulted. Further exchange of raw materials reflected individuals' or families' desires over and above what was needed for basic provisioning.

151

Inequalities of wealth between households and individuals tended to be minimal; first, because of the limited sources of wealth, and secondly, because Plains society was governed by production-for-use. The latter placed political and economic emphasis on group consumption rather than the creation of surplus for increased individual wealth. Wealth differences tended to be leveled out, via "big man" giveaways which was the only route to prestige, and which further underscored the egalitarian structure of early Plains society.

19th CENTURY RELATIONS OF PRODUCTION

The buffalo hide trade seemed to grow in direct proportion to the changes wrought by the horse in the hunt. That these two were very well suited to one another is evident in the changes they jointly were able to effect.

The Impact of the Horse

At once a technological factor and a commodity, the horse presented profound possibilities to a pedestrian hunting people. As a means of transportation it afforded overland travel with increased loads in ways never before dreamt of. It likewise increased the efficiency of the hunter who could prevent the quarry from escaping. Moreover, the hunter could now travel to the game rather than try to lure it to the pound. Both as a commodity and a technological factor it was controlled by individual males. As a commodity the horse came to hold the position of a "special purpose currency" being equated with bridewealth, fines, most trade goods.

Unlike most technological factors, however, the horse was not internally reproduced. Only two Plains societies reproduced their herds via procreation (the Comanche and Nez Perce). All others experienced a chronic shortage with the result that raiding (another male-dominated institution) became the major economic institution.

Hunting was increasingly individualized. The chase method supplanted the earlier pound and cliff drive as the paramount form of hunting. It emphasized individual hunters rather than groups (Denig 1930:504; Flannery 1953:56; Ewers 1955:305; Roe 1955:258). Mobility enhanced, a mounted hunter could advance into a herd, select the animal desired and dispatch it through the chase. While the new method did at times utilize large groups of hunters, it no longer did so out of necessity or efficiency, but rather because seasonal concentrations of buffalo brought together large numbers of tribesmen. The logistical task which ensued involved restraining over-zealous hunters increasingly capable of acting on their own. What was changing in the 19th century was access to and ownership over wealth (in either a crude state--hides; or a finished state--horses and trade goods).

As essential as collective efforts were to the pound method of hunting, and as the dead buffalo in the pound were the result of many efforts and many arrows, the arrow as a property marker stood for nothing. The kill was collectively owned. Eighteenth century production and distribution relations were synonymous, but the horse and chase method of hunting shattered this unity. Rooted in individual effort and ownership, this new set of production relations also utilized different property relations: individual ownership over the kill. By the mid 19th century this pattern had emerged as dominant: the hide, tongue, and choice cuts of meat now belonged to the man who killed the animal (Parkman 1911:264; Denig 1930:531; Tabeau 1939:199; Flannery 1953:64). Paralleling these developments, the arrow as property marker in the kill also became recognized.

The absence of women from the 19th century hunt was conspicuous. It was now the domain of men (as raiders and hunters), and women along with horses and buffalo hides were to occupy positions in the chain of wealth now forming.

Men were also discriminated against. The ability to gain wealth and position was determined by individual merit: individuals as raiders, hunters, and gatherers of wives who could transform hides into exchange commodities. Youth, daring, and self concern were key ingredients (Denig 1930:474; Richardson and Hanks 1945:56; Ewers 1955:188).

Implications of the Hide Trade

The hide trade began in earnest around 1820, though interest in hides had been gradually building since the turn of the century. Once entrenched, it fed naturally into Plains production relations.

New goods were introduced through trade with Euro-Americans. Metal goods, guns, ammunition, and a host of personal items (including alcohol) provided the initial incentive for nomads to trade. These goods, however, merged with the potential impact of the horse and buffalo chase methods to exacerbate wealth differentials, and ultimately status and prestige. Social fragmentation also came about as a result of the dependency relations which had formed. Ewers (1959:96) indicated that Blackfoot households would at times abandon their encampment or band when the leader held back his gifts to the poor. Hassrick (1964:97) discussed Teton Dakota kin groupings (tiospaye) as having been more self contained in the 18th century.

Changes in Labor

The new technology, and prosperity, had the effect of more strictly dichotomizing labor between the sexes, with men hunting and women gathering. Additionally, Flannery showed that men became "procurers" of raw materials, while women became "processers" (1953:51). This increased degree of specialization of labor held dire consequences for women.

The trade with Americans and Europeans created a demand for hides that far outstripped the Native Americans' capacity to produce under the traditional units of domestic production. Changes in labor resulted, and one of the most telling is that women's labor time in processing ballooned. The size of the trade is revealing for its demands upon both men and women. Culbertson (1952:91) reported that in 1850 over 100,000 hides were shipped down to St. Louis from this area alone, and that at least three times that many were in circulation among the tribes of the Upper Missouri. From 1850 to 1883 the hide trade rose meteorically (Burlingame 1940; Roe 1951; Bartlett 1974). To reduce the millions of buffalo to a few thousand in the span of thirty years was an act of unprecedented carnage, requiring a lust for profit as well as cooperation from many sources. The Upper Missouri tribes clearly possessed neither the time nor inclination to slaughter that many animals; and to this end they were ignobly assisted by a host of white hunters and sportsmen. Nevertheless, the demands on their domestic mode of production had increased beyond the point where the household unit (man and wife) could comfortably accommodate the situation.

With the exception of being removed from the hunt, women's labor remained identical to that of the 18th century. Aside from the complete array of domestic duties (child care, cooking, gathering wood and water, setting up and taking down the lodge, manufacturing clothing for the family, and fashioning the lodge itself), women were also responsible for gathering plant life and tanning hides.

The rise in the hide trade dramatically increased the time she spent tanning hides. Taking into account her domestic duties, Hassrick estimates that it took one woman approximately ten days to tan a single buffalo robe (1964:183). Denig claimed that, if freed from other tasks, a woman could tan a hide in three days (1930:541). Calculating over the course of a season, a woman could produce between 20 and 30 hides (Flannery 1953:73; Ewers 1959:110).

Providing the raw materials for women proved far less time consuming for men. A single run at a herd of buffalo, Ewers calculated, would take between 30 minutes to an hour (1955:150). On average, a hunter mounted on a decent buffalo horse could net four to five animals (Ewers 1955:150). Flannery (1953:61) claims seven or eight buffalo is more likely. Plotted over a season, a camp of 15 to 20 men (average number for an encampment) could bring in over 1000 buffalo (Hornaday 1887:465). While crude, the data clearly point to the relative ease with which men could provide women with raw materials. Given these figures, the average man could easily supply at least two women with enough hides to tan.

The rise in demand for tanners resulted in increased polygyny (Dorsey 1892:226; Maximilian 1906:V.23:110; McClintock 1910:189). Bridewealth was now calculated almost exclusively in horses, further reinforcing potential wealth differences since now only successful raiders could get wives (as well as access to buffalo) (Goldfrank 1945; Richardson and Hanks 1945). Even polygyny, however, was not a sufficient answer to the labor shortage. Two additional methods were noted: the capture of women from other tribes,[3] and the use of women punished for committing adultery (Maximilian 1906:V.23:110).[4]

Thus while a woman's labor was at a premium her position in the political economy was in jeopardy: she labored more, but enjoyed it less, so to speak. The new forms of wealth in horses and trade goods fed back on a system that was predisposed to those who were already well-heeled. It allowed men to spend less time on non-wealth producing tasks so that they might expend their energies on more fruitful tasks. Rather than getting bogged down in their wealth, or satiated by it, the combination of traits (horse to buffalo to wives to trade goods) allowed economic disparities to proliferate. Established men were now in a position to pay for work which was not directly related to wealth accumulation (e.g. paying older men to make arrowheads and common weapon repairs--Densmore 1918:439; Ewers 1959:123). Young boys were used to tend to herds (Parkman 1911:248; Denig 1930:505) further freeing their owners from a laborious task.

The economy was shifting away from a preoccupation with subsistence to production-for-exchange; and with it the production relations between the sexes had altered. The overall prosperity concealed an erosion of women's position through her being increasingly circumscribed to a few tasks related to processing and domestic production. On the other hand, men were increasingly free to pursue wealth.

Control Over Goods

While women were never to completely lose their position in the political economy, their removal from crucial spheres of production adversely affected their ability to control status bearing goods. Certain goods (and the discrepancies) may have been traditional, but others perhaps resulted from the European trade era. A survey of some of them is revealing.

Apart from the land and its basic resources, and

156

situations of extreme scarcity, most things were individually owned. Tools, as well as most commonplace goods were privately owned (Dorsey 1892:225; Wissler 1910:22; Thompson 1916:264; Denig 1930:463). Here, control was simply a matter of manufacturing the item: women and men produced and controlled what they wanted. Valued goods were another matter. Generally, the more valued the good, the more likely that it would be male owned, and where both sexes owned the same things men tended to own more of them. Horses, for instance, were in theory and fact owned by both sexes. The data, however, reveal that horses owned by women were the least valued mounts (packing or transport horses), while men owned the prized war, race, and buffalo horses (Schultz 1935:30-31; Flannery 1953:66; Ewers 1955:28). Hides were also owned by women but only after they were given to them by men, and only those that were used for domestic purposes. Control over the use of trade hides was firmly in the hands of men (Flannery 1953:82; Denig 1961:155; Kurz 1970:216; Boller 1972:301-302); so that even when women were trading at the posts they were acting in the capacity of agents for their men rather than autonomously.

In the establishment of trade, both before and after trade had been completed, substantial amounts of goods were distributed (Culbertson 1952:83). The control of these goods fell to the men as well (Lewis 1942:45; Fidler 1967:V.26:279; Tomison 1967:V.26:51).

One of the more startling contradictions between legal rights and political economic practice deals with the destruction of property for committing certain offenses. The lodge, one of the most valuable items in Plains society was manufactured and owned by women (Densmore 1918:437; Flannery 1953:44; Ewers 1955:159; DeSmet 1969:V.4:1028). Keeping in mind the respect that exists for private right, it is puzzling that the punishment for a man hunting without permission was the destruction of his property: his horse, weapons, and lodge being most frequently mentioned (Densmore 1918; Flannery 1953; Ewers 1955; DeSmet 1969). To whom, then, does the lodge belong? The contradiction may be explained if we view women as subsumed by men so that their ownership is superseded by his.

RISE OF MALE SODALITIES

Unlike Moore's (1974) study of Cheyenne society, in which tension existed between the earlier matrilineal and later patrilineal foci, the societies in my analysis were not matrilineal. They were essentially bilateral, tending slightly towards a male orientation. The 19th century saw the gender balance shift noticeably in favor of male institutions. Raiding and hunting rose in importance and, in doing so, served as the backbone of male ascendancy. Any examination of the loss of women's status position must also look at the rise of the male position. However, both male and female shift in the political economy was but a subset of the larger economic and political picture of the society as a whole.

The loss of much of women's position (in the hunt, property relations, and control over goods) is masked by the general rise in repoductivity in the hunting-raiding sector of society. The horse clearly brought about a revolution in transportation (Mishkin 1940), hunting and raiding. The entire society prospered from the increased trade that came about as new forms of production (internal) and trade (external) merged. If women occupied a more circumscript role in production it was while enjoying the new prosperity. Hunting was now more assured. Metal pots, knives and axes had obvious advantages over stone and pottery. Iron arrowheads were infinitely better than stone counterparts. Guns were superior weapons of war. And the host of cosmetic products provided welcome relief in the world of self-presentation and fashion. However, the continued enjoyment of these goods demanded the shift to an economy geared for exchange, which in turn assumed dependency on foreign trade.

Internally, the new prosperity prompted the more specialized use of men and women; dividing major tasks between them, they developed procuring and processing subspecialties. Other institutions changed as well; two in particular deserve analysis: (1) military sodalities; and (2) the rise of individualism.

The Rise of Individualism and the Provisioning Crisis

The 19th century relations of production were marked by the potential for individualized production and private property relations. Both of these were present in the earlier era but were secondary in provisioning the society. The increased importance of these economic factors brought about a minor crisis in provisioning of all members of the group. The increased importance of soldier societies during the 19th century helped offset the potential for individualisms, and in the course of doing so had the effect of increasing men's position in the society at large.

The view of production taken in this study is that of Marx's in the Grundrisse (1973). For him every act of production had a form of distribution attached to it. Distribution, for Marx, is a societally recognized phenomenon which is woven into each act of production so as to go unquestioned by the actors. He distinguished distribution from exchange--a flow of goods and/or services subsequent to distribution. In exchange, people take what gets distributed to them (via production) and transact commodities based on their individual desires or needs. Thus, distribution is societal, unconscious, and determined by law or custom; while exchange is individual, conscious, and determined by whim or need. As originally envisioned, exchange follows distribution, both of which are completed in the act of consumption. This causes the cycle to be repeated.

In the 18th century production was governed by collective relations and property rights. Translated into Marx's model, this means that Plains societies were provisioned effectively by their cycles of Production-Distribution-Exchange-Consumption. Each lodge and its occupants were provided for as a result of the collective mode of production and distribution. Individual exchange was carried out but was entirely secondary to distribution; i.e. it was not necessary for survival.

The 19th century with its constellation of traits, all of which favored individualism and private property, created a problem in provisioning members of society who, as a result of not owning the necessary requisites to wealth, were unable to provision themselves. With the ability of collective distribution diminished, the brunt of provisioning increasingly fell to the subsequent layer of circulation: exchange. In one sense the exchange component was ideally suited to the 19th century since it was rooted in individualism. But, precisely because of this it had difficulty in provisioning the group.

Individual access to game and rights over game precipitated this shift, and disparities in wealth between individuals and between families grew as a consequence (Parkman 1911:283; Flannery 1953:92; Ewers 1955:162; DeSmet 1969:V.4:964). Dependency between people of wealth and the poor added a dimension to the provisioning problems. Blackfoot scholars point out that the institutionalization of the loaning of horses by wealthier individuals, rather than resolving the discrepancy added to it. Because horses were loaned with interest they barely kept the borrower's head above water (Lewis 1942:54; Goldfrank 1945:18; Richardson and Hanks 1945:55).

Self interest is the hallmark of the exchange level of circulation in Marx's scheme. Ewers (1955:240) presents an interesting case along these lines. He cites the instance of a young man, who having killed a buffalo, was butchering it. Coming towards him was an elderly couple. He saw them but they had not as yet seen him. He lay down as if dead, and when the elderly couple finally came upon him and his buffalo they tried in vain to revive him. Had they come upon him while he was butchering they would have been entitled to a share of the game, but fearing the young man dead they ran back to the village. No sooner were they out of sight when the young man got up and continued to butcher his kill.

While extreme, this example is nevertheless illustrative of the dilemma faced by those who could no longer be provisioned by the old standards of society. To overcome these tendencies a number of institutions were invented or elaborated upon. One such device was known among the Teton as the "Challenge Stick" (Mirsky 1967:410). A small wooden object carved in the likeness of a desired object was thrown into the tent of a rich man by his poorer colleagues. It served as a reminder that it was the duty of the more affluent to share with others. The

160

very presence of such an institution underscores some of the points I have made.

Hassrick (1964:176) writes of another means by which the poor might gain access to meat. "Tail Tieing" was a ritual in which those unable to engage in the hunt could tie the tail of a buffalo being butchered by a successful hunter. While the hunter had first choice, he could not refuse meat to others in accordance with this ritual. However, as Hassrick goes on to point out, there was a stigma attached to those who had to resort to tail tieing. This would have been unnecessary under the older pound method of distribution.

Other means by which individuals could secure goods from the rich was by presenting them with a small present. The nature of gift-giving was graduated so that the wealthy were required to give something befitting their status (Ewers 1955:255).

Goldfrank (1943:75-76) notes that among the Teton Dakota the Hunka ceremony--a ritual adoption along family lines--gradually merged with the "favorite child" ceremony. This fusion was in response to the marked increase in individualism of the 19th century. The upshot of the merger was that the occasion was used to distribute substantial amounts of goods throughout the society. Giveaways and Ghost Owning--two other ceremonies which occasioned wealth distribution--also became more prevalent in response to the provisioning crisis.

Male Sodalities

The erosion of the collective mode of production spawned the increased use of other mechanisms to provision society. The role of men's soldier societies also underwent changes in response to this need.

Soldier societies were men's sodalities, found throughout the Plains (Grinnell 1892:220; Densmore 1918:313; Bradley 1923:279; Denig 1930:544; Henry the Elder 1966:282). Their presence in the 18th century is documented in some of the earlier accounts (Hendry 1907:45; LaVerendrye 1927:334; Henry the Elder 1966:230). While we know little of their origins we

do know a bit about their functions. Most travelers
and early ethnographers saw fit to mention the ceremonial and policing duties that soldier societies performed (Hendry 1907:330; McClintock 1910:465; Denig
1930:622; Flannery 1953:40).

Though soldier societies helped to integrate and
manage Plains life through their social and ceremonial
functions, their role in the political economy has
been overlooked. The data warrant thinking of at
least four economic functions for them: (1) the regulation of access to resources; (2) the maintenance and
initiation of crucial economic strategies; (3) their
role as redistributional agents for scarce goods or
resources; (4) their role in calling for goods needed
to sustain themselves. These collectively aided in
distributing goods throughout the society, and so
aided in ameliorating the effects of an individualized
economy.

The membership of soldier societies was recruited
along age lines among the Gros Ventre and Blackfoot,
and individually among the Teton Dakota and
Assiniboines. In either case, being a member of a
sodality heightened male bonding. Bonding was
furthered by the institutionalized friendships (called
Kolas among the Teton Dakota) that occurred in Plains
society (Flannery 1953:39; Ewers 1959:105; Hassrick
1964:20). These dyads were entered into voluntarily
and lasted a lifetime. Their intensity and loyalty
advanced the comradery that formed the building blocks
in societies.

Often interpreted as simply "policing," the role
played by soldier societies in the hunt is really one
of assuring equal access to resources. Also of
interest is their role in the regulation of access to
resources other than the buffalo herds (McClintock
1910:464). The well documented performance of sodalities in the hunt includes an economic component in
addition to policing. By assuring each mounted hunter
a chance at the herd they were securing the maximum
opportunity of most households (Maximilian
1906:V.23:115; Densmore 1918:313; Lewis and Clark
1969:V.1:168).

A second function is the working out of crucial
economic strategies. In certain instances a strategy,
such as suing for peace ("Smoking"), or the summer

buffalo hunt, the sodality played the role of initiators. We have already pointed this out in the case of the buffalo hunt, but in the less frequently mentioned "smoking" strategy their role has not been discussed. Where two political and/or economic entities come together for the purpose of declaring peace (and to facilitate needed exchange of goods) soldier societies were used to begin deliberations and facilitate their undertaking.

> Peaces are made between wild tribes by the ceremony of smoking and exchanging presents of horses, and other property; sometimes women. The advantages are well calculated on both sides before overtures of peace are made (Denig 1930:404).

Securing a cessation of hostilities, as mentioned by the trader Denig, might be a motive; it might also be used as a means of establishing trade (Boller 1972:138). More often, however, it was a strategy designed to obtain gifts (Bradbury 1906:113; Ewers 1937:18; MacKenzie 1961:346). Later in the century it would be used with U.S. officials to secure annuities.

In whatever guise it was used, it was soldier societies who governed the proceedings (Denig 1930:442, 470; Kurz 1970:219). In carrying out these duties the soldier society acted in tandem with the political consensus arrived at by chiefs and councils.

The most important function carried out by these sodalities was the redistribution of goods and resources, especially those that were scarce or irregularly occurring. When subsistence was in doubt, it was to soldier societies that the political authorities turned to assure fair rationing. McClintock reports an instance among the Blackfoot in which sodalities were charged with the regulation of women gathering berries. Since this was a situation of scarcity, it fell to the soldiers to appropriate and ration out the berries (1910:464). In all situations pertaining to the exchange of gifts between groups it was sodalities which oversaw the distribution of goods (Culbertson 1952:470; Kurz 1970:219).

As units of consumption, sodalities called upon the community for aid. In this respect they also insured the redistribution of goods. The Gros Ventre

"Begging Dance" and the Assiniboine "Dance of the Provision Stealers" were but two of many instances of ritualization of the request by sodalities for aid. In the Gros Ventre case the sodality would use their distinctive begging songs as they advanced upon one of the rival sodalities' lodge (Flannery 1953:41). In this way goods were kept circulating through the band. The Assiniboines case uses a ceremonial ploy in which soldiers go through camp and secretly appropriate items for which the owners must pay a ransom to have them returned (Denig 1930:564). Even day-to-day food was solicited from the band. While soldiers were also members of households and hunted, when serving in any official capacity the band would provide for them. Densmore (1918:322) mentions that the Teton Dakota "Strong Hearts" sodality went around the village requisitioning food for the day. This service was often given by the encampment or band for periods ranging, in one instance, up to a year (Lowie 1909: 94).

In so far as sodalities are functioning parts of the group, they both serve and depend on the group. The political functions the sodalities provide are openly acknowledged by the group, and in return they are provided for in most ways. The economic functions, however, are not so easily discernable. They rarely are directly involved in hunting, trading, raiding and so appear outside of the relations of production. But they perform vital duties in that they assure access to the primary resources, and distribute goods. In the context of the crisis of provisioning emerging in the 19th century the sodality worked to take up the slack left by the erosion of the collective mode of production and distribution. It provided. As a byproduct these sodalities raised the already rising position of men vis-a-vis women.

CONCLUSION

Changes in the political economy of the 19th century Plains continued to address fundamental questions: provisioning the group; establishing the guidelines for prestige; regulating access to resources; maintaining coherent groups (both on the band and tribal level); and continuing to be responsive to the need for sensitivity to ecology. However, the introduction of new production factors, orientations to subsistence and distributional models, and a new basis of wealth brought changes in almost every Plains institution. The new mode of production favored men over women, young over old, the individual over the group. Economic strategies such as trading, raiding, individualized hunting, and 'smoking' emphasized individual males and privately held rights in property. The buffalo hide trade also lifted the economic ceiling which had governed Plains nomadic production. The prosperity which followed solved old problems such as subsistence shortages, but created new ones: provisioning people who no longer had an active role in crucial economic spheres. The emerging "have-nots" became dependents thereby underwriting the status of wealthier members.

Individualized production-for-exchange, however, continued alongside a framework of collective ownership over resources and was still curbed by the requirements of functioning in a kin-based society. This prevented a full fledged turn to privatizing the economy and society. The resulting tension between collective and individual modes of production was somewhat ameliorated by: group-wide prosperity; the creation of alternatives to the defunct 18th century mode of ownership; the frenetic pace of the hide trade; and the stepped up warfare against American intruders. Within this 19th century Plains version of "life in the fast lane," women's relative loss of political economic position was lost sight of.

FOOTNOTES

1. Relations of Production represent those social relationships that are found in the act of production of goods. Marxists commonly see these relations as part of the substucture which also includes the factors involved in production (e.g. resources, technology, etc.). However, relations of production go beyond mere social relationships to include political authority, property relations, and the relationships between them.

2. Lewis (1942), Richardson (1945), and Ewers (1955) have all made some astute comments on the impact of these things upon Plains Indian women, but no one has taken on a systematic analysis.

3. In the 18th century captives were taken and traded to the British. The marginal subsistence of Plains nomads would not allow them to tax their reserves by taking on captives to any large degree.

4. This latter method, while not perhaps consciously formulated, had the effect of creating a significant number of women, who, repudiated by their husbands because of sexual indiscretions and disfigured had no way of earning their keep except to do whatever labor was demanded of them. Maximilian (1906:V.23:110) claims that in every dozen lodges he would find anywhere from 8 to 10 of these women.

REFERENCES CITED

Albers, Patricia C. (1982a) Sioux Kinship in a Colonial Setting. _Dialectical Anthropology_ Vol. 6, pp. 253-270.

_____ (1982b) Sioux Women in Transition: A Study of Their Changing Status in Domestic and Capitalist Sectors of Production (in this volume).

Bartlett, Richard A. (1974) _The New Country: A Social History of the American Frontier, 1776-1890_. London: Oxford University Press.

Bloch, Maurice (Ed.) (1975) _Marxist Analysis in Social Anthropology_. New York: John Wiley & Sons.

Boller, Henry A. (1972) _Among the Indians: Four Years on the Upper Missouri 1858 to 1862_. Milo Quaife, ed. Lincoln: University of Nebraska Press.

Bradbury, John (1906) _Bradbury's Travels in the Interior of America in the Years 1809 to 1811_. R.G. Thwaites, ed. _Early Western Travels_, Vol. 6. Cleveland: Arthur H. Clark Co.

Bradley, James H. (1923) Characteristics, Habits, and Customs of the Blackfoot Indians. _Montana Historical Society Contributions_, Vol. 9, Helena.

Burlingame, Merrill G. (1940) The Buffalo in Trade and Commerce. _North Dakota Historical Quarterly_, Vol. 3, No. 4, Bismark.

Catlin, George (1973) _Letters and Notes on the Manners, Customs, and Conditions of the North American Indians_ (2 Volumes). New York: Dover Books.

Chardon, Pierre (1932) _Chardon's Journal at Fort Clark 1834-1839_. Annie Able, ed. Pierre: Department of History for the State of South Dakota.

Cocking, Matthew (1908) Journal of Matthew Cocking, from Fort York to the Blackfoot Country, 1772-1773, Lawrence Burpee, ed. Ottawa: Royal Society of Canada Transactions, Sec. II.

Culbertson, Thaddeus (1952) Journal of an Expedition to the Mauvaises Terres and the Upper Missouri in 1850, John McDermott, ed. Smithsonian Institution Bureau of American Ethnology, Bulletin No. 147, Washington.

Denig, Edwin (1930) Indian Tribes of the Upper Missouri. John Ewers, ed. Washington, D.C.: Annual Report of the Bureau of American Ethnology.

_____ (1961) Indian Tribes of the Upper Missouri. John Ewers, ed. Norman: University of Oklahoma Press.

Densmore, Francis (1918) Teton Sioux Music. Smithsonian Institution, Bureau of American Ethnology, Bulletin #61, Washington, D.C.

DeSmet, Father (1969) Life, Letters, and Travels of Father DeSmet (4 Volumes), Chittenden and Richardson, eds. New York: New York Times Press.

Dodge, Richard I. (1970) Our Wild Indians. Freeport, New York: Books for Libraries Press.

Dorsey, J.O. (1892) Siouan Sociology. Annual Report of the Bureau of American Ethnology, Washington, D.C.

Etienne, Mona, and Eleanor Leacock, Eds. (1980) Women in Colonialism. New York: Praeger.

Ewers, John C. (1937) Teton Dakota: Ethnology and History. Berkeley, California: U.S. Department of the Interior, National Park Service.

_____ (1955) The Horse in Blackfoot Culture. Smithsonian Institution Bureau of American Ethnology, Bulletin #159, Washington, D.C.

_____ (1959) The Blackfoot: Raiders of the Northwestern Plains. Norman: University of Oklahoma Press.

Ewers, John C. (1968) <u>Indian Life on the Upper Missouri.</u> Norman: University of Oklahoma Press.

Fidler, Peter (1967) <u>Journal of Peter Fidler - Chesterfield House.</u> London: Publication of the Hudson Bay Record Society, Vol. 26.

Flannery, Regina (1953) <u>The Gros Ventre of Montana.</u> Washington, D.C.: Catholic University Press.

Friedl, Ernestine (1975) <u>Women and Men: An Anthropological Perspective.</u> New York: Holt, Rinehart, and Winston.

Frison, George (1978) <u>Prehistoric Hunters on the High Plains.</u> New York: Academic Press.

Godelier, Maurice (1977) <u>Perspectives in Marxist Anthropology.</u> London: Cambridge University Press.

Goldfrank, Esther (1943) Historic Change and Social Character: A Study of the Teton Dakota. <u>American Anthropologist</u>, Vol. 45, No. 1, Washington, D.C.

_____ (1945) <u>Changing Configurations in the Social Organization of the Blackfoot Tribe During the Reserve Period.</u> Monographs of the American Ethnological Society, University of Washington Press, Seattle.

Grinnell, George Bird (1892) Early Blackfoot History. <u>American Anthropologist</u>, Vol. 5, No. 2, Washington, D.C.

Hassrick, Royal B. (1964) <u>The Sioux: Life and Customs of a Warrior Society.</u> Norman: University of Oklahoma Press.

Hendry, Anthony (1907) <u>York Factory to the Blackfoot Country: The Journal of Anthony Hendry, 1754-1755,</u> Lawrence Burpee, ed. Royal Society of Canada, Ser. 3, Vol. 2, Sec. 2, Ottawa.

Henry, Alexander (the Elder) (1966) <u>Travels and Adventures in Canada and the Indian Territories Between the Years 1760 and 1776.</u> Ann Arbor: Ann Arbor Microfilms.

Henry, Alexander (the Younger) (1898) New Light on the History of the Greater Northwest (2 Volumes), Elliot Coues, ed. Minneapolis: Ross and Haines Inc.

Holder, Preston (1970) The Hoe and the Horse on the Plains: A Study of Cultural Development Among North American Indians. Lincoln: University of Nebraska Press.

Hornaday, William T. (1887) The Extermination of the American Bison. Annual Report of the U.S. Natural Museum, Washington.

Jablow, Joseph (1950) The Cheyenne in Plains Indian Trade Relations, 1795-1840. American Ethnological Society Monographs, No. 19. Seattle: University of Washington Press.

Kelly, Francis (1973) My Captivity Among the Sioux Indians. Secaucus, N.J.: Citadel Press.

Klein, Alan M. (1977) Adaptive Strategies and Processes on the Plains: The 19th Century Cultural Sink. Ph.D. Dissertation, Department of Anthropology, SUNY-Buffalo, Buffalo, New York.

_____ (1980) Economic Analysis on the Great Plains: The Marxist Complement. In: Anthropology on the Great Plains, Margot Liberty and Raymond Woods, eds. Lincoln: University of Nebraska Press.

Kurz, Rudolph (1970) Journal of Rudolph Friederich Kurz, J.N.B. Hewitt, ed. Lincoln: University of Nebraska Press.

La Verendrye, Pierre (1927) Journal and Letters of Pierre de Varennes de La Verendrye and His Sons, Lawrence Burpee, ed. Toronto: Publications of the Champlain Society, No. 16.

Leacock, Eleanore (1954) The Montagnais 'Hunting Territory' and the Fur Trade. Washington, D.C.: American Anthropological Association Memoirs #78.

Leacock, Eleanore (1978) Women's Status in Egalitarian Society. Current Anthropology, Vol. 19, No. 2, pp. 247-275, Chicago.

Lee, Richard B., and Irvin DeVore, eds. (1968) Man the Hunter. Chicago: Aldine Publishers.

_____ (1980) Kung San. London: Cambridge University Press.

Lewis, Oscar (1942) The Effects of White Contact Upon Blackfoot Culture. American Ethnological Society Monographs #6, University of Washington Press.

Lewis, Meriweather, and William Clark (1969) The Journals of Lewis and Clark, Nicolas Biddle, ed. New York: New York Heritage Press (original edition 1904).

Lowie, Robert (1909) The Assiniboines. American Museum of Natural History Anthropological Papers, Vol. 4, Pt. 1, New York.

M'Gillivray, Duncan (1929) The Journal of Duncan M'Gillivray, Arthur Morton, ed. Toronto: University of Toronto Press.

MacKenzie, Charles (1961) The Missouri Indians: A Narrative of Four Trading Expeditions to the Missouri. In: Bourgeois de la Compagnie du Nord Ouest, L.F. Masson, ed. New York: Antiquarian Press.

Marx, Karl (1973) Grundrisse. New York: Vintage Books.

Maximilian, Prince of Wied (1906) Travels in the Interior of North America. In: Early Western Travels, 1748-1846, R.G. Thwaites, ed., Vol. 23. New York: AMS Press (reprinted 1966).

McClintock, Walter (1910) Old North Trail. London.

McElroy, Ann, and Carolyn Mathiason, eds. (1979) Sex Roles in Changing Cultures. Occasional Papers in Anthropology, Vol. 1, Department of Anthropology, SUNY-Buffalo, Buffalo, New York.

Meillassoux, Claude (1974) _Anthropologie Economique des Gouro de Cote d'Ivoire_. The Hague: Mouton.

Mishkin, Bernard (1940) _Rank and Warfare Among the Plains Indians_. American Ethnological Society Monographs #3. Seattle: University of Washington Press.

Mirsky, Jeanette (1967) The Dakota. In: _Co-operation and Competition in Primitive Society_, Margaret Mead, ed. Boston: Beacon Press.

Moore, John H. (1974) Cheyenne Political History, 1820-1894. _Ethnohistory_, Vol. 21, No. 4, pp. 329-359, New York.

_____ (1980) Plains Ethnography and the Ethnology of Kinship. In: _Anthropology on the Great Plains_, Margot Liberty and Raymond Woods, eds. Lincoln: University of Nebraska Press.

Murphy, Robert (1970) _The Dialectics of Social Life: Alarms and Excursions into Anthropological Theory_. New York: Basic Books.

Oliver, Symmes (1962) Ecology and Cultural Continuity as Contributring Factors in Social Organization of the Plains Indians. _Publications in Archaeology and Ethnology_, Vol. 48, No. 1, University of California Press.

Parkman, Francis (1911) _The Oregon Trail: Sketches of Prairies and Rocky Mountain Life_. New York: Scott, Foresman and Co.

Ray, Arthur (1974) _Indians of the Fur Trade_. Toronto: University of Toronto Press.

Reiter, Rayna, ed. (1976) _Toward an Anthropology of Women_. New York: Monthly Review Press.

Richardson, Jane, and Lucien Hanks (1945) _Observations on Blackfoot Kinship System_. American Ethnological Society Monographs #9. Seattle: University of Washington Press.

Roe, Frank G. (1951) _The North American Buffalo_. Toronto: University of Toronto Press.

Roe, Frank G. (1955) The Indian and the Horse.
Norman: University of Oklahoma Press.

Rosaldo, Michele, and Louise Lamphere, eds. (1974)
Women, Culture, and Society. Palo Alto:
Stanford University Press.

Schultz, Willard (1935) My Life as an Indian.
New York: Bantam Books (reprinted 1972).

Secoy, Frank (1953) Changing Military Patterns on
the Great Plains. American Ethnological Society
Monographs #21. Seattle: University of
Washington Press.

Strong, William Duncan (1941) Environment and Native
Subsistence Economies in the Central Great
Plains. Smithsonian Institution Miscellaneous
Collections, Vol. 101, Washington, D.C.

Tabeau, Pierre A. (1939) Tabeau's Narrative of
Loisel's Expedition to the Upper Missouri,
Anne Able, ed. Norman: University of
Oklahoma Press.

Terray, Emmanuel (1972) Marxism and 'Primtive'
Society. New York: Monthly Review Press.

Thompson, David (1916) David Thompson's Narrative,
1784-1812, Richard Gover, ed. Toronto:
Champlain Society.

Tomison, William (1967) Journal of William Tomison.
Hudson Bay Record Society, Vol. 26, London.

Turnbull, Colin (1966) Wayward Servants. London:
Eyre and Spotteswood.

Umfreville, Edward (1954) The Present State of
the Hudson's Bay Company, Steward Wallace, ed.
Toronto: Ryerton Press.

Wedel, Waldo (1961) Prehistoric Man on the Great
Plains. Norman: University of Oklahoma Press.

Wissler, Clark (1910) The Material Culture of the
Blackfoot Indian. American Anthropologist,
Vol. 16, pp. 1-25.

CHAPTER 8

SIOUX WOMEN IN TRANSITION:

A Study of Their Changing Status in Domestic and Capitalist Sectors of Production

Patricia C. Albers
University of Utah

The changing status of women under colonial domination is a widely discussed and debated issue. If
any conclusion is to be reached from recent studies on
the subject, it would be that the historical experiences of women in colonial settings are not uniform
(Hamamsy 1957; Spindler 1962; Boserup 1970; Mintz
1971; Lamphere 1974, 1977; Van Allen 1974; Bossen
1975; James 1975; Leacock 1975, 1978, 1979; Okonjo
1975; Remy 1975; Aguiar 1976; Deere 1976, 1979;
Elmendorf 1976; Garrett 1976; Rothenberg 1976; Vidal
1976; Quinn 1977; Russell-Wood 1978; Safiotti 1978;
Apodoca 1979; Burkett 1979; Dole 1979; Henderson 1979;
Leis 1979; McElroy 1979; Nowack 1979; Urdang 1979;
Etienne and Leacock 1980).

The effects of colonialism on female status are
varied, and often contradictory, even within a single
population. This is revealed in two recent articles
(Bysiewicz and Van de Mark 1977; Maynard 1979) on the
changing status of Sioux (Dakota)[1] women. Shirley
Bysiewicz and Ruth Van de Mark, on the one hand, maintain that the status of Sioux women has declined
during reservation times. In arguing their case,
these two authors identify several areas where sexual
inequality has increased and become institutionalized
within reservation communities: the areas include
segregation in job opportunities and wages, discrimination in legal rights, as well as exclusion from
federal and tribal government positions. Eileen
Maynard (1979), on the other hand, reaches an entirely

different conclusion. Focusing attention on the role of women in the family and household, Maynard takes the position that female status has risen during the modern era. More specifically, she claims that Sioux women have gained an economic advantage which has enabled them to wield considerable influence and power in their own communities.

The contrasting views on the contemporary status of Sioux women is not a case of one position being right and the other wrong. Nor is it a case of observation and interpretation being biased by opposing premises. Instead, the disagreement derives from the fact that each of the authors (Bysiewicz and Van de Mark 1977; Maynard 1979) have examined separate aspects of female economic and political involvement. In concentrating attention on the changing status of Sioux women within more restricted realms of their participation, neither of the authors recognized the obvious contradictions in the nature of female status in modern reservation settings. Had a wider perspective been taken, the contradictions might have been illuminated and, possibly, even explained.

The contradictory nature of female status in Sioux reservation settings raises two separate but related questions: (1) how has this contradiction emerged and manifested itself in modern times? and (2) what can the contradictory experiences of Sioux women tell us about the impact of colonialism on female status more generally? Using data drawn from my field research with women living on the Devil's Lake Sioux Reservation in North Dakota[2], my purpose in this paper is to arrive at some answers to these questions.

STATEMENT OF THE PROBLEM

In the literature that deals with women under colonialism,[3] there is a growing recognition that changes in the status and role of women have been a direct result of capitalism (Boserup 1970; Van Allen 1974; James 1975; Leacock 1975, 1978, 1979; Remy 1975; Aguiar 1976; Deere 1976, 1979; Rothenberg 1976; Safiotti 1978; Burkett 1979; Etienne and Leacock 1980). Capitalism has had a major impact not only on the nature of women's work within and outside a domestic setting but also on the power and influence women are able to exercise in managing their labor and in controlling material goods. The realization that capitalism is directly implicated in the changing position of indigenous women raises two important questions: (1) how and to what degree have female work experiences changed under capitalism? (2) what has happened to the role of domestic production (that is, production of use-values) in the process? Even though there is a general consensus that these are critical questions to ask, there is little agreement on the answers.

One approach to these questions involves a dualistic perspective. This particular point-of-view presumes that domestic and capitalist sectors of production are independent of each other. This division is not merely heuristic in scope but represents, in fact, an epistemological premise. Many of those who follow this approach take the view that there is a universal cleavage in human societies, commonly known as the public-private dichotomy. On the public side is a sector based on commmunity-wide associations of a jural-political nature, whereas the private side is identified by domestic relations which are familial in character. In writings where this sectorial split is used, it is generally presumed that the public sector is male-dominated and organizes, as well as controls, the diverse, and at times conflicting, interests of female-centered household groups (Ortner 1974; Rosaldo 1974; Sanday 1974).

Adherents of the dualistic approach maintain that with the advent of capitalism the separation of these two spheres and the domination of the public over the private becomes more pronounced.[4] They also argue that productive activities once concentrated in the domestic sphere are eventually appropriated by the capitalist sector of production. With these changes, women's work in the domestic sector becomes less essential, and as a result, it is devalued (i.e. it loses prestige). This kind of reasoning is supported, in one way or another, by a wide range of scholars (Michaelson and Goldschmidt 1971; Schultz 1971; Oakley 1974; Minge-Klevana 1978, 1980). As I see it, the "dualistic" perspective has two essential drawbacks.

One problem is empirical. If one takes the dualistic argument to its ultimate conclusion, not only does one have to presume a universal structural split along public-private lines but one also has to suppose an inevitable decline in the status of women under capitalism. Suppositions such as these, in my estimation, are deficient. While it is clear that in many, perhaps the majority, of cases, there is a rigid sectorial split in human societies, and while it is also true that in a large number of situations women have lost ground under capitalism, there are significant exceptions. For instance, evidence on the Iroquois suggests that a public-private dichotomy did not exist as conventionally defined. Even more interesting, the data indicate that in the early years of mercantile expansions into the New World, the status of women actually increased (Randle 1951; Rothenberg 1976, 1980; Nowack 1979). Unless the Iroquis situation is viewed as totally aberrant, there is no way to comprehend, much less explain this circumstance, with a dualistic paradigm.

The empirical weakness of dualistic approaches is rooted in more basic theoretical flaws. When it is presumed that the capitalist sector of an economy acts as a monolithic determining or causative force on other modes of production, one consequence is an absence of any attempt to understand the dynamics and organization of the articulation between capitalism and domestic production. The dualistic approach is almost entirely unidirectional, with dominance emanating from the public to the private sphere or from the capitalist to the domestic sector. Questions of change are presented in a unlineal fashion, ignoring the dialectical realities of the encounter which, among other things, includes the resistance and challenge of those who labor under capitalism, either in the home or the marketplace. In failing to grasp the nature, dynamics, and historical specificity of this articulation, the explanatory power of dualistic approaches is severaly impoverished.

Another perspective, which will be identified here as "holistic," also distinguishes between domestic and capitalist sectors of production. But here the separation is only categorical and heuristic. From an epistemological standpoint the sectors are interrelated so that the dynamics of each are mutually determined. In the holistic approach, production in the domestic sector is pivotal (though not necessarily dominant in a causal sense) to the entire capitalist production process. Not only does it carry out a wide variety of provisioning tasks necessary to maintain and reproduce a given class structure; but, in the case of those "who work for capitalism," it plays an important role in keeping wages depressed and increasing profits (Seccombe 1974; Sacks 1975; Fee 1976; Deere 1976, 1979; Garrett 1976; Sudarkasa 1976; Saffioti 1977, 1978; Himmelweit and Mohun 1977). Notwithstanding the fact that domestic labor is devalued in many social (class) ideologies[5], it is nevertheless essential to the continuance of capitalist production and reproduction.

In holistic approaches, the status of women and the division of labor by sex are made intelligible only through an understanding of (1) how women and their communities (classes) are linked to the capitalist production process; and (2) how this linkage influences the way(s) in which provisioning tasks are organized in the domestic sector. But even though it is clear that these are important issues to consider, it is also obvious that the answers are grounded in the historical specificity of a people's existence during the period of capitalism's encroachments.

A primary advantage, in my view, of using a holistic approach is that it allows for an understanding of the articulations between domestic and capitalist sectors of production, and in doing this, it offers a more powerful model for comparing differences in the dynamics and organization of these articulations. Thus far, studies which have followed a holistic paradigm have dealt primarily with the situation of the working-class in the geographic centers of capitalism (Seccombe 1974; Fee 1976; Himmelweit and Mohan 1977). There are a growing number of studies, however, which are using this paradigm in the analysis of workers on capitalism's geographic peripheries, notably Africa and Latin America (Van Allen 1974; James 1975; Remy 1975; Deere 1976, 1979; Garrett 1976; Sudarkasa 1976; Saffioti 1978). The evidence from this research indicates that there are important differences between the situations of working peoples in the centers and peripheries of capitalism. Paramount among these differences is the fact that in the peripheries domestic production, involving both men and women, is more attenuated because the wages workers receive are insufficient to provision themselves and their households. This fact influences both the particular character of domestic production, and the distinctive entry of men and women into the capitalist production process.

The contemporary Sioux present another interesting case study of the articulations between a domestic economy and capitalism. This case, however, does not fit neatly into the frameworks that are now being used in the analysis of industrial or agrarian working classes. The relationship of the Sioux to capitalism and the organization of their domestic production presents certain unique aspects which differentiate their situation from what has been described elsewhere. Although discussed in more detail later, the differences are: (1) the unique relationship of the Sioux and other reservation-based peoples to capitalism as a result of their federal trust status; and (2) the distinctive features of their social formation which are based on an historically developed pattern of kinship.

It is my position that the way in which domestic production is organized in Sioux reservation communities has been mutually determined by their historically specific social formation and their unique place in the national political economy. In particular, these two forces have had a profound impact on the experiences of Sioux women within both a domestic and a capitalist producing sector. As I argue in the remaining portions of this paper, the experiences of Sioux women in these two spheres of production have changed over the last century as a result of wider transformations in the articulations between their indigenous economy and capitalism. By understanding these articulations and their changes, I maintain that the contradictory status of Sioux women in modern times becomes intelligible.

THE ETHNOGRAPHIC SETTING

The Devil's Lake Sioux Reservation in northeastern North Dakota was established in 1867 under a treaty agreement between the United States government and the Sioux that settled there. These Sioux included Sisseton and Wahpeton who had been exiled from their homelands in Minnesota after hostilities

with White settlers, as well as Yanktonnai who origi-
nally lived in the eastern regions of Dakota
Territory. A sizeable community of Chippewa has also
lived on the reservation since the late nineteenth
century. Although enrolled on the Turtle Mountain
Reservation in northcentral North Dakota, these
Chippewa were assigned lands adjacent to those of the
Sioux. In 1968, when I first began my research at
Devil's Lake, there were approximately 1,700 American
Indians living on the reservation. Besides those of
Sioux and Chippewa ancestry, there were people of
Arikara, Mandan, Hidatsa, Cree, and Winnebago
background who established homes at Devil's Lake
through marriages with Sioux enrolled on the reser-
vation.

Like its counterparts, the Devil's Lake Sioux
Reservation occupies a trust status vis-à-vis the
United States. Under the Treaty of 1867, the federal
government agreed to assume trust responsibility over
the people and property under reservation jurisdiction
(Meyer 1967:220-225). This trust responsibility has
placed the Devil's Lake Sioux, and other reservation
populations, in a unique position in the nation's
political economy. Unlike most other Americans, the
Sioux's links to the capitalist production process are
monitored almost entirely by the machinery of the
state. Over the past century, the federal government
has defined the conditions of Sioux land-ownership,
wage-labor, and private as well as corporate entre-
preneurship. In addition, the government has stipulated the grounds under which the Sioux receive
welfare assistance when other avenues to the nation's
economy are closed, as they have been many times in
the past.

The policies that govern federal trust responsibility over native land and people were developed
ostensibly to work on behalf of Indian interests.
Yet, the history of the last century has demonstrated
quite clearly that federal policies have not benefited
the American Indian. Instead, these policies have
worked ultimately in the interest of non-Indian
entrepreneurs and corporations (Jorgensen 1971, 1972,
1978; Ruffing 1979).

Since the beginning of the reservation era, the
Devil's Lake Sioux have been on the margins of the
U.S. political economy. Not only have they been

181

alienated from the means to produce their own livelihood, but they have been denied competitive access to
the capitalist production process as wage-laborers and
entrepreneurs. The net effect of this process has
been the impoverishment of the Devil's Lake Sioux as
individuals and as a tribal community.

In order to survive under such conditions the
Devil's Lake Sioux have developed an attenuated sector
of domestic production. This includes a wide range of
activities which provision the Devil's Lake Sioux
either through their own efforts or through earnings
derived from the capitalist sector of production. The
internal organization of their domestic sector and its
relationship to the capitalist production process have
not been stable. Significant changes have occurred
over the last century that have had a profound impact
on the life experiences of Sioux women living on the
Devil's Lake Reservation. In the following pages, I
describe these changes during three historical periods
in the post-reservation era.

The Early Reservation Period: 1870-1910

From the beginning of the reservation era,
federal policy excluded Sioux women from those areas
where the interests of native communities and capitalism intersected. Not only were women excluded from
the treaty negotiations under which Sioux land was
ceded and reservations were established, but they continued to be discriminated against in all subsequent
federal policy initiatives.

A major plan of the federal government at the end
of the nineteenth century was to transform the Sioux
into self-sufficient farmers, able to feed themselves
and market their surplus crops. The agrarian plan
that the government instituted was indisputably Anglo-
American, and at every stage of its implementation, it
excluded Sioux women from a viable role in agricultural production.

What is ironic about this entire process is the
fact that in pre-reservation times cultivation was
primarily the work of Sioux women (Pond 1908:342-345;
Skinner 1919:167). From the standpoint of those
attempting to "civilize" the Sioux, such a division of

labor ran contrary to every precept they held about the proper (i.e., natural) place of women. The fact that Sioux women engaged in strenuous labor, as in planting and harvesting, only reinforced the notions of many early missionaries and government agents that Sioux men were "savages" forcing women to work as "beasts of burden" (Neill 1872:234-235). Given this attitude, every effort was made to reverse the Sioux's customary division of labor in crop production.

The reversal was accomplished, in part, by the fact that agriculture involved techniques different from the traditional horticultural practices of the Sioux. Beginning as early as 1828, when the predecessors of the Devil's Lake Sioux lived in Minnesota, missionaries attempted to teach Sioux men agricultural skills as an essential feature of their proselitizing efforts (Stipe 1968:141-178). Later, after 1867, this training was taken over by federal agents hired to teach the Sioux agriculture. At Devil's Lake, the federal government developed farms (known as agency farms) where Sioux men were forced to work in order to receive the food commodities and annuities (i.e., garments, kerosene, metal tools) awarded in treaty settlements.[6] As part of this program, a system of rewards was established whereby men who worked the hardest and most consistently received a larger share in the annuity distributions (Meyer 1967:228-230).

As Sioux men became proficient farmers, they were assigned plots of lands to work for themselves. In addition, they were awarded the equipment, stock, and seeds necessary for an agricultural production process. By virtue of this distribution pattern, Sioux women were effectively excluded from agriculture. Not controlling the means of production, women were not in a position to decide either how reservation lands would be used or how the products of farming would be distributed. But, then, Sioux men did not have much control either since their entire involvement in agriculture was being monitored by the federal government.

Sioux men did have an advantage over women, however, in so far as they were the ones who had prior access to the resources upon which a family's livelihood was based. As part of its plan to "familialize" the Sioux--that is, to transfer economic and political power from the extended kin group to the nuclear family--the federal government instituted a practice whereby it distributed resources to each household head (which by the government's definition was always male) rather than to duly appointed band leaders as it had done in the past. This plan was instituted in several different ways, and in all cases, it discriminated against Sioux women (Wilcox 1942:26-27).

Popular opinion to the contrary, the Devil's Lake Sioux's early attempts at farming were fairly successful. Despite the precariousness of farming in the drought-ridden northern Plains, the Sioux at Devil's Lake managed to produce a marginal subsistence and at times even marketed surplus crops (Meyer 1967:224-239; Albers 1974:109-111). Under federal supervision, the Devil's Lake Sioux initially cultivated root crops, especially potatoes, turnips, and carrots. Later, they were encouraged to invest more of their labor in farming the major cash-crop of the region, wheat. The marketing of cash-crops from privately-owned plots was supervised by the federal agent, who not only arranged the sales but also distributed the profits among Sioux farmers. The profits, however, were not distributed in cash but in the form of food commodities and annuities purchased by the government from private sources. Generally, goods consigned from federal storehouses were distributed to the male head-of-the-household.

Although the federal government divided the products of Sioux labor on a household basis, the Sioux continued to work their lands collectively and to share their provisions among a wider group of kin. The kin groups that pooled their labor and provisions were organized along agnatic lines. Generally, a man, his sons, and sometimes grandsons formed the nucleus of a cooperative work group, and along with their wives and unmarried daughters, lived together in the same or closely adjacent log houses.

The kin groups, called tiošpaye[7] in Sioux, were a constant and elementary feature of Sioux social organization, but their membership was not stable. Lacking iron-clad rules of residence and collaboration along kin lines, the Sioux often shifted their tiošpaye attachments (Albers n.d.:20-21). This shifting could either be initiated by men or women, and in pre-reservation times, there was considerable variation in the composition of tiošpaye in terms of their emphasis on agnatic or uterine ties. Much of

184

this variation was seasonal and linked to the productive activities that were important at a given point in the year (Albers n.d.:28-32). But in post-reservation times, agnatic ties dominated largely as a consequence of the patrilateral bias in the land allotment patterns of the federal government, and also as a result of the agnatic emphasis in all other areas of federal distribution.

In the agnatically-based tiošpaye, men were the ones primarily responsible for tending the live-stock and cash-crops. However, government efforts to the contrary, Sioux women also engaged in crop cultivation. Not only did they assist men in agricultural activities, but they also maintained their own gardens where they grew staple root crops as well as native varieties of corn, squash, and beans (Wilcox 1942:73, 92).

What contribution these gardens made to Sioux diets is not clear from early government reports. At the very least, this gardening offered a supplemental and more varied food supply than what was being provided in the food commodity distributions of the federal government. There is also some evidence (Wilcox 1942:95) that in the early nineteenth century, this gardening gave Sioux access to goods and some cash from sources other than the federal government. Even more importantly, the food contributions of females seems to have been significant for the Sioux during times when the more vulnerable cash-crops failed as a result of drought or a depressed market. Roy Meyer (1967:232) notes that, in a number of different years, agency reports indicate that the Sioux were reduced to living off "parched corn and wild turnips," foods produced primarily by women.

Aside from their respective efforts in food cultivation, Sioux men and women continued to engage in a wide range of foraging activities. In the summer months, women devoted considerable labor to digging wild prairie turnips, picking June berries, choke cherries, as well as wild plums, and gathering a wide range of other plants for food and medicine. These gathering activities contributed a major portion of the Sioux's summer food supply. Men, on the other hand, hunted the abundant supplies of waterfowl in the region, they stalked deer and other game, they trapped small mammals like rabbit, beaver, and muskrat, and finally, they fished in local rivers and fresh water lakes. Although much of this subsistence activity was frowned upon by federal agents and missionaries, who believed it encouraged the Sioux to retain their traditional ways, it could hardly be prevented when the yields from farming were not sufficient to feed a family through an entire year and when government food commodities did not make up the difference (Wilcox 1942:73, 92).

Foraging, subsistence farming, and annuities from cash crop production were not always sufficient, even in good years, to provide the food and other commodities that Sioux households needed. In order to maintain and expand their consumption base, the Sioux engaged in additional work activities within and outside the household.

Beginning in the late nineteenth century, the federal government provided Sioux households with annuities for work areas other than cash-crop production. The government hired people to work as police, to cut timber for cooking and heating, to erect schools, storehouses, and other agency buildings, as well as to provide labor in a wide range of menial tasks (e.g., janitorial) which maintained the physical operations of local government and church bureaucracies. Again, these jobs and the annuities they provided were granted exclusively to Sioux men (Meyer 1967:230-233).

The federally imposed segregation of Sioux work activity in the capitalist sector of the reservation economy was mirrored in all educational programs, whether run by the church or the government. The "civilized" learning experiences of Sioux men were aimed at developing the skills needed for wage-labor or small family-farm production. Reservation boarding schools maintained their own industrial work shops where the basic techniques of carpentry were taught, and they owned farms where young Sioux men learned essential agricultural methods.

Sioux women, in contrast, were trained to become efficient homemakers. They were taught a wide variety of domestic skills including baking, canning, quilting, knitting, crocheting, and of course, housecleaning. In the earliest years of reservation settlement, these skills were taught to Sioux women by the wives of missionaries and federal agents. In later years, this training was continued through the instruction of government field matrons (a role equivalent to the modern county extension agent) and in the meetings of church religious societies, such as the St. Mary's Society of the Catholic Church. Eventually, such teaching became the primary responsibility of the domestic science curriculum in boarding and day schools on the reservation.

Although Sioux women were excluded from major annuity and cash-producing activities such as farming, they did earn money in early reservation times. Largely through their own initiative, Sioux women entered into the cash-economy (that is, the capitalist sector) by way of petty commodity production. Aside from selling some of their garden produce to neighboring Whites, they manufactured a wide variety of textile commodities suitable for sale or trade in an off-reservation marketplace. In this manufacture, Sioux women not only used traditional industrial and decorative skills (e.g., beadwork, quillwork), but they also employed such newly learned techniques as quilting, crocheting, and lacemaking. With few exceptions, such as the lacemaking enterprise of Sioux and Chippewa women in Minnesota (Duncan 1980), petty commodity production offered native women meager earnings. Data that Katherine Duncan (1980:34) gathered from a BIA report indicate that in 1912 Indian women who made beadwork for sale received slightly less than $7.00 per annum for their labor. But even though the earnings from petty commodity production were small, they did provide Sioux women with an income over which they had full control.

The industrial and decorative skills that Sioux women utilized in their petty commodity production were also an essential aspect of the work they performed for their own households. By the turn of the twentieth century, Sioux women were supplying their households with textile items as diverse as clothing, bedding, curtains, and carrying bags. In their textile production, Sioux women adopted ingenious ways of making traditional items out of new materials. They also became adept at transforming second-hand clothing and yard good scraps into usable as well as artful objects, such as quilts (Albers and Medicine 1980).

In addition to the work that created new products, female labor was engaged in the preservation and preparation of food as well as in the physical maintenance of the homesite. Sioux women preserved food, including the products of male subsistence, through traditional drying techniques and newly learned canning processes. They cut wood needed for cooking and heating. They hauled water. They cooked food. And they cleaned the household areas the family lived and worked in.

In their respective work activities, Sioux men and women scheduled their labor separately. Neither sex controlled or directed the pace, intensity, or direction of the other's work patterns. Among both sexes, work activity was carried on alone or in small work groups who pooled their labor through simple as well as complex forms of cooperation. Contrary to conventional opinions on the matter, female cooperative work patterns were not always repetitious and organized for purposes of socializing. Many of the tasks they performed in the early reservation period, and continue to perform today, involved an internal division of labor where work activities were divided according to age, knowledge, and expertise. In harvesting corn, for example, it is critical, soon after the cobs have been removed from the stalks, to have the cobs shucked, their kernels boiled and dryed in order to preserve the sugar content and fresh flavor of the corn. When efficiently organized, this labor process usually involved three or more women, each of whom performed a different task. Similarly, in the tanning and decoration of hides, as in the more recent manufacture of quilts, Sioux women divided their labor into different tasks within a larger work process. In quilting, for example, some women concentrated on cutting the quilt patches, others devoted themselves to piecing the patches together, while others worked on quilting the patched top to its filling and back (Albers and Medicine 1980).

Not only did each sex manage their own labor activity, but they also controlled the distribution of the products that resulted from this labor. In early reservation times, and even today, men did not exercise any control over the products of female subsistence and industrial activity. Likewise, women did not have any say in how men divided, shared, traded, or sold the products of their labor efforts. However, when women entered into a production process originating with men, as in the butchering and cooking of meat, they had rights to make decisions about the product's distribution.

In early Sioux households, the ideal relationship between men and women was based on principles of complementarity. Under these principles, the members of each sex were expected to be proficient in their respective work activities and self-sufficient as well. Work autonomy and prior claims on the products of one's labor, however, did not mitigate against voluntary sharing between the sexes. For just as each sex was accorded a certain degree of independence from the other, men and women were expected to be generous and willingly share the products of their respective labors.

The complementary basis of relationships between the sexes was consistent with a wider Sioux ethos, which idealized and dialectically engaged mutually distinct moral imperatives. One set of imperatives stipulated that kin, affinal as well as consanguinal, should be responsible for each others' welfare. Not only should they be generous with their food and other material possessions, but they should also willingly cooperate and be helpful in their day-to-day activities. Another set of imperatives, however, stressed the personal integrity (autonomy) of kin. Here no one, regardless of sex or age, had the right to forcefully impose their will on another. Thus, no person had the right to command or appropriate the possessions of another (or the products that someone produces) without that individual's permission, nor did a person have the right to engage others in labor through coercion whether physical or verbal (Albers 1982).

It should be noted at this point that although many early observers took great pains to describe male brutality against women, the use of physical force in bringing about female compliance was not, nor has it ever been, sanctioned in Sioux communities. That such brutality occurred speaks not to an ideology which condones the use of violence but rather to the disastrous effects of alcohol-abuse which was increasing at a rapid rate in early reservation settings (Medicine 1980).

In their essential character, the moral precepts that governed relationships among Sioux kin were egalitarian and not compatible with European notions of dominance and subordination. Notwithstanding the efforts of missionaries and government agents to the contrary, the Sioux did not develop and institutionalize an ideology based on the notion of male providers and female dependents. But even though the Sioux maintained, at least theoretically, egalitarian ideas about relations between men and women, the realities of their life experiences in early reservation times made it very difficult to put these into practice.

The new situation that Sioux women found themselves in gave them less opportunity to be autonomous and exercise influence than they had in the past. Denied access to annuity distributions and other means of livelihood coming from the federal government, Sioux women had no means to assert their independence except within the confines of their own self-generated subsistence and handicraft activities. Increasingly, the balance of power leaned toward Sioux men who, by virtue of federal fiat, held a prior claim on a household's provisions and its means of production.

Sioux women, however, did not become totally powerless or passive under their new circumstances. Not only did they continue to exercise influence over their own work activities and the products these created within a household setting, but they still monitored some of the distribution taking place between households. Sioux women were free to share or barter what they owned and produced with others. Women traded their wares among themselves, with the men of their community, and with outsiders. When relatives stayed at Sioux homesites on extended visits and when families held honoring rituals (i.e., naming ceremonies, memorial feasts), women supervised much of the food distribution and the giving of material goods (i.e., quilts, moccasins) produced by their labor. Thus, even though Sioux women had become dependent on men for commodities obtained from federal sources, they were able to maintain some autonomy through their own productive efforts.

Another area where Sioux women exhibited some degree of independence was in the dissolution of a marriage. As in pre-reservation times, the first marriage of a Sioux woman was usually arranged by her family, especially her father and brothers. Although the selection of her first mate was governed by interests other than her own, she was not compelled to remain in this union. Not uncommonly, Sioux women left their first husband. Removed from their own kin circles at marriage, especially the close companionship of their sisters and female cousins, Sioux women often experienced a sense of profound isolation in the tiošpaye of their spouse. Whether a woman was treated badly or was simply lonely in her husband's home, she could leave and return to her consanguinal kin. It is important to emphasize that no one, not even a father or brother, could force a woman to stay in a marriage where, for whatever reason, she was unhappy. That Sioux women could, and frequently did, leave spouses under their own volition is an important indication of their autonomy.

To the dismay of many early missionaries and government agents, Sioux marriages were notoriously brittle. They were dissolved easily by either a man or a woman, and there were no stigmas attached to those who were divorced. Although the family laws of the federal government, combined with the teachings of missionaries, attempted to curb the high rate of divorce in Sioux communities, these were never very successful. The Sioux simply practiced common law marriages, and therefore, avoided the fetters of divorce regulations.

Sioux women also retained influential roles in certain indigenous ceremonies, like the Medicine Dance and Sun Dance, whose rituals continued to be performed in early reservation times. In these ceremonies, women occupied prestigious positions which were vital to the ritual conduct of a ceremony (Skinner 1920; Wallis 1947). In addition, Sioux women continued to acquire supernatural powers that gave them talent in their decorative arts, that enabled them to cure, and that provided them luck in gambling (Wallis 1947). But as some of the traditional ceremonies gave way under the influence of Christianity and the Native American Church,[8] much of the sacred power and prestige that women had held began to diminish.

The area where Sioux women lost the most ground was in the political dealings between their communities and the federal government. In the pre-reservation era, Sioux women played an active role in the affairs of their bands and villages. They were empowered with the authority to police community gatherings. They held formal roles in supervising the distribution of meat from collective hunts. And finally, they had institutionalized mechanisms for making their interests known in the meetings of the tiyotipi, or soldier's lodge.[9] But this all changed in the reservation setting because of the federal government's discriminatory practice of dealing only with Sioux men in matters of community-wide concern.

The practice of conducting diplomatic and trade negotiations exclusively with men was not a new feature in Indian-White relationships. It was a long-standing pattern which can be traced back to the eighteenth century when European traders chose certain native men to intercede in the dealings between the fur companies and Sioux communities (Landes 1968: 66-94; Stipe 1968:214-221). In later years, this practice was continued in the federal government's early encounters with the Sioux. The Sioux men who became intermediaries acquired a base of power that had not existed before the arrival of Whites. By virtue of the fact that these men held a prior claim on commodities coming from fur traders and government representatives, they were able to wield considerable influence in their own communities.

In the early reservation period, the Sioux men who functioned as intermediaries were the nuclei around which neighborhood and community districts were formed at Devil's Lake. Since it was through these men that negotiations were conducted and annuities distributed, they became a central source of provisions for those who followed them. But when the federal government divested these men of their power, largely through the policy of distributing provisions to the head of every household, the confidence they once inspired among their followers began to wane. Increasingly, these men became token figures who had no authority and no special advantages vis-à-vis the rest of the population. In fact, no Sioux male had any real community-wide power. It was the federal government, not the Sioux people, who ruled in early reservation times. That Sioux women were excluded from the token leadership positions that existed in their communities was probably of little consequence. Since these positions conferred no power, women would have had nothing to gain by holding them.

It is important to emphasize that in early reservation times there was no community-wide political base among the Devil's Lake Sioux. Local level authority and power were fragmented along family and household lines, where men as well as women could exercise influence. What power each sex exerted was not absolute but relative to the contributions that each made to the support of their households and families. Thus, while it is clear that many traditional avenues of female influence were closed in the community at large and confined to a domestic arena, it is also obvious that most areas of male power were similarly restricted.

There were some Sioux women, however, who were able to transcend many of the political and economic constraints imposed on their people. Ironically, the pathway to independence for many of these women was through their marriages to Whitemen. Just as it occurred a century before the Devil's Lake Sioux Reservation was established, a few Sioux women married traders, government agents, and soldiers who worked among their people. Unfortunately, this entire historical experience has not been systematically explored in the literature on the Sioux, although Jennifer Brown (1980) has documented its development and consequences within the setting of the Canadian fur-trade. Over the period in which these marriages occurred, they ranged from tenuous unions where Sioux women were abandoned by their husbands to enduring conjugal relationships. In the early reservation period, the vast majority of long-lasting marriages involved situations where White husbands homesteaded land that was open for sale on the reservation and/or worked lands that their wives owned. At least two of the Sioux women who married Whitemen during this period gained notoriety for their independence and influence in the local Indian as well as White community. They achieved their notoriety largely by working and managing the farms their husbands had left them when they died. Since these farms were not under federal jurisdiction, the government had no authority to prevent the women from taking over the farming operations. Uninhibited by the constraints that other Sioux people faced in their agricultural endeavors, as a consequence of federal interference, these women kept their farms going, even in the most difficult times. Although the autonomy that these women gained was exceptional, even by non-Indian standards of the time, they pioneered a pattern of female independence that would become more widespread among the Sioux in later years.

Transition: 1910-1945

By the beginning of the twentieth century, important changes were taking place in the Devil's Lake Sioux's relationship to the sector of capitalist production that would have an immeasurable impact on their economic and political viability in the future. The most important changes were related to federal policy on the trust status of Sioux lands. Within a few decades after the Devil's Lake Sioux Reservation was established, much of the treaty land was lost to the railways. By 1892, more land was alienated as a result of the General Allotment Act. Under the provisions of this legislation, whatever land remained after allotment was placed in the public domain where it was sold eventually to the railways and White settlers. In subsequent years, additional lands were lost either through the outright sale of private holdings or through the growing federal practice of leasing native lands to outside interests (Meyer 1967:221-241).

The federal practice of leasing Sioux lands was predicated on a common but fallacious belief that Indian men were not suited temperamentally for farming. The argument, as it was customarily presented, held that because Sioux men were warriors and hunters they never had any inclination to be farmers (MacGregor 1946). But despite the fact that this entire argument could be challenged by abundant evidence to the contrary, it gained wide appeal and became a primary justification for withdrawing support for agrarian development on Sioux reservations.

There is no question that by the second decade of the twentieth century the practice of agriculture among the Devil's Lake Sioux was rapidly declining. What led to the decline was not a lack of initiative but rather a lack of necessary capital. Putting aside the consequences of severe drought conditions in the northern Plains, there was the even more serious problem that the Devil's Lake Sioux could not use their land as collateral to borrow private capital for investments in equipment, stock, and seeds. In previous years capital had been advanced from the land settlement funds of the Sioux. But as these funds became depleted, the federal government was not interested in providing its own capital to nurture the growth of Sioux farming. Instead, it advocated a policy of selling and leasing Sioux land to neighboring White farmers who had the capital to develop it (Meyer 1967:318-327).

The growing practice of leasing Indian land had an unanticipated economic advantage for some Sioux women. For now, just like men, they could accrue direct cash benefits from the lands in their names. But in order for Sioux women to get these benefits directly, they had to be divorced, widowed, or single and living alone or with dependent children. They also had to be over eighteen years of age. The lease monies of married women were credited to the agency books of their husbands and those of minors to their father's account (Wilcox 1942:27). Notwithstanding the fact that married women did not receive their lease incomes directly, Sioux husbands generally respected their wives' prior claim to this money. In fact, married women could, and many did, use these incomes as a leverage in advancing their interests within the household.[10] Women who were separated or divorced could petition the federal agent to have the funds dispensed in their names.

As time went on, the size of some female landholdings increased through inheritance, and consequently, there were fewer disparities between men and women in land-ownership. By the 1940's, several women had as much, if not more land, than many men on the reservation, and, thus, were in a position to make substantial contributions to the livelihood of their households.

While there was an increasing parity between men and women in land-ownership, the ability of the land to sustain its owners was declining. From the beginning, the leasing arrangements that the federal government made with outsiders were notoriously unfair. Rather than awarding leases on a proportion of the profits the land yielded, the federal government established fixed rent payments. The prices of leases were well below fair-market value, and as late as 1968, good wheat-growing land was being leased for less than <u>ten dollars an acre per annum</u>!

The increasing difficulty of living off lease-incomes was not only a product of low rents but also a consequence of the fact that the average amount of land held under the ownership of single parties was declining rapidly. In exceptionally hard years, which were not uncommon in the early twentieth century, many Sioux were forced to sell all or major portions of their land-holdings to survive. Thus, in later years, these Sioux had no lease-income. In addition, there were growing numbers of young adults who did not own land, either because they had not inherited any as yet or else because there was nothing to inherit. But even those who acquired lands through inheritance were finding that they received only a small portion of the rent payment on a given parcel of land. The original allotments had become increasingly fractionated because of the federal practice of dividing landed-property among all rightful heirs. In the end, land became less of an asset for the Sioux men and women who held title to it.

The declining ability of the land to support the Devil's Lake Sioux on either a cash or productive basis forced increasing numbers of people to rely on federal relief and wage labor. Aside from its food commodity distributions, the federal government did not have a systematic or steady welfare program for the Sioux until the mid-1930's when Congress passed the Child Welfare and Social Security Acts. Before that time, only emergency relief funds were available for families in dire straits, but the process of gaining access to them was a humiliating experience and frustrated by bureaucratic red-tape. Besides this, the funds were not sufficient to provide families with even the bare necessities.

Wage-labor, on the other hand, offered more substantial incomes <u>when</u> jobs were available. Throughout the early half of the twentieth century, the federal government continued to be the primary employer of native peoples. Except for a short period when the Works Project Administration was in effect during the 1930's, the job situation on the Devil's Lake Sioux Reservation was dismal. Federal jobs were few in number, low in pay, and often temporary in duration. Some employment in the form of farm labor,[11] construction, and domestic work was available in surrounding White communities. But, again, the pay was low and the work was temporary.

In this period, hiring patterns continued to be sex-segregated. Within the reservation, federally supported jobs, including those under the WPA, were given almost exclusively to males. Except for a few occupations that involved domestic work, there was little employment available to Sioux women either in the federal government or in the surrounding White communities. Even clerical jobs were not open to Sioux women because they lacked the appropriate training. As in the previous era, the boarding and day schools' curricula for women emphasized domestic science and prepared them to be housewives rather than wage-laborers.

As the agrarian program of the federal government collapsed and the Sioux turned to lease-incomes, relief, and wage-labor as their principal means of livelihood, many profound changes occurred in reservation social formations. One of the most important changes was the destruction of the closely-knit and agnatically-oriented tiošpaye. Except for a few tiošpaye who were able to maintain sizable landholdings and work them collectively, the vast majority were breaking down and becoming reconstituted along other lines. Increasingly, tiošpaye were landless and residentially dispersed kin groups which were organized bilaterally. Unlike in the past, when these groups functioned as viable production units, they were now becoming loosely-organized distributive networks in which their members shared individual incomes and the commodities these bought (Albers 1974, 1982).

The process by which Sioux tiošpaye changed was complex and can only be highlighted here. By the 1920's, the land-based assets of the Sioux were mostly in the hands of the older generation. Young adults, for the most part, were landless. For a short time, some of the older generation were able to support their landless descendants by combining lease-incomes with subsistence production. But as the purchasing power of lease-incomes declined, the older generation became less able to support its adult offspring as it had done in the past. Increasingly, the young adults, especially the men, were moving to the agency, mission, and commercial communities on the reservation to search for employment. Those who acquired stable

197

jobs remained in these communities, while the ones with temporary work continued to return to their families' rural homesteads where they were given support while unemployed.

But with the migration of the young people away from the rural family homesteads, the older generation were less able to continue the subsistence and petty commodity production they had carried on in the past. Not having a stable pool of labor to rely upon in this production, they were also forced to leave their rural homesteads and move to the nucleated settlements that were now growing around the agency, mission, and commercial centers of the reservation. In these settlements, all Devil's Lake Sioux became more dependent on a cash economy. Rather than providing some of their own livelihood through self-generated subsistence production, they now purchased the bulk of their necessities through cash-earnings. The non-Indian stores in these settlements became the primary source of the Sioux's provisioning needs rather than being agents for the occasional purchase of staples and luxury goods.

The younger generation was caught in an economic limbo where they were being driven into a job market which could not absorb them on a steady basis. With wage-labor uncertain and federal relief meager, young couples could not support themselves and their dependents alone. The vast majority of men did not have enough work to maintain a family, and most women could not get work. Under these untenable circumstances, couples had two options. On the one hand, they could depend on the support of either spouse's kin, providing that there were relatives to provision them. Or, on the other hand, they could separate and thereby insure that at least the wife and offspring had support through ADC (Aid to Families with Dependent Children). In either case, couples were faced with severe economic strains which increasingly eroded the viability of their marriages. The economic uncertainty that the Devil's Lake Sioux now faced made the already brittle nature of conjugal relationships even more fragile. There were, of course, enduring marriages among the Devil's Lake Sioux, but, in most instances, these were possible only because there was a stable and sufficient economic base to support them, either through jobs, lease-income, and/or the help of a wider kin group.

In these times, it was increasingly more difficult for Devil's Lake Sioux to maintain their traditional ideal of complementarity in the relationships between men and women. The economic contributions of each sex to the provisioning of the household and the relative power that each exercised in a domestic setting became more variable. When men alone, or with the aid of their kin, maintained a household, they generally had more influence than in situations where the couple was being supported by the wife's earnings or that of her kin. The chances that a woman and/or her relatives would provide the bulk of a household's support were now increasing not only because of the changing pattern of land-ownership but also because women could draw upon an independent source of support, namely welfare.

In effect, what was happening in the first half of the twentieth century was that federal policy, especially as it pertained to land, had created conditions which undermined household stability and the influence of men in domestic settings. Gradually, women were gaining the ascendancy simply because they were in a better position to acquire the necessities upon which a household depended. The autonomy women were now beginning to realize did not afford them any real freedom, however. They were still dependent. Maybe they no longer relied on a spouse to assist them in provisioning a household, but they were still under the control and domination of the federal government.

Although the influence of Sioux women in the household was growing stronger, they still did not have any major role, at least formally, in the politics of the reservation. Legally, they continued to be fettered by anachronistic policies established in early reservation times (Bysiewicz and Van de Mark 1977). Politically, they were not given access to positions where decisions were made about the welfare and future of their communities. That women continued to remain outside the formal political arena was still not a great disadvantage. For in this period, as in the previous one, the "leadership" positions that men occupied continued to be mere "tokenism." Whether self-proclaimed or appointed by the federal government, Devil's Lake Sioux leaders received no special compensation for their services, nor did they have any material foundation upon which to dispense "favors" in their communities. They were powerless figureheads, who often derived their sense of prestige only from the clergy or the federal officials they served. Sometimes, they inspired confidence among their own people. But more often than not, they were as incapable of influencing the course of the reservation's future as the most politically isolated and alienated people on the reservation.

Modern Times: 1945-1972

In the years after World War II, the Devil's Lake Sioux Reservation fell even deeper into poverty. About all that saved the Sioux from total economic collapse were temporary jobs, paltry forms of federal relief, and their own ingenious survival strategies within the domestic sector of production. Statistics gathered by the federal government (House Committee on Interior and Insular Affairs 1953, 1962; Economic Development Administration 1971) indicate that the Devil's Lake Sioux Reservation ranked as one of the most depressed reservations in the northern Plains when judged in terms of family/per capita incomes, tribal revenue, and rates of unemployment/under-employment.

In the modern era, unearned incomes from land-leasing have not been a viable source of livelihood for their owners. Only a small proportion of the Devil's Lake Sioux hold title to land, and of those who do, an even smaller number receive rents in excess of a few hundred dollars per year. For the Devil's Lake Sioux who receive welfare assistance, which includes the bulk of the elderly population and many of the younger people, there are no gains from land-ownership because monthly welfare payments are adjusted downward according to a person's annual lease earnings. In effect, the Devil's Lake Sioux have become disenfranchised from their landed-property, and for all intents and purposes, the land has little direct economic value for its owners on either a pro-ductive or a cash basis (Albers 1974:134-135).

In the decade after World War II, a growing pro-portion of the Devil's Lake Sioux had come to rely on wage-labor for their livelihood. But employment was becoming more difficult to secure on or near the reservation. The local farm jobs that had provided them with summer work had largely disappeared as grain production became more mechanized. Unlike the period under the WPA, there was no longer a wide range of federal "make-work" jobs on the reservation. What federal employment was available provided work for less than five percent of the adult population. Construction, janitorial, and domestic work in surrounding White towns was decreasing as these rural communities were becoming more impoverished themselves.

The only major source of employment in the area was work in the potato and sugar beet fields of the Red River Valley in North Dakota. Every fall, large numbers of Devil's Lake Sioux, men as well as women, would migrate to this valley to work. The job was temporary, the pay was low, and the living conditions were abysmal, but for many it was a lifeline--the difference between survival and starvation. When the fall harvest was over, some returned to the reservation and tried to stretch their meager earnings through the cold and relentless North Dakota winter. Others, however, remained in the Red River Valley cities of Fargo and Grand Forks where they tried to get work as domestics, janitors, and short-order cooks. A few traveled further, to Chicago, Minneapolis-St. Paul, and Omaha, seeking jobs. After staying in these urban areas a few months or even years, they would return to the reservation in hopes of finding work or the support of some kin.

The trend in off-reservation migration, which the Devil's Lake Sioux had initiated themselves, was eventually promoted by the federal government and institutionalized under job training and relocation programs. Through these programs, the Devil's Lake Sioux were sent to urban areas far removed from the reservation. While some made a successful adjustment to their new urban situation, the vast majority did not. They returned to the reservation where there were no jobs, only to be relocated again to a different city and training program.

Like the federal job policies of the past, the work training and relocation programs instituted in the 1950's and 1960's were discriminatory--aimed almost exclusively at male employment. The opportunity to learn skills appropriate to participation in

201

the capitalist sector of production continued to be a
male prerogative. As the federal government attempted
to funnel men into jobs, even if unsuccessfully, it
awarded women welfare subsidies under ADC. Instead of
giving women a chance to become occupationally skilled
and potentially self-sufficient, the federal government continued its practice of making women dependent
on the state.

While welfare subsidies were available to most
Sioux women, they were rarely sufficient to support a
household. When work opportunities became available,
many Sioux women took them. The jobs they were able
to engage in, either on the reservation or in
surrounding White communities, were clearly sex-typed.
They included work as domestics, nurses' aides, cooks,
and clerical workers. As in the nation at large, the
pay that Sioux women received for this work was
generally lower than the earnings that men received
from their jobs. Even when women carried on the same
work as men, as happened when both sexes worked alongside each other in the potato and sugar beet fields,
female wages were lower.

When I began my fieldwork in the late 1960's,
steady jobs on the Devil's Lake Sioux Reservation were
few in number. The depth of job depression was
revealed in figures compiled by the Economic
Development Administration (1971) in 1970. These
figures indicate that nearly sixty percent of adult
Devil's Lake Sioux between the ages of 18 and 55 were
unemployed, while ninety-five percent of the remaining
40 percent were underemployed. The reason that so
much of the work force was underemployed at this time
had to do with the nature of the federal "make-work"
projects being instituted on the reservation. A great
many of these projects hired people on a part-time
basis, while others offered short-term work, which
lasted only as long as it took to complete a project
(e.g., housing and road construction) or only through
the duration of a social service or development grant.

In the 1970's, however, steady employment opportunities expanded at Devil's Lake, not only as a
result of the building of a factory on the reservation
but also through jobs that the tribe created from
funds originating in federal programs and land claims'
settlements.[12]   Unfortunately, this expansion has not
kept up with the reservation's rising population

growth, nor have the wages in the new jobs kept abreast of inflation.

In the last decade, Devil's Lake Sioux women have been entering the labor force in increasing numbers. Although many still work in the domestic-oriented jobs of the past, a greater number of female workers are now engaged in other kinds of occupations. They are working in jobs as diverse as social service counseling, elementary and secondary school teaching, assembly-line production at the reservation's New Brunswick plant, and the administration of programs under federal agencies like CAP (Community Action Program). Only in recent years, and largely through the assistance of tribal funds, have there been opportunities for women to learn technical skills necessary for a wider base of participation in the capitalist sector of production. Much of the training that women are receiving through such educationally-oriented groups as the United Tribes of North Dakota, remains sex-typed, but there are a number of on-the-job teaching programs which are not. Devil's Lake Sioux women still face job discrimination, especially when it comes to wages, but it is important to emphasize that the employment gap between male and female has narrowed in recent times.

Although I did not survey the entire reservation between 1968 and 1972, my data indicated that women had a more continuous source of income. Even excluding those women who received welfare assistance, the data suggest that females worked at jobs longer than men. The longevity of female wage-workers seems to have been more a matter of the kinds of occupations they entered rather than a result of some difference between Sioux men and women in their work initiative. Whereas the jobs available to females were fairly enduring, those which men tended to enter were linked to projects (e.g., construction) that were transient in nature.

Although more widely based profiles (House Committee on Interior and Insular Affairs 1953, 1962) on Sioux men and women indicate that a higher proportion of men work than women, and that when they work their earnings are greater, such evidence belies the fact that most of the occupations men have traditionally worked in entail temporary employment. In addition, it obscures the fact that men are discriminated against when it comes to receiving welfare assistance, and that it is women who have the primary economic advantages here. Until very recently, most Sioux men were not eligible for any kind of stable unearned income from federal or state sources. Since most of them did not work long enough or in the types of jobs that pay unemployment compensation, they rarely received any kind of unearned benefits. Only men disabled in war, from work, or by age were able to receive a steady income through welfare sources. Indeed, if one were able to compare more recent annual incomes of men and women through earned and unearned sources, the pattern would likely indicate three things: (1) that the spread in male incomes has been much wider than that of females; (2) that for the majority of the population the averaged annual income of women has probably been on a par with that of men; and (3) that female earnings have been much more stable than those of men.

No matter what type of income disparities exist between men and women, the livelihood of most Devil's Lake Sioux has been substandard. Considering all sources of earnings, the average family income of Devil's Lake Sioux in 1970 was $3,200 (Economic Development Administration 1971:216). My data indicate that although most per capita incomes clustered in the neighborhood of $1,500 to $5,000 per annum, the range was from less than $100 to more than $10,000 a year. Not only were the earnings of most Devil's Lake Sioux well below the poverty limits for that time, but they were also erratic as a result of the transient character of employment in the area (Albers 1974:123–139). This meant that the amount and distribution of individual earnings was in a continual state of flux. It also meant that since women tended to receive steady earnings through welfare, men were the ones who experienced the greatest income fluctuations.

Along with important changes in their economic circumstances, the Devil's Lake Sioux have witnessed important shifts in the nature of reservation politics during the modern period. In the 1950's, the Devil's Lake Sioux finally incorporated themselves under the provisions of the Indian Reorganization Act which was passed by Congress in 1934 (Meyer 1967:339–343). Through their incorporation, Devil's Lake Sioux were able to elect leaders to represent them in negotiations with the federal government. Until the early seventies, however, positions in tribal government did not confer any great advantage on those who held them because the tribe was impoverished.

The fact that the Devil's Lake Sioux Reservation was impoverished had a very important impact on the complexion of local politics. Unlike other Sioux reservations, where sizable economic assets were at stake and where leaders exercised considerable power through their control over tribal funds, there was little at stake in the elections at Devil's Lake except who was going to assume petitionary positions on the tribal council. Maintaining a tribal office at Devil's Lake was determined by the strength of a leader's support in the electorate; and this, in turn, was conditioned by that leader's success in marshalling federal revenue for jobs, housing, and development. For much of the period after its incorporation, the Devil's Lake Tribe and its leaders were virtually dependent on the largesse of the federal government. Since federal funding was, and still is, meager and erratic (determined by vascillations in the state of the national economy and by the changing policies of federal administrations), tribal leaders did not have a firm financial base from which to develop, much less wield, any sort of real power. Consequently, there was a continual turnover in the people who held tribal leadership positions (Albers 1974: 314-322).

It should be noted that this situation changed during the 1970's. Through the influx of sizable funds from land claims' settlements and increased revenue for development from the federal government, the Devil's Lake Sioux Tribe had a much improved fiscal base. The tribe was able to pay good wages, comparatively speaking, not only to its leaders but also to a wide variety of people who held administrative positions in tribal government and who worked under various programs financed with money from the federal government.

What is most interesting about the changing complexion of reservation politics since the mid-fifties is the fact that a growing number of women have run for and been elected to tribal offices. In addition, women are being hired in a wide variety of tribally-supported jobs including important administrative positions. Although the number of women entering tribal government is small compared to men, it represents a major advance over what existed in the 1950's when women had virtually no access to formally acknowledged political positions. A central question which needs to be considered is why, after being excluded from the tribal political arena (which is most directly associated with the capitalist production process) for so many years, are women now playing such an important and growing role in this aspect of reservation life? In order to answer this question, it is necessary to examine the experience of Sioux women in the domestic sector of production.

Many of the changes that were beginning to occur in the domestic sector of production before World War II have become fully manifested in the modern era. One of the areas where change has been most obvious is in the work activity of the household. In the last several decades, there has been a progressive decline in the Devil's Lake Sioux's involvement in subsistence and handicraft activity, particularly of the sort that is aimed at domestic use.

Today, less than five percent of the population raise livestock or cultivate gardens. The decline in subsistence farming has been a consequence of many factors, but two stand out. On the one hand, the increasing entry of the Devil's Lake Sioux into the wage-labor market has been incompatible with food production activity, especially when jobs require people to leave the reservation for prolonged periods of time. But even when employment does not take Devil's Lake Sioux away from the reservation, it still reduces the amount of time they can devote to subsistence farming. On the other hand, the vast majority of Devil's Lake Sioux do not own land, or else their homes are far removed from the lands that they might rightfully cultivate. In the nucleated settlements that have grown around the agency, mission, and commercial centers on the reservation, the new federal houses are crowded so close together that there is no space to put in garden plots or raise animals. Only those Sioux who own land and have houses built on their property are in a position to engage in subsistence farming on a sustained basis.

Reliance on foraging has also declined in recent years. Although it is still practiced, it is not carried on as systematically or as regularly as it was in the past. Whether or not Devil's Lake Sioux forage is conditioned not only by natural fluctuations in the availability of wild animals and plant foods in the area. It is also influenced by a household's access to transportation needed for reaching sites where food is located and by its ownership of equipment (e.g., guns) necessary for foraging production. Hunting, gathering, and fishing do offer supplemental food for many households at Devil's Lake, but the contributions from these activities are highly erratic from one year to the next.

Along with a drop in food production, there has been a substantial decline in the handiwork of men and women. Fewer women, today, make their family's clothing and the wide range of other household objects they produced in the past. Increasingly, Sioux women are acquiring these goods through the cash economy. Their cash economy, however, is not tied primarily to local retail establishments. Instead, it is linked to the weekly rummage sales at local mission and neighboring White communities. Searching for inexpensive and quality items in clothing, appliances, toys, dishes, and furniture is a major "foraging" activity of contemporary Sioux women.

Most of the handicraft labor, that Sioux women still engage in, is devoted to the making of costumes and objects (e.g., star quilts) for ceremonial use. The number of women who produce beadwork for sale to outsiders, however, is declining. For many, the time and labor that must be put into this work is not worth the meager earnings derived from it. Consequently, much of the fine beadwork that is now made is produced either for family members or as a favor to friends and distant kin. Only in the 1970's was it worthwhile for some women to engage in handicraft activity. Largely through the development of a special Community Action Program (CAP) for the elderly, minimum hourly wages were paid for the production of quilts, shawls, and beadwork which were sold locally. This project has now been disbanded as a result of federal cutbacks.

Today, most of the work that is performed in Devil's Lake Sioux households is custodial in nature. There is a customary division of labor between men and women in household tasks, but the division is not rigid. Many tasks such as cutting wood, hauling water, and doing yard work are interchangeable. By and large, however, women take care of most of the housecleaning and food preparation, while men repair and maintain cars as well as perform a wide range of household carpentry tasks. Although childcare is most often in the hands of women, men also share in this responsibility. Generally speaking, whichever parent, grandparent, or elder sibling is around the household will tend to the children who need care and watching.

More so than in the past, the modern households of the Devil's Lake Sioux are provisioning units organized around the pooling and sharing of cash earnings and the commodities these buy. Every adult is expected to contribute what they can to a household's maintenance. This not only involves offering assistance in cash or kind (e.g., groceries, fuel) but also providing labor in any of a variety of household chores. Relatives who have no source of income and who cannot contribute provisions are welcome in Sioux households as long as they are willing to offer assistance in household chores. When kin move into a household and contribute neither labor nor goods, their presence is begrudgingly tolerated, if not openly resented. The addition of a non-supporting member can easily become burdensome in households that already exist on very marginal grounds. One way that those in need of suport avoid overtaxing a household and creating conflict is to constantly shift their place of residence. In doing this, these Sioux effectively distribute the responsibility for their support among a wide range of kin, and as a consequence, they diminish the possibility of jeopardizing the survival of any single household in their kinship network (Albers 1982).

A very significant change in the modern era is the increasing role that women play in the provisioning of households through their own earnings. In the vast majority of cases, incomes that women receive through wage-labor and relief represent a substantial contribution to their household's welfare. Female earnings equal or exceed the contributions of men in forty percent of the households that I have evidence for, and they constitute the sole source of support in another twenty percent of the sample. The households where women make no cash contribution are small in number, making up less than ten percent of the total.

Not only do women make substantial contributions

to the livelihood of a household, but they also
control how their earnings are going to be spent in
meeting household needs. As in the past, Devil's Lake
Sioux continue to respect, at least ideally, the prior
claim that people have to the products of their labor.
Neither sex controls the earnings of the other. What
each sex contributes to a household's provisions is
decided on a voluntary basis, and how much is given is
determined largely by their respective incomes. When
both husband and wife have stable earnings, expenses
are divided according to what each income is able to
cover. Otherwise, financial obligations are settled
primarily by the spouse who has the most constant
income, which is often the wife. When a husband's
earnings are erratic, as they frequently are, his
income offers a household temporary luxuries above and
beyond the staple commodities provided by the wife.

Since there is such variation and fluctuation in
the amount and dependability of incomes between the
sexes, there is also a highly varied and shifting pattern of male and female influence in household
affairs. While the number of households where female
incomes dominate is growing, this has not been associated with the emergence of a pattern of female
tyranny over the sexual politics of the household.
The greater economic autonomy of women has given them
more weight in the day-to-day decisions of their
households, and it has also given them more opportunities to establish households independent of any
support from men. To be sure, there are many households where women exert more influence than men, but
this is not always a stable situation. It can be
altered easily through such circumstantial factors as
a shift in the relative income of a husband and wife.
An ideology based on the domination of one person over
another, regardless of sex or age, has no more appeal
among the Sioux today than it had in the past. The
relative power that any person exercises in a household is subtly expressed and suggested by the degree
to which others voluntarily consent to or comply with
such influence. The use of force whether physical or
verbal does not bring about control. Instead, it
usually initiates a fissioning process which in the
case of a husband and wife leads to divorce or separation.

Along with changes in the functioning of households, there have also been significant shifts in

household composition. Today, the size and membership of households at Devil's Lake are not only varied but they are ever-changing as well. Household composition is very fluid, not only as a result of changes in the domestic cycle but also as a consequence of the fluctuating economic and demographic conditions under which the Devil's Lake Sioux live (Albers 1982).

A large proportion of the households at Devil's Lake still conform to an extended family pattern. As in the past, marriages remain brittle, and affinal links do not provide a stable foundation for the building of enduring household relationships. The consanguinal ties which are emphasized in modern household formations, however, are much more viable than they were in earlier historical periods.

In a growing number of households, the emphasis is uterine rather than agnatic. There has been an increasing tendency for daughters to remain in or near the households of their parents after marriage. The reasons for this uterine emphasis are many, but probably the most important factor is the inability of young men to assist in the support of a wife and family. Young couples usually begin their marriages living in the household of the husband's kin, when these relatives can offer support. The wives, however, are often uncomfortable in this type of arrangement because it places them in a position of dependency and powerlessness. This not only makes young women feel isolated but it also breeds conflict with their affines. Eventually, most women return home either alone or with their spouses. Today, there is an increasing number of unmarried or separated women who live with their children in the households of their parents.

The fragile, and potentially antagonistic, relationships between affines has always been acknowledged by the Sioux. As a way to reduce dependency and the conflicts that this can generate between affines, the Sioux have encouraged young couples to establish separate households whenever possible. While nuclear family households have been an ideal among the Sioux since pre-reservation times, this type of arrangement has not been easy to achieve because of the shortage in housing on the reservation. In recent years, however, the number of new houses has grown at a rapid rate, and many people are establishing nuclear family and single parent households. But while the greater availability of housing has given young families more opportunities for privacy and autonomy, they cannot become independent households unless they have the means to sustain themselves. Generally, it is not until adults reach their thirties that they are in secure enough positions, economically, to form a separate household.

Although Sioux households strive towards self-sufficiency through the combined contributions of their members, many of them fail in this effort. One of the ways that households can remain viable and independent units in the face of economic decline or collapse is to become embedded in wider networks of support where kin pool, share, and barter their labor as well as cash-earnings. Mutual aid among kin living in different households is just as important today as it was in the past.

In the daily provisioning of their households, Sioux women have many opportunities to call on their kin for assistance. Kin, especially consanguines, may be relied upon to give cash, food, and other material goods when these are needed. They may also be depended upon to help in childcare, household chores, sewing, quilting, gardening, gathering, or any other kind of domestic activity where collaboration is solicited. Exchange of labor and resources among kin are open-ended--with reciprocity being indefinite both from the standpoint of time and value. Although expectations of return are vaguely stipulated, those who receive assistance are expected to reciprocate when they are able to do so and/or when a request is made.

There is a definite but informal order in the intensity of sharing relationships among kin. In the giving and receiving of aid, the most intense relationships a woman maintains are with her parents and children. The next important source of mutual support is a woman's sisters, then her brothers, and finally more distantly removed kin (that is, relatives beyond the boundaries of a tiošpaye which is usually reckoned no further than the second collateral line from ego). Since kinship is determined bilaterally, assistance may be sought from kin on either the maternal or paternal side. This order in the giving and receiving of assistance is followed whenever possible. There are many situations, however, in which it cannot be followed because the people who are customarily relied upon are not in a position to give. In reality, reciprocity among kin is very flexible and situationally defined. Sharing relationships regularly shift according to changes in the number of co-resident kin and also as a result of fluctuations in the distribution of incomes among them (Albers 1974).

Among female kin, the giving and receiving of assistance is a daily occurrence. Although the direction and intensity of this mutual aid may vary from one moment in time to another, cooperation and sharing are elementary aspects of interhousehold associations between female kin. This type of collaboration is especially pronounced in situations where there is a high ratio of females among a set of siblings. In two cases at Devil's Lake where there were a large number of sisters in a family, the women formed enduring and tightly-knit support networks. In addition, these women lived in nearby households that were closely situated to the parental home. Their husbands' kin, for the most part, lived in more removed locations at Devil's Lake or on other reservations. These two cases clearly constitute an instance of matrifocality, but they do not represent a generalized pattern.

There are also situations at Devil's Lake where the sex-ratio among a set of siblings favors males, and here the emphasis in residence is usually agnatic. In a few of these cases, the wives, as the Devil's Lake Sioux would put it, "went more for their husband's side," which is to say that they defined their support alliances to correspond with those of their spouse. Yet the vast majority of women who lived in an agnatically-oriented setting continued to seek their primary support from their own kin, especially sisters. And for all intents and purposes, a pattern of dual support networks developed in most agnatic residential formations.

In situations where there is no bias in the sex-ratio of siblings, the patterns of residence and mutual support are much more variable. There are cases where brothers and sisters, along with their spouses, live in close proximity to the parental home, and the cognatic orientation in residence gives rise to support networks that have no particular orientation along either agnatic or uterine lines.

The variability in the organization of residence and mutual support networks at Devil's Lake defies easy generalization. One thing is clear, however, and that is, no matter how residence and mutual support are patterned, women play a very important role in the sharing and cooperation that goes on between households. There are two important reasons for this. One reason derives from the division of household labor between men and women. Given the work they perform in the household, women are simply in a better position to monitor the distribution of food and other necessities that circulate widely in interhousehold networks. The second reason is directly related to the fact that a growing number of Sioux women now have autonomous incomes which they are able to distribute as they see fit. At their own discretion, women may give, voluntarily or upon request, provisions to any member of their kin group who needs them. Although husbands often tease their wives about this support, especially when it becomes burdensome, they rarely intervene and ultimately defer to the decisions of their wives on this matter. Conversely, women may disapprove of their husband's generosity to his kin, but they generally do little about it unless it interferes with the welfare of the household. Thus, as Sioux women have gained increasing economic independence, they have also achieved greater influence in monitoring the circulation of provisions within and between households.

In cases where women have considerable wealth (relatively speaking, of course), they often serve as the nucleus of a kin-based support network. In such a position, these women exercise considerable influence because they control the distribution of provisions upon which others are dependent. In a few instances, Sioux women have come to achieve the influence and respect accorded to certain men in former times, and they have done so precisely because their wealth supports, directly or indirectly, a large number of kin. But even when women are not wealthy in reservation terms, they can still gain the confidence and admiration of others through their generosity and willingness to help others with what they have.

The important role that women now play in monitoring the distribution of food and other necessities in an interhousehold setting extends to the ceremonial arena as well. Today, Sioux women have an influential place in supporting ceremonies organized by family groups, as well as those sponsored on a community-wide basis.

In modern times, as in the past, an important responsibility of Devil's Lake Sioux is to publically acknowledge the major achievements and life cycle transitions of their kin. To this end, the Sioux hold special honoring ceremonies accompanied by feasts and give-aways. The elaborateness and prestige of these ceremonies is largely dependent on the contributions that women make. Much of the preparation that goes into a feast and give-away is in the hands of females.

Women are the ones primarily responsible for building what the Devil's Lake Sioux call "collections," that is, an accumulation of gifts to be distributed to guests who attend the honoring ceremony. It is interesting to note that most of the gifts that are given are household goods, which include blankets, towels, potholders, pillowcases, fabrics, as well as Tupperware and enamelware dishes. In addition, items of apparel are given, and these include dresses, shirts, moccasins, medallions, shawls, feathered-headdresses, and the like. And finally, cash is a ubiquitous gift in the give-away. Most of the objects that are given at these ceremonies are either made by women or purchased with their earnings. In fact, the most prestigious items given and displayed at an honoring is the star quilt, which is made exclusively by women (Albers and Medicine 1980). Women not only contribute much of what is distributed at a give-away, but they also decide to whom the gifts will be given. As in household provisioning, men and women determine independently, or through mutual consensus, the use and distribution of that which each produces. Although it may look like men are controlling give-aways, because they generally assume the role of speaker, eyapaha in Sioux, and make the announcement at an honoring ceremony, the public appearance is deceptive. The fact of the matter is that behind every successful give-away are women who make and/or buy most of the goods distributed and who therefore determine to whom the gifts will be given.

Women are also the ones who do most of the work in preparing the food that is distributed at an honoring feast. Besides, much of the food that is

214

prepared is purchased with their own earnings or produced through their labor in gathering and gardening.
Even when men donate money to buy food and contribute
livestock or wild meat, women do most of the cooking
and serving of food. In their role as food servers,
women directly control what is distributed, the size
of the portions, and to whom it is given.

The central role of women in the distribution of
food and gifts at honoring ceremonies also holds true
in celebration activities sponsored by local communities or voluntary associations like Omaha Clubs.
Powwows, which are the most actively supported
community-wide celebrations at Devil's Lake, are organized by a group called the "committee." Committee
members are either appointed or elected to their positions. Among the Sioux, the customary practice is to
place children in these positions, although their
parents assume the responsibility of the office.
Whether a committee position is bestowed on an adult
or a child, the sex of the occupant may be either male
or female. Whichever sex holds a committee office,
lines of authority and power in organizing a powwow
reside in that office. Consequently, women can assume
influential roles in powwow activity either directly
or on behalf of a child who is honored with a committee position.

At Devil's Lake, there are several women who have
become well-known and respected for their support of
ceremonial activities. Their notoriety is not confined to their own reservation but is regional in
scope. Whenever these women travel to celebrations on
other reservations, their influence and respect is
acknowledged by the host committee whose members give
them the most prestigious gifts in their give-aways.
One Devil's Lake Sioux woman, in particular, was
widely admired for her generosity and the support she
gave to ceremonial activity. The esteem people gave
her was clearly acknowledged when she recently passed
away and hundreds of people from several different
reservations in the United States and Canada attended
her funeral.

It is true that few women hold the prestigious
position of the _eyapaha_ at celebrations and that no
Devil's Lake Sioux woman has performed this role. It
is also true that women do not receive the same
acclaim and prize monies that men do in competitive

powwow dancing. Nor do women occupy leading positions in certain religious ceremonies, especially those of the Native American Church, although they do hold a very important and honored position in the Sun Dance. Inequities of this order are not considered really significant among most Sioux women, for none exclude them from participation in any ceremonial activity and from gaining prestige in their own right. It is in the modern give-away, which accompanies most contemporary ceremonies, that Sioux women exercise the leading role and gain the greatest influence, and for most of them this avenue of prestige is sufficient. Indeed, contemporary Sioux women achieve as much influence and respect for the ceremonial activities they dominate as men do in theirs.

Understanding the influence and control Sioux women exercise in the social networks organized for provisioning and ceremonial purposes helps to explain why women are now achieving greater recognition within a community-wide political realm. Since the 1950's when an elected tribal government was formed on the Devil's Lake Sioux Reservation, women have played an important role in directing the course of political action. Their influence in mobilizing and monitoring political support is inseparable from their contributions in ceremonial and interhousehold provisioning. This is because the social arena where kin share and collaborate in their domestic and ceremonial affairs overlaps, and in some instances is virtually identical with, the major fields of political action on the reservation. While it is true that the tribal government is organized around formal offices and rules, which are defined in terms of Western jurisprudence, it is also clear that what goes on in tribal government is directly influenced by the support and challenge of kin-based networks on the outside (Albers 1974:314-323).

To a large extent, tribal politics and domestic politics are the same. The social formations which dominate the everyday life of most Sioux are defined by kinship and organized around the interests of separate but related domestic groups or tiošpaye. In the situation that the Devil's Lake Sioux have found themselves during the last century, their primary political interests have been defined in terms of gaining access to an adequate means of livelihood for all households on the reservation. The issues that tribal leaders have been faced with in recent years are dominated by domestic concerns that have been critical to both men and women.

Therefore, it is not surprising that political involvement is _ipso facto_ domestic in nature. Nor is it fortuitous that women use their mutual aid networks for generating support when they or their kin (male or female) seek political office. Through their kinship channels, women censure and exert pressure on the direction and effectiveness of decisions made in tribal government. Through these same channels, they influence the course of tribal elections and even force the removal of people from political office. While women may not have gained parity with men in terms of the number of elected and administrative offices they hold, they certainly have achieved equality of influence in the social networks that support or challenge tribal government.

The recent rise in the influence of Sioux women is clearly a consequence of their more stable and independent economic positions vis-a-vis the capitalist sector of production. In this position, they have been able to provide a more constant and reliable source of support in the provisioning of their households and in the assistance that they offer their kin. The erratic nature of wage-labor, particularly the jobs that men have traditionally entered, has made it difficult for many men to provide steady support for their own household or to extend help to other households. Not having independent sources of income, these men have had to rely on others in the community to provide for them. Often, this aid comes from females, either a wife, mother, sister, or even daughter. Under conditions such as these, it is not surprising that the balance of power should shift increasingly in favor of women.

The ascendancy of female influence, however, is also a consequence of an historically based pattern of relationships among the Sioux. This pattern, which is defined by the language of kinship, emphasizes egalitarian relationships based on mutual sharing and cooperation. It is a pattern which, at least ideally, accords all people a degree of autonomy and the right to exert influence through their own work and example. Whether or not this independence is realized has largely been a matter of circumstance, especially the

217

nature of wider historical forces that have dominated the Sioux in post-reservation times. The persistence of an egalitarian pattern among the Sioux, as I argue in detail elsewhere (Albers 1982), has not been the result of some form of ideological lag, but rather, this pattern continues precisely because it works in the situations under which Devil's Lake Sioux live in the modern era. Forced to survive on meager and erratic earnings from sources over which they have had little control, the Devil's Lake Sioux's primary security has been their kin. By sharing and pooling their labor and provisions, the Devil's Lake Sioux effectively transform the disparities and fluctuations of their incomes into a more equitable and stable environment for consumption. That women occupy a pivotal role in this transformation is not only a consequence of the more stable nature of their incomes but also a result of the kinds of provisioning tasks they have traditionally performed in their households.

CONCLUSION

During the last century, major changes have taken place in the role and status of women living on the Devil's Lake Sioux Reservation. The changes have resulted from a dynamic interaction between a capitalist sector of production that is organized in terms of a class hierarchy and the generation of surplus-value (profit) and a domestic sector of production that is patterned around kinship and the creation of use-value.

When the Devil's Lake Sioux Reservation was first established, its Sioux inhabitants brought with them an historically developed system of social relationship based on centuries of past experience. Within this system, women as well as men had rights that guaranteed them control over their own production and the fruits of their labor. Under federal domination, these rights were all but destroyed except in those areas where the Sioux were able to manage their own subsistence production. These areas of resistance, so to speak, were dominated by the work activity of women in gardening, gathering, and handicrafts. Sioux men, on the other hand, were being drawn into a capitalist production process as laborers in government farms. Through this labor, Sioux men gained exclusive control over commodities on which their family's livelihood, in part, depended. Denied access to the tools of agriculture, to agency-based jobs, and to annuity distributions, Sioux women were effectively cut off from direct participation in those areas where the reservation was tied to the capitalist sector of production. But while they were excluded from direct involvement in the capitalist sector as wage-laborers, female contributions in subsistence food production and handicrafts were essential in maintaining their households with provisions beyond the paltry annuities offered by the federal government.

In the early reservation era, federal domination was not merely a form of paternalism as it has often been described. Rather, it was, and still is, an active element in the capitalist production process. By taking the surplus gains from Indian land, livestock, and crops and using these to purchase annuities from private business, the federal government was not only depriving the Sioux of control over their means of production but it was also denying them control over the consumption of products which they had labored for. In this situation, Sioux men were just as oppressed and exploited as Sioux women. The manner by which each was exploited was clearly different, but the fact remains that the land and labor of men, as well as women, was being appropriated to support a growing federal bureaucracy and its investments in the nation's private enterprises. Although men did gain a temporary advantage over women through their prior claim on provisions coming from the capitalist sector, they did so at considerable cost to their own independence. What does it mean to exercise power over a family's support when the provisions, themselves, are not under your control?

The influence that Sioux men exercised in early reservation times was really never their own because it was ultimately granted or denied through the federal government in compliance with wider corporate interests. In running farming operations on the reservation, the government stood in competition with the private interests of the developing agrobusiness. Ultimately, the government withdrew and turned Sioux land over to the private sector. With this shift, whatever value land had had to the Sioux on a cash or productive basis began to decline. With this decline the labor-power of Sioux men in agriculture was also devalued. There was nothing, however, in the reservation's capitalist sector of production to replace it. From the 1920's until modern times, many Sioux men were placed in an economic limbo where they had neither steady jobs nor unearned forms of income to support themselves, much less a family. Nor did some of them have a small plot of land on which to produce a meager subsistence. In this vacuum Sioux women began to emerge as an important source of support in the provisioning of their households and wider kin groups. While their ascendance was created, in part, by a more extensive federal relief program under ADC, it also resulted from their own past history in household production. In the years after World War II, as more women gained access to steady incomes through welfare or employment, the balance of power in the Sioux household, and in wider community settings, increasingly shifted to women.

What is especially ironic is that the very programs that the federal government has established to make the Sioux dependent on the capitalist production process have created, simultaneously, the basis of their relative autonomy. Not being able to live off the small annuities or cash incomes made available to them through private and federal sources, the Sioux have been forced to develop a wide range of strategies within a domestic sector of production that would insure their survival. These strategies, including the intensification of subsistence production and the "stretching" of provisions through distributive mechanisms based on sharing, had always been under women's control. As the pattern of income distribution changed in the direction of women, they assumed an increasingly important role in monitoring the provisions essential to their own households and those of their kin. And when federal policy in modern times began to lean towards supporting tribal self-governance and corporate enterprise, it was not a major leap for women to use the strategies they had developed in their domestic provisioning to influence the course of "self-determination."

What the past century of Sioux female experience suggests is that the domination of a capitalist mode of production does not lead inevitably to a decline in the status of women in their own class or community.

Clearly, Sioux women have never been accorded the same rights as men within the capitalist production system. But, even in early reservation times, it would be inappropriate to say that Sioux women lost status. Rather, what happened is that they never received, at least initially, the same income-producing opportunities as men. But did this really represent a "decline" in status for women, when the process by which men acquired an income involved their direct exploitation by another class? Notwithstanding the fact that Sioux women were excluded from "equal" participation in the areas where the reservation was linked to a wider capitalist production process, they did maintain some autonomy (no matter how limited) within a domestic sector of production. The autonomy that Sioux women retained in this sector, and that was later expanded through federal welfare policy, has created what appears to be a contradiction in their status.

The contradiction originally revealed in the study of Shirley Bysewicz and Ruth Van de Mark (1977) as well as in the work of Eileen Maynard (1979) is mentioned in the beginning of this paper. These two articles suggest that while Sioux women have a high status within the realm of their domestic and family affairs, they have a low status when judged in terms of their involvement in the political economy of the reservation. The data that have been presented here clearly indicate that such a contradiction has existed, if one divides the reservation into jural-political and family-based sectors. But when the machinations of tribal government are examined more carefully in terms of the elective process, council decision-making, and the dispensation of "favors" in the form of housing, jobs and the like, it is not so easy to draw a line between these sectors. In the modern situation of the Devil's Lake Sioux, at least, a contradiction exists between the rights of Sioux women in the broader political economy of this country and their prerogatives within the affairs of their family. But, since the interests of family and community are virtually indistinguishable in the operations of tribal government, there is no real contradiction here. For whether women hold a formal office or not, they have a direct and influential access to the political process that goes on in their communities.

221

The contradiction between the status of Sioux women in their own communities and in the political economy at large is a result of the peculiarities of the role that domestic production plays in reservation settings. This, in turn, is a product of the unique way in which reservations have been linked to the capitalist production process. It is the peculiar nature of this linkage, combined with the Sioux's own historically developed pattern of social relationship, that gives Sioux women a base of influence in their own community, while it denies them a means for power in the society at large. This contradiction will continue as long as Sioux people remain in a marginal and dependent position, and as long as they continue to survive in this position through an attenuated and community-based pattern of domestic production.

As I have demonstrated in this paper, the changing, and at times seemingly contradictory, status of Sioux women is made intelligible only when examined in relation to the shifting articulations between domestic and capitalist sectors of production in reservation settings. To separate the two sectors in a dualistic fashion, identifying one as private and another public, confuses rather than reveals what is happening in situations where a capitalist mode of production penetrates and alters an economy that was traditionally based on the production of use-values. In the case of the Sioux this penetration occurred as early as the seventeenth century when mercantile companies from Europe engaged them in fur-production. From that time on, there have been many changes in the social formations of the Sioux. But throughout the period of capitalist penetration, there has remained in Sioux communities an attenuated sector of production which is organized around kinship and the creation of use-value. Since the formation of reservations, Sioux people have become increasingly marginal to the capitalist production process. Having been excluded from an active and permanent place, as wage-laborers or entrepreneurs, in capitalist production, they have come to live under conditions that foster a domestic pattern of production aimed at maintaining people on the fringes of capitalism rather than preparing them for active participation in the system. In this situation, capitalism does not fashion the domestic sector in its own image as it does with most working-class people. Instead, as in the case of the Devil's Lake Sioux, the domestic sector is organized by the conditions of political-economic marginality as these have been combined, in a dialectical fashion, with the Sioux's own traditional patterns of relationship. Here Sioux women have retained a degree of autonomy and have come to occupy an influential position in their own communities.

ACKNOWLEDGEMENTS

I wish to thank the National Institute of Mental Health and the Wenner-Gren Foundation for their financial support in carrying out part of the field research upon which this paper is based. I would also like to acknowledge my gratitude to William James for his editorial and theoretical assistance and to Ursula Hanly for her careful typing of the original manuscript. Finally, and most importantly, I wish to thank the Devil's Lake Sioux for the support and hospitality they extended to me while I did my research. In particular, I wish to dedicate this paper to the memory of my fictive sisters, Emma Woods Adams and Mary Woods Hopkins, as well as my friends, Theresa Dunn Leftbear and Martha Leftbear Glaser who in their life epitomized the independence, courage, and generosity of Sioux women.

FOOTNOTES

1. The ethnic terms, Sioux and Dakota, are interchangeable names for the same American Indian group.

2. Eighteen months were spent doing fieldwork on the Devil's Lake Reservation over a four year period from 1968 to 1972. Additional fieldwork on this reservation was conducted in the summers of 1977, 1978, and 1980.

3. The expression "colonialism" has many different meanings. Originally, it was used to identify a situation where European nations took over and administrated the lands of indigenous peoples. More recently, it has come to refer to a situation where Western capitalism dominates the political economy of subordinated peoples and nations.

4. Recent criticism of the public-private split indicates that in many situations this division is a false dichotomy since domestic production and familial relations are community-based. Consequently, a number of anthropologists, like Rayna Reiter (1975), argue that this dichotomy is appropriate only in situations that post-date the emergence of the state.

5. It is very likely that the devaluation of domestic work is more related to the emergence of an elite class, who do not engage in this type of production, than it is to some gender specific quality of the work itself.

6. When Sioux lands were ceded under treaty, the federal government agreed to provide compensation in the form of a cash settlement to be used for per capita annuities and developmental purposes (e.g., education, farming).

7. The inner-most circle of an individual's consanguinal kin is called the tiospaye. Usually, it includes all relatives who are removed from ego by no more than two collateral lines. Among modern Sioux, this term is used almost exclusively to refer to a genealogical reference group. But in the past, it also had a residential connotation, referring to a group of kin who lived in close proximity.

8. The Native American Church is a post-reserva-

tion religion which among the Sioux is heavily infused with Christian elements. This religion was introduced to them in the early twentieth century. Although Sioux women have always been able to participate in this religion, they have never led or conducted the ceremonial rites.

9. The involvement of Sioux women in pre-reservation community affairs is reported in four major sources (Riggs 1893; Pond 1908; Landes 1968; Stipe 1968).

10. When a woman's husband spent her lease money in an irresponsible way, she had the right to request that the funds be transferred to her directly.

11. It is interesting to note that the farmers who leased the land of the Devil's Lake Sioux were often the same ones who hired the Sioux as wage-laborers during the summer months. In a couple of cases, Devil's Lake Sioux actually worked as wage-laborers on the land allotments they owned.

12. In the mid-1970's, the Devil's Lake Sioux, along with several other Sioux reservation populations, were awarded a settlement of several million dollars as a reimbursement for lands dispossessed in Minnesota after 1862. A portion of this money was paid to the tribe collectively, while the rest was divided in per capita payments.

REFERENCES CITED

Aguiar, Neuma (1976) The Impact of Industrialization
on Women's Work Roles in Northeast Brazil. In:
Sex and Class in Latin America, J. Nash and H.
Safa, eds., pp. 110-128. New York: Praeger
Press.

Albers, Patricia (1974) The Regional System of the
Devil's Lake Sioux. Unpublished Ph.D.
Dissertation, University of Wisconsin-Madison.

_____ (1982) Sioux Kinship in a Colonial Setting.
Dialectical Anthropology 6:253-269.

_____ (n.d.) Santee (Eastern Dakota). Handbook of
North American Indians, Vol. 14, The Plains (in
press).

Albers, Patricia, and Beatrice Medicine (1980)
Star Quilts. Native Arts West, Vol. I,
pp. 9-15 (also in this volume pp. 123-140).

Amin, Samir (1976) Unequal Development: An Essay
on the Social Formation of Peripheral Capitalism.
Translated by B. Pearce. New York: Monthly
Review Press.

Apodaca, Maria Linda (1979) The Chicano Woman: An
Historical Materialist Perspective. In: Women
in Latin America, pp. 81-100. Riverside, Ca.:
Latin American Perspectives.

Bodley, John (1975) Victims of Progress. Menlo
Park, Ca.: Cummings Publ.

Boserup, E. (1970) Woman's Role in Economic
Development. New York: St. Martin's Press.

Bossen, L. (1975) Women in Modernizing Societies.
American Ethnologist 2:587-601.

Brown, Jennifer (1980) Strangers in Blood.
Vancouver: University of British Columbia Press.

Burkett, Elinor   (1979)   In Dubious Sisterhood:
Class and Sex in Spanish Colonial South America.
In: Women in Latin America, pp. 17-25.
Riverside, Ca.:   Latin American Perspectives.

Bysiewicz, Shirley and Ruth Van de Mark   (1977)   The
Legal Status of Dakota Women. American Indian
Law Review 3:255-312.

Deere, Carmen Diana   (1976)   Rural Women's Subsistence
Production in the Capitalist Peripherey.   In:
Women and the Economy. The Review of Radical
Political Economics, Vol. 8(1), pp. 9-17.

_____   (1979)   Changing Social Relations of Pro-
duction and Peruvian Peasant Women's Work. In:
Women in Latin America. Riverside, Ca.:   Latin
American Perspectives.

Dole, Gertrude   (1979)   Amahuaca Women in Social
Change. In: Sex Roles in Changing Cultures,
A. McElroy and C. Matthiasson, eds. Occasional
Papers in Anthropology 1:111-122.

Duncan, Katherine   (1980)   American Indian Lace
Making. American Indian Art 3:29-35.

Economic Development Administration (EDA)   (1971)
Federal and State Indian Reservations: An
Economic Development Administration Handbook.
Washington, D.C.:   U.S. Government Printing
Office.

Elmendorf, Mary Lindsay   (1976)   Nine Mayan Women:
A Village Faces Change. New York: Schenkman
Publishing Co.

Etienne, Mona and Leacock, Eleanor, eds.   (1980)
Women and Colonization: Anthropological
Perspectives. New York: Praeger.

Fee, Terry   (1976)   Domestic Labor: An Analysis of
Housework and its Relation to the Production
Process. The Review of Radical Political
Economics 8:1-8.

Frank, Andre G.   (1969)   Latin America: Underdevelopment or Revolution. New York: Modern Reader.

Garrett, Patricia (1976) Some Structural Constraints
    on the Agricultural Activities of Women: The
    Chilean Hacienda. Paper presented at the
    Wellesley Conference on Women and Development.

Hamamsy, Laila S. (1957) The Role of Women in a
    Changing Navajo Society. American Anthropologist
    59:101-111.

Hassrick, Royal (1944) Teton Dakota Kinship System.
    American Anthropologist 16:338-347.

Henderson, Behjat (1979) The Effect of Modernization
    on the Roles of Iranian Women. In: Sex Roles in
    Changing Cultures, A. McElroy and C. Matthiasson,
    eds. Occasional Papers in Anthropology
    1:143-154.

Himmelweit, Susan, and Simon Mohun (1977) Domestic
    Labor and Capital. Cambridge Journal of
    Economics 1:15-31.

House Committee on Interior and Insular Affairs (1953)
    Investigation of the Bureau of Indian Affairs.
    U.S. Congress House Report No. 2503, 82nd
    Congress, 2nd Session.

_____ (1962) Indian Unemployment Survey.
    Committee Print 3, 88th Congress, 1st Session.

James, William (1975) Subsistence, Survival and
    Capitalist Agriculture: Aspects of the Mode of
    Production Among a Colombian Proletariat. Latin
    American Perspectives 3:84-95.

Jorgensen, Joseph (1971) Indians and the Metropolis.
    In: The American Indian in Urban Society, J.O.
    Waddell and O.M. Watson, eds. Boston: Little,
    Brown and Co.

_____ (1972) The Sun Dance Religion: Power for
    the Powerless. Chicago: University of Chicago
    Press.

_____ (1978) A Century of Political Economic
    Effects on American Indian Society, 1880-1980.
    Journal of Ethnic Studies 6:1-82.

Klein, Laura (1976) "She's one of us, you know":
    The Public Life of Tlingit Women: Traditional,
    Historical, and Contemporary Perspectives.
    Western Canadian Journal of Anthropology
    6:164-183.

Knight, Rolf (1978) Indians at Work: An Informal
    History of Native Indian Labor in British
    Columbia, 1858-1930. Vancouver: New Star Books.

Lamphere, Louise (1974) Strategies, Cooperation, and
    Conflict Among Women in Domestic Groups. In:
    Woman, Culture, and Society, M.Z. Rosaldo and
    L. Lamphere, eds. Stanford: Stanford University
    Press.

_____ (1977) To Run After Them: Cultural and
    Social Bases of Cooperation in a Navajo
    Community. Tucson: University of Arizona Press.

Landes, Ruth (1968) The Mystic Lake Sioux:
    Sociology of the Mdewakantonwan Santee. Madison:
    University of Wisconsin Press.

_____ (1971) The Ojibway Woman. New York: W.W.
    Norton and Company.

Leacock, Eleanor (1975) Class, Commodity, and the
    Status of Women. In: Women Cross-Culturally:
    Change and Challenge, R. Rohrlich-Leavitt, ed.,
    pp. 601-616. The Hague: Mouton Publishers.

_____ (1978) Women's Status in Egalitarian
    Society: Implications of Social Evolution.
    Current Anthropology 19:247-276.

_____ (1979) Women, Development, and Anthropologi-
    cal Facts and Fictions. In: Women in Latin
    America, pp. 7-16. Riverside, Ca.: Latin
    American Perspectives.

Leis, Nancy (1979) West African Women and the
    Colonial Experience. In: Sex Roles in Changing
    Cultures, A. McElroy and C. Matthiasson, eds.
    Occasional Papers in Anthropology 1:167-176.

McElroy, Ann (1979)   The Negotiations of Sex-Role
    Identity in Eastern Arctic Culture Change.   In:
    Sex Roles in Changing Cultures, A. McElroy and
    C. Matthiasson, eds.   Occasional Papers in
    Anthropology 1:49-60.

McGregor, Gordon   (1946)   Warriors Without Weapons.
    Chicago: University of Chicago Press.

Maynard, Eileen   (1979)   Changing Sex Roles and Family
    Structure Among the Oglala Sioux.   In: Sex Roles
    in Changing Cultures, A. McElroy and C.
    Matthiasson, eds.   Occasional Papers in Anthro-
    pology 1:11-20.

Medicine, Beatrice   (1978)   The Native American Woman:
    A Perspective.   Austin, Texas: National Edu-
    cational Labortory Publishers.

_____ (1980)   Out of the Mirage: Current Research
    and Interpretations of Women in Northern Plains
    Societies.   Paper presented at Festschrift for
    John Ewers, Smithsonian Institution, Museum of
    Man.

Michaelson, E.J., and W. Goldschmidt (1971)   Female
    Roles and Male Dominance Among Peasants.   South-
    western Journal of Anthropology 4:330-352.

Meyer, Roy W.   (1967)   A History of the Santee Sioux:
    United States Indian Policy on Trial.   Lincoln:
    University of Nebraska.

Minge-Klevana, Wanda   (1978)   Household Economy During
    the Peasant-to-Worker Transition in the Swiss
    Alps.   Ethnology 17:183-196.

_____ (1980)   Does Labor Time Decrease with
    Industrialization?   A Survey of Time-Allocation
    Studies.   Current Anthropology 21:279-298.

Mintz, Sidney   (1971)   Men, Women and Trade.
    Comparative Studies in Society and History 13:
    247-269.

Neill, Edward   (1872)   Dakota Land and Dakota Life
    (1850-1856).   Minnesota Historical Society
    Collections 1:205-240.

Nowack, Barbara (1979) Women's Roles and Status in a Changing Iroquois Society. In: Sex Roles in Changing Cultures, A. McElroy and C. Matthiasson, eds. Occasional Papers in Anthropology 1:95-110.

Oakley, Ann (1974) The Sociology of Housework. New York: Pantheon.

Okonjo, Kamene (1975) The Role of Women in the Development of Culture in Nigeria. In: Women Cross-Culturally: Change and Challenge, R. Rohrlich-Leavitt, ed. The Hague: Mouton.

Ortner, S.B. (1974) Is Female to Male as Nature to Culture? In: Woman, Culture and Society, M.Z. Rosaldo and L. Lamphere, eds. Stanford: Stanford University Press.

Pond, Samuel (1908) The Dakotas or Sioux in Minnesota as they were in 1834. Minnesota Historical Society Collections 12:319-501.

Quinn, Naomi (1977) Anthropological Studies on Women's Status. In: Annual Review of Anthropology, Bernard J. Siegel, ed. Volume 6:181-225.

Randle, Martha (1951) Iroquois Women, Then and Now. In: Bureau of American Ethnology Bulletin No. 149, W. Fenton, ed. Washington, D.C.

Reiter, Rayna (1975) Men and Women in the South of France: Public and Private Domains. In: Towards an Anthropology of Women, R. Reiter, ed., pp. 252-282. New York: Monthly Review Press.

Remy, D. (1975) Underdevelopment and the Experience of Women: A Nigerian Case Study. In: Towards an Anthropology of Women, R. Reiter, ed. New York: Monthly Review Press.

Riggs, Stephen R. (1893) Dakota Grammar, Texts and Ethnography. In: Contributions to North American Ethnology, James O. Dorsey, ed. Department of the Interior, United States Geographical and Geological Survey of the Rocky Mountain Region 9:1-232.

Rosaldo, Michelle (1974) Woman, Culture, and
    Society: A Theoretical Overview. In: Woman,
    Culture, and Society, M. Rosaldo and L. Lamphere,
    eds. Stanford: Stanford University Press.

Rothenberg, Diane (1976) Erosion of Power: An
    Economic Basis for the Selective Conservatism
    of Seneca Women in the Nineteenth Century.
    Western Canadian Journal of Anthropology
    6:106-118.

_____ (1980) The Mothers of the Nation: Seneca
    Resistance to Quaker Intervention. In: Women
    and Colonization: Anthropological Perspectives,
    M. Etienne and E. Leacock, eds., pp. 63-87.
    New York: Praeger.

Ruffing, Lorraine (1979) The Navajo Nation: A
    History of Dependence and Underdevelopment. The
    Review of Radical Political Economics 11:25-37.

Russell-Wood, A.J.R. (1978) Female and Family in the
    Economy and Society of Colonial Brazil. In:
    Latin American Women: Historical Perspectives,
    A. Lavrin, ed., pp. 60-100. Westport: Greenwood
    Press.

Sacks, K. (1975) Engels Revisited: Women, the
    Organization of Production, and Private Property.
    In: Toward an Anthropology of Women, R. Reiter,
    ed. New York: Monthly Review Press.

Safiotti, Heleieth (1977) Women, Mode of Production,
    and Social Formations. Latin American
    Perspectives 4:27-37.

_____ (1978) Women in Class Society. New York:
    Monthly Review Press.

Sanday, Peggy R. (1974) Female Status in the Public
    Domain. In: Woman, Culture, and Society, M.Z.
    Rosaldo and L. Lamphere, eds. Stanford:
    Stanford University Press.

Schultz, Theodore, ed. (1971) Economics of the
    Family: Marriage, Children, and Human Capital.
    Chicago: University of Chicago Press.

Seccombe, Wally (1974) The Housewife and Her Labor Under Capitalism. New Left Review 83:3-24.

Skinner, Alanson (1919) A Sketch of Eastern Dakota Ethnology. American Anthropologist 21:164-174.

_____ (1920) Medicine Ceremony of the Menomini, Iowa, and Wahpeton Dakota, with Notes on the Ceremony Among the Ponca, Bungi Ojibway, and Potawatomi. Indian Notes, Museum of the American Indian, Heye Foundation 3.

Spindler, Louise (1962) Menomini Women and Culture Change. American Anthropological Association, Memoir 91.

Stipe, Claude (1968) Eastern Dakota Acculturation: The Role of Agents of Culture Change. Unpublished Ph.D. Dissertation, University of Minnesota.

Sudarkasa, Niara (1976) Female Employment and Family Organization in West Africa. In: New Research on Women and Sex, D. McGuigan, ed. Ann Arbor: University of Michigan Center for Continuing Education of Women.

Urdang, Stephanie (1979) Fighting Two Colonialisms: Women in Guinea-Bissau. New York: Monthly Review Press.

Van Allen, Judith (1974) Modernization Means Dependency, Women in Africa. The Center Magazine 7(3).

Vidal, Isabel (1976) The History of Women's Struggle for Equality in Puerto Rico. In: Sex and Class in Latin America, J. Nash and H. Safa, eds., pp. 202-215. New York: Praeger.

Wallerstein, Immanuel (1974) The Modern World System. New York: Academic Press.

_____ (1974) The Rise and Future Demise of the World Capitalist System: Concepts for Comparative Analysis. Comparative Studies in Society and History, 16(4):387-415.

Wallis, Wilson D. (1947) The Canadian Dakota.
Anthropological Papers of the American Museum
of Natural History 41(1).

Washburn, Wilcomb (1975) The Assault on Indian
Tribalism: The General Allotment Law (Daws Act)
of 1887. New York: J.B. Lippencott Company.

Wilcox, Lloyd (1942) Group Structure and Personality
Types Among Sioux Indians of North Dakota.
Unpublished Ph.D. Dissertation, University of
Wisconsin-Madison.

PART IV

FEMALE IDENTITY

CHAPTER 9

MALE AND FEMALE IN TRADITIONAL LAKOTA CULTURE[1]

Raymond J. DeMallie
Indiana University

The traditional Lakotas are popularly considered to typify a society in which men dominated over women, a male-oriented society in which sexual inequality was the cultural norm. The most popular summary of Lakota lifeways, Royal B. Hassrick's The Sioux: Life and Customs of a Warrior Society (1964), emphasizes sexual inequality by analyzing Lakota culture from a psychological perspective. According to Hassrick, "the Sioux man was conditioned to consider woman as an adversary"; further, "If Sioux men considered women as adversaries, as foes to be conquered and quelled, Sioux women were no less straight forward in their opinion of men as dangerous predators" (1964:111, 123). He characterizes the relationship between the sexes as one of "innate hostility" and "innate distrust" (1964:123-124), and suggests sexual frustration as the basis for this "not-too-happy situation" (1964:126). Hassrick's interpretation stresses the consistency of the male role as aggressive warrior and hunter, even in the domestic situation.

This paper reexamines the relation between the sexes from the perspective of the cultural symbols that defined masculinity and femininity for the traditional Lakotas. This is an exercise in historical ethnography, based primarily on accounts written or dictated by a number of Lakota people between 1887 and 1960. The basic sources are the writings of George Bushotter (1887), George Sword (ca. 1909), Thomas Tyon (ca. 1911), and Ella C. Deloria (ca. 1929-1960). Additional data are taken from standard historical and anthropological sources, as well as from fieldwork among the contemporary Lakotas.

237

SEXUAL DIFFERENTIATION

In symbolic terms, the distinction between male and female was the single most important attribute for defining an individual in Lakota culture. Sex differences were emphasized in virtually every aspect of life. Masculinity and femininity were marked most importantly by behavioral differences. Sexual division of labor was very rigid and it may be said that behavior itself was the most important criterion differentiating male from female. George Sword (ms.) characterized this division of labor in these words:

> The work of men was as follows: they took part in fighting the enemy; that was a great honor. They hunted buffalo; they shot deer; they hunted for wild animals for food; they went to the hill to scout for buffalo.

> The work of women was: they packed every bit of household equipment each time the camp moved; they alone guarded all these things during the march. When they stopped to make camp the women again unpacked everything alone and erected their tipis. They laid out all the bedding; they gathered and brought in firewood; they brought water; they cooked, they passed out the food; they took care of all the children. They made all the utensils needed to manage the household. They even made the tipis; they themselves dressed the robes for their tipis. They made all the bedding; they were in entire charge of all food, once it had been obtained and brought home by the men.

Sword leaves no doubt that the work of men was considered to be more glorious and highly honored than the work of women. But it is equally clear from his account that Lakota women were accorded a full measure of respect for the performance of the work appropriate to their sex. The sexual division of labor was a simple fact of life, taken as natural. Ella Deloria wrote (1944:40):

> A woman caring for children and doing all the work around the house thought herself no worse off than her husband who was compelled to risk his life continuously,

238

hunting and remaining ever on guard against enemy attacks on his family.

The sexual division of labor was strictly upheld. Women doing the work of their husbands, or men doing the work of their wives, prompted ridicule from other Lakotas. It was dishonorable for both partners (Deloria ms. 1:134). Walker wrote (1982:63-64) that it was women who most insisted on preserving this division of labor. "If a man was found doing what was considered women's work, the women would ridicule him and attempt to dress him in women's clothes."

Deloria recorded many details of behavioral differences between men and women that extended into almost every area of life. Males and females were always expected to behave according to different patterns and to have different demeanors. Men were expected to be aggressive, women to be passive. Men were expected to boast of their deeds, and groups of men were expected at times to talk and laugh boisterously. Women on the other hand felt it immodest to talk too much when men were present, although they were expected to join in conversations with men if they had something to contribute. Only old women occasionally abused this right by talking too much. When women spoke, men did not look directly at them. Women talked freely among themselves, but never became boisterous in the manner of men. Loud laughter on a woman's part was immodest and was associated with sexual promiscuity. A man proved his masculinity by avoiding all womanish subjects in conversation. Thus even a wife's pregnancy was not a topic to be discussed by a man; it would be undignified and embarrassing (Deloria ms. 1:27-28, 92, 304).

Men and women had slight but significant differences in speech patterns. They used different greetings, different exclamations, different words for calling attention to things, and different suffixes to indicate commands and questions. Thus at the verbal level there was constant marking of the speaker's sex.

Men and women had different ways of sitting. Men (and children) sat with their legs crossed, while women after puberty sat with their legs folded to the side. If a woman sat like a man she was considered immodest (Walker 1917:146). Sitting and sleeping arrangements within the tipi were also differentiated by sex. The side left of the door as one entered was the male side, and the right side was the female side (Deloria ms. 1:86; see also Walker 1982:40).

Anger and shame were expressed differently by the sexes. Men would leave the camp and go to war, sometimes with the avowed intention of loosing one's life in battle. Vestal records the extreme case of Sitting Bull's father, Jumping Bull, who tried to throw his life away in battle because of a toothache (1957:46). Leaving the camp was not a usual option for women. They might commit suicide by hanging or they might "pout" (wacinko), a culturally-recognized psychological state in which the person sat motionless, refusing to eat or speak (Lewis 1975). In the past this was evidently solely a woman's reaction to stress, although it has been reported for men as well during the reservation period.

POWER

Sword's description of the sexual division of labor omitted two important areas of life: religion and medicine on the one hand, leadership and government on the other. Both were primarily men's concerns.

Men were the shamans and doctors, the seekers-after-visions and the controllers of relations with the powers of the universe. Men's visions gave them power to heal, to go to war, and to hunt. Women were only peripherally involved in these matters. Women were important and essential participants in religious ceremonies but they were never the directors of them.

Although women did not go on the vision quest, some women nonetheless had visions. These might give them power to use herbs to cure bodily ailments, to act as midwife, or to make charms (mahpiyatola, "little blue clouds" [Deloria ms. 1:330]) to protect growing children. Visions might also provide inspiration and power to execute quill or beadwork designs. These designs represent a type of power that was uniquely female, manipulating the power of color as well as of form. According to Walker (1982:107), in doing beadwork Lakota women originally mixed together the various colors of beads to be used in a design, picking out each bead individually as it was to be used. He wrote:

240

This is because glass beads are made by white men who do not know how to control their potencies and by mixing the beads their potencies are equalized so that no bead may have the power to overcome other beads, and the potency of the design will not be disturbed.

Women who were expert at quill and beadwork evidently formed a society that met occasionally for feasts and public displays of their work. According to Wissler (1912:79), this association was founded by a Double Woman dreamer, and it was the Double Woman who first taught Lakota women to dye quills and to do quillwork, and who gave individual women the power to do fine quillwork (Wissler 1902:123; 1912:93). The Double Woman dreamers sometimes enacted their dream publicly. As they walked through the camp flashing mirrors, they caused both men and women to fall prostrate and to spit up black earth or plant material. While in a trance so induced, a Double Woman dreamer might obtain power to make shields and war medicines (Wissler 1912:94). However, the power of the Double Woman was also associated with evil, as discussed below.

In addition to the Porcupine Quill Workers, Wissler also mentions other women's societies (1912:76-80, 98-99): the Praiseworthy Women (Winyan tapika), a wakan society for young women, evidently virgins; the Owns-Alone, a feasting society of women over the age of forty who had only known one man; the Tanners, an association of women who made tipi covers; and the Women's Medicine Cult, a wakan society of women who had experienced animal visions, and who were said to have gathered annually to prepare war medicines and shields and to predict the outcome of war parties. The Double Woman dreamers, Porcupine Quill Workers, and the Women's Medicine Cult may possibly all have been aspects of a single woman's society.

Women's power, on the whole, was associated with domestic matters, while men's power dealt with the dangers of life outside the camp circle. The Double Woman dreamers and the Women's Medicine Society would seem to represent a unique female contribution to a cultural domain that was usually entirely controlled by men. The explanation may be that all these women were Double Woman dreamers, women who because of their dream were masculine in their behavior and who might be considered as forming an intermediary category between male and female (discussed further below).

Paralleling the religious domain, the overt forms of government were also all in the hands of men. Men only were chiefs, and the councils were attended only by men. Membership in warrior societies was restricted to men, although a few women were singers for some of the societies. There was no developed tradition of warrior women among the Lakotas.

The council was probably the most significant male institution. Ella Deloria discussed the council lodge as a symbol of Lakota society (1944:39-40; ms. 1:71-72, 29). It was, she wrote, "a lively place," with much coming and going. However, the men who were members of the council were only those of "mature judgment"; it was they who came to the council lodge to "deliberate and plan and philosophize." These were men of "hospitality and generosity," whose good deeds "weighted their words and earned them the right to be listened to whenever they spoke."

The council lodge was the central institution for the expression of Lakota wisdom and virtue. It was a place where men gathered to confer about the welfare of the people as a whole. Deloria tells us that to honor the men, women brought the best food they had to the council lodge, then hurried away to let the men eat and deliberate. She wrote (1944:39):

> But don't assume they were chased off. They left because it was considered unwomanly to push one's way into a gathering of the other sex; it was unmanly for men to do so under opposite circumstances. Outsiders seeing women keep to themselves have frequently expressed a snap judgment that they were regarded as inferior to the noble male. The simple fact is that woman had her own place and man his; they were not the same and neither inferior or superior.

MASCULINITY AND FEMININITY

From earliest childhood youngsters were closely watched to be certain that they behaved according to ways proper for their sex. Children were corrected when they played games of the opposite sex or when they used linguistic forms inappropriate for their sex. Homosexual play between children was not tolerated, and Deloria wrote that a child suspected of such practices could acquire a reputation, rightly or wrongly, that would last into adulthood (ms. 1:344, 355-357). Much childhood play seems to have been restricted to playmates of the same sex, and once children reached adolescence, strict segregation of the sexes was enforced. Some girls were watched so closely that they were virtually unknown to the young men of the camp. They never went anywhere without a chaperon and never mingled in crowds (Deloria ms. 1: 379, 381).

During childhood, boys were frequently lectured on the importance of acting like men. Parents worried if their sons showed an inclination for girlish games and mannerisms. Such boys were liable to grow up to be winkte, "berdaches," men who dressed and behaved as if they were women. The word winkte, according to Bushotter, means "would be a woman" (ms. 215). These individuals were considered to be very unfortunate; the greatest tragedy that could befall a Lakota male was to become winkte. However, they were not necessarily held to be personally responsible for their status. These boys had dreams that caused them to become winkte. The nature of these dreams is poorly recorded, although Wissler reported that several of his informants told him that the dream was of a wakan woman, while one man said that the dream was of a particular buffalo spirit, the ptewinkte (1912:92). Nothing is known of the latter; Bull Ring translated this term for Buechel as meaning a fat and dry buffalo cow (1970:449). Wissler (1912:95) also recorded that the boy might dream of a male messenger who takes him to a tipi. He is told to enter: one side of the tipi has skin-dressing tools and the other has bows and arrows. In this case the choice evidently was left to the boy to select the symbols of the lifestyle he desired. Among the Omahas, a boy sometimes dreamed of the spirit of the moon who would trick him into taking a woman's pack strap instead of a bow, thus dooming him to the status of berdache

(Fletcher and LaFlesche 1911:132).

Apparently the life of a winkte was not happy. It is said that there never were very many of them. Lakota winter counts mention a winkte who committed suicide by hanging, culturally defined as the woman's form of suicide (Howard 1960:375). Winkte were believed to be very wakan, and in many ways their status in life was similar to the heyoka, the Thunder dreamers who because of their visions made people laugh by acting and speaking backwards. Both men and women might be heyoka.

According to Bushotter, winkte "lived the life of women" (ms. 104). Some became famous for the excellence of their quill and beadwork, for they were believed to have special power for artistic creation. At least some married men in polygamous unions; others lived alone in tipis of their own. Iron Shell told Hassrick that after a winkte had had sexual relations for the first time, his parents would put up a tipi for him (1964:122). (The term winktepi means "sodomy" [Riggs 1890:577].) These homosexual relationships were recognized but disapproved (Bushotter ms. 101, 215; Mirsky 1961:417). Again, Iron Shell told Hassrick that if a man had relations with a winkte he would regret it after death for he would have to live outside the main camp circle, with the murderers, and be tormented by the winkte. Hence Iron Shell's grandfather had cautioned him to leave the winkte alone (1964:122). The implication seems to be that men before marriage were likely to be tempted by the winkte into sexual relationships.

The winkte, Bushotter wrote, "spent their time making people laugh." They conferred funny, frequently obscene, nicknames on people (ms. 104, 215). Blue Whirlwind told Hassrick that if a winkte names a child, the child would grow up without sickness. Only boys received such nicknames (1964:122-123). Winkte called each other "sister" and called everyone else "cross cousin." Most of the time they dressed as women, although in some instances winkte apparently lived part of the time as men, and part as women, and engaged in the pursuits of both sexes. According to R. and G. Laubin, winkte sometimes went to war and were believed to bring luck to the war party (1977:366). A winkte predicted the defeat of Captain William J. Fetterman's command by the Lakotas and their Cheyenne allies at Fort Phil Kearny in 1867 (Hyde 1957:147).

Winkte in a sense was a mediating category between male and female. This becomes clear in an account recorded by Ella Deloria of the death of a winkte (ms. 2:3-5). The people were faced with the problem of whether men or women should prepare the body for burial. The final decision was to request an old married couple to do the work jointly, and meanwhile a scaffold was built so that the body would be disposed of honorably.

The point to be emphasized is that in the understanding of the Lakotas, the status of winkte was not an escape for those boys who failed at the rigors of warfare and hunting.[2] Most of the evidence suggests that boys never made a conscious choice to become winkte. They were embued with a supernatural power that made them wakan in this special way and marked them off from other members of society. Unfortunately, there seems to be no recorded life history of a winkte to give a fuller understanding.

Significantly, there is a comparable status for women who behaved in masculine ways. These women were believed to have dreamed of the Double Woman (Winyan Nunpapika), causing them to act with masculine demeanor and to do men's work. Like the winkte, they also became extraordinarily proficient at porcupine quill and beadwork, and they possessed the power to cast spells on men and seduce them. They were said to be very promiscuous, to live alone, and on occasion to perform the Double Woman dreamer ceremony publically, acting out their dream. They were believed to be very wakan, and some of them became doctors (Tyon in Walker 1980:165-166).

Wissler recorded that a woman who dreamed of the Double Face Woman (Anog Ite) became a prostitute. He was told that in the distant past these women wore a small hoop with feathers attached around the periphery. "In this figure the ring is the vulva of the woman and feathers about it are the symbol of the penis. This has long been out of use" (Wissler 1902:107). However, both Wissler (1902:124) and Walker (1917:166) confused the Double Face Woman with the Double Woman; the former is described as having two faces, one beautiful and one ugly, while the latter is

245

described as two women joined together by a rope from which dangles a baby (cf. Dorsey 1894:473, 480). Probably the symbol described by Wissler was the sign of a Double Woman dreamer.

According to Wissler (1912:93-94), at the end of a dream of the Double Woman, she runs away as a black-tail doe, thus further identifying Double Woman/Double Face with the Black Tail Deer Woman (Sintesapela win), who enchants and seduces hunters when they are away from camp, causing them to become mute and sometimes to die (cf. Tyon in Walker 1980:167). In one form of the dream as described by Wissler, a woman is conducted to a lone tipi; inside sit two deer women. The dreamer must choose whether to enter the lodge along one side, lined with a row of skin-dressing tools, or the other, lined with a row of parfleche headdress bags. The deer women urge the dreamer to choose the latter. The former portends riches and a usual woman's life, while the latter symbolizes the life of a prostitute.

George Sword, talking to Wissler, emphasized the aspect of choice on the part of the Double Woman dreamer. Wissler wrote (1902:124):

Sword gives the following:

The two women are of opposite character. One is very industrious, neat, virtuous; the other idle, extravagant and a prostitute. In the dream the pair are seen to come from a lodge, from which two roads branch out. One road leads to virtue and industry; the other in the other way. The women speak as one and say: "Which way shall I go?" It seems that the dreamer leads them to make the choice, or makes it for them. At last they come to the end of the road. Now they give advice according to the road they chose. This advice makes or mars the dreamer. If the road to virtue is chosen, the dreamer is granted great skill in needlework and is also a wakan woman. . . .

Sword explains that this is to represent the struggle that goes on in one between the right and the wrong. The two women so bound together are the personification of the two selves. Often a woman who had received the advice from the evil woman would not listen to reproof or advice of friends, saying that such was her dream and so would she do.

A contemporary story of a Double Woman dreamer from Standing Rock Reservation runs as follows (DeMallie ms.):

A woman could dream of the Double Woman and they would teach her songs. One such woman used to live here. She could do the quill or beadwork on one side of a pair of moccasins, place it against the blank one, sit on it, sing the song, and both would be done. Or she could even just put the quills between the moccasin blanks, sit on them, sing the song, and it would be finished, whatever it was. But this woman died a terrible death because of her evil life and while dying she cried and screamed.

The Double Woman dreamer, to the extent that she might choose a lifestyle distinctly masculine (by not marrying, behaving aggressively, and solicitng promiscuous intercourse) and yet have some socially-recognized rationale for her behavior, places her in a parallel position to the winkte. The two are not the obverse of one another, but both represent intermediate categories between male and female, symbolized by active and disapproved forms of sexuality and by the production of the finest quill and beadwork. Unfortunately, even less is known of the Double Woman dreamers than of the winkte. However, it is clear that the female (life-giving) power of these women was symbolically dead. This is expressed by the baby seen dragging from the rope that joins the Double Woman together, symbolizing the loss of power to nurture life.

Whether there ever were any number of Double Woman dreamers is unknown, although it seems unlikely. According to Mirsky (1961:417), using Deloria's data, those rare women who acted in the ways of men "left the group and wandered by themselves," presumably to be killed or captured by an enemy. Perhaps these were women who lacked the sanction of the Double Woman dream.

For the Lakota boy, fear of becoming winkte was the ultimate incentive to make him strive to be manly.

247

Bushotter wrote that, when he was a boy, "My whole preoccupation was to be brave." He recorded at some length advice given to him by his father (ms. 101):

> My father continually gave us good
> advice. . . . He made us train wild horses.
> He taught us to have strong hearts for war.
> My father made me specially do many difficult
> things. My father told me to practice with
> the bow. . . . He told me to think about
> the things I would do on the warpath. "Son,
> a man who lives desiring to do difficult
> things will be very brave. He who is brave
> becomes famous, but he who is foolish, his
> name also becomes famous." When I was afraid
> of something they would say, "Why, my son is
> brave! He will pay no attention to his hurt!
> This is what I used to think, but now I see
> that my son will be a winkte! . . . Come on!
> If you are unable to flee from the enemy by
> swimming among cakes of floating ice, or if
> you are unable to charge the enemy, from
> that very time you must dress like a woman
> and live like a foolish woman."

Such advice makes clear the ways in which Lakota boys were trained. Ella Deloria (ms. 1:369) recorded a story from a man named Makula whose father awoke him one snowy morning to announce that buffalo were near. He told his son: "Come, come! Women may stay warm in their beds at a time like this but real men must go forth!" This inspired Makula to join his first buffalo chase, and he came back with a calf. Deloria commented as follows:

> It was the reference to his maleness that
> challenged him. For to be compared to a
> woman was the worst possible insult, whose
> effect was to drive many a boy into assuming
> a man's role regardless of danger and possible
> death. Even as small boys they were reminded
> from time to time by fathers and grandfathers
> that "Winica yelo" [You are male!]. And . . .
> they were argued into good behavior by their
> male collaterals, or dared to take risks--
> "because they were male." If a small boy
> cried, they remarked, "Here is a girl crying,"
> and that was enough. Courage and endurance
> were thus inculcated and induced.

The symbolic difference between men and women might be seen to center around courage, or "hardness of heart." Bushotter's father would tell him: "That which is female is weak of heart, but that which is male must carry about a heart of stone" (ms. 101). This in turn is a reflection of the division of labor, men's concerns being directed outside the camp and women's concerns within the camp.

Women played a large part in inspiring men to bravery. Mothers encouraged their sons to be brave and instructed their daughters to respect their brothers, and do favors for them, because they would have to go fight the enemy and their lives were liable to be hard and short. Women's demands for the revenge of loved ones slain by the enemy was a further stimulus bolstering the warrior ethos.

Yet there was always an implicit contradiction between everyday camp life--the preserve of women--and the cultural emphasis on warfare. As a boy grew up he was constantly exhorted to be brave and to look forward to going to war in order to seek honor. He was told that it was better for him to lie dead on the field of battle than to stay at home like a woman. But families hated to see their sons go to war. Red Fox related the following experience, which must have occurred during the 1860s (Densmore 1918:375):

> My mother was a good and beautiful woman.
> She wore her hair in long braids and I
> remember how she looked as she said, "If
> my son ever goes on the warpath I shall take
> a lariat and hang myself." I was a very
> little boy, and it made a great impression
> on me, as my mother intended it should do.
> Of course, she did not really mean it, but
> she did not want me to run away and go with
> a war party. Yet that is exactly what I did.

Going to war was a usual prerequisite for marriage: it was proof of manhood and could provide horses needed to offer to the girl's family. Yet warriors attempted to prevent young men from courting prematurely for fear that they would want to spend too much of their time at home. Among the Yanktons, and long ago, probably among the Tetons as well, there was a society known as <u>wimnašni</u>. Members could have no dealings with women until they had won four feathers for their deeds in war (Deloria ms. 1:371). Nicollet recorded that the <u>wimnášni</u> sometimes gave public feasts at which the young men affirmed their virginity (1976:270). According to Wissler (1912:77) these were the same feasts at which women swore their virginity. Both sexes swore the oath by reaching into a hole dug in the earth and by biting a knife (for women) or an arrow (for men).

COURTSHIP AND MARRIAGE

Marriage among the Lakotas, according to Deloria (ms. 1:118-121), was of three kinds. The first was marriage by elopement. In such a case the young couple ran away together before any exchange of gifts between their families to sanction the relationship. They usually began their married life with the man's family. The second type was mutual agreement, by which both families exchanged presents and the couple usually began their married life with the woman's family. The third type of marriage was by purchase, in which the man gave a large quantity of goods to the woman's family. This was the most highly honored type of marriage since it symbolized the great value placed on the woman. Walker recorded that the standard value was equivalent to six buffalo robes, and that the woman would ever after boast that her husband had paid the price for her (1917:148; 1982:51). It seems likely that such marriages were neolocal, and perhaps were most frequently second marriages in polygynous unions.

Marriage was definitely considered a joint enterprise. Only after marriage did a couple get to know one another (Deloria ms. 1:133). One Dakota father told his son, "Treat your wife with pity [compassion] for a woman is not a slave" (Deloria ms. 1:367). However, some men beat their wives. Deloria wrote that such behavior might occur if "the wife was inhospitable, ugly-tempered, flirtatious, actually unfaithful, [or] cruel to her step-children" (ms. 1:137). Deloria emphasized that these were all faults that the wife could correct; men did not beat their wives for faults over which they had no control.

On the whole, marriage was an equal partnership,

with neither spouse babying the other (Deloria ms. 1: 134). Men and women owned material goods separately; everything pertaining to the home was owned by the woman, and she might own livestock as well (Deloria ms. 1:134). Husbands and wives did not ordinarily address one another as "my wife" or "my husband," and referred to one another in the third person. According to Deloria, spouses were not considered to be related to each other (ms. 1:134). After a long life together an old couple might seem to transcend the sexual difference between them and address one another as kola, the male term for a special friend (Deloria ms. 1:149).

Although the ultimate decision as to whether a girl should marry a particular suitor was the responsibility of her male relatives, particularly her brothers, in theory and normally in practice, girls were allowed to make their own decisions as to whom to marry (Deloria ms. 1:121).

Divorce was simple in Lakota society and could be initiated by either husband or wife. The tipi belonged to the woman and the children usually went with their mother in the case of divorce (see Walker 1982:41-44, 55-57). Sometimes men threw away their wives (wiihoyeyapi) at a warrior society dance (Deloria ms. 1:143). This was considered a great deed since it deprived the man of the comforts of life. White Bull recorded that in his youth he had two wives who were so jealous of one another that they gave him no peace; he solved the problem by giving them away to a fellow member of his warrior society at a public dance. However, he wished to keep his child, and this caused such problems that the mother of the child eventually returned to him (Vestal 1934:213-216). Men who took too many women in succession, not keeping any of them very long, were called wicawitkowinla, "men crazy over women" (Riggs 1890:569). The implication would seem to be that such men were overly interested in sexual relations.

Polygyny was common in traditional Lakota society. Two wives in polygynous marriages were the usual number, although Deloria heard of a Santee who had nine. Four, she said, was considered many (ms. 1:137). Walker recorded data on twenty-four polygynous families at Pine Ridge during the early twentieth century (Cook and DeMallie, in press). In each of

these families there were two wives; in six of the
families the wives were sisters, and in one they were
cousins. (These references are undoubtedly to biological relationships, so more of these co-wives may
have been related to each other according to the
Lakota kinship system.)

Plural marriages were ideally agreeable to all
parties since the wives would be able to share the
household duties between them. However, jealousy over
the husband's attention was a common theme. Women in
a polygynous marriage were believed to get along
better if they were sisters. One of Deloria's informants told of wanting to adopt her co-wife as a
sister, and being happy to accept her into the marital
relationship (ms. 1:61). Polygyny was in no way considered demeaning to women, and later wives were
accorded just as much honor at their marriage as was
the first.

Eventually, marriage was the expected status for
most Lakota people. For men it was an economic
necessity in order to maintain a household, and if a
widower did not remarry he was accused of being stingy
(Deloria ms. 1:146). Some women never married and
instead devoted themselves to the care of a relative.
Lakotas did not marry too young. In a sample of 122
mid-nineteenth century marriages, Walker found the
average age at marriage for women to be twenty-two
years, with seventeen the youngest and twenty-eight
the oldest (the latter being a woman who had borne two
children before marriage) (Cook and DeMallie, in
press). According to Deloria, men were about the same
age as their wives, or ideally a little older (ms. 1:
138).

Since marriage and warfare made diametrically
opposed demands on a man, it is perhaps understandable
that courtship became for at least some men a kind of
surrogate warfare. Women were cautioned to be wary of
men, and a definite system of flirting and at least
feigned resistance on the girls' part added spice to
the standardized courtship ritual. As the man enve-
loped a girl in his blanket--a custom called wioyuspa,
"catching a woman"--she was supposed to appear bored
and uninterested, and to remain always suspicious of
his motives. Deloria records that a girl would not
answer yes to any question that might be put to her by
a suitor for fear that he would tell others that she

had said "yes" to him (ms. 1:104). A symbolic sanction on courting behavior was the belief that if a girl engaged in petting and necking, her breasts would become large (Deloria ms. 1:378).

An unscrupulous man might try to get a girl to run away with him, then abandon her in the wilderness, a practice called manil eḣpeyapi. Some men counted their triumphs over women in the same way that they counted their coups, and they would compose mocking songs (wioweṡtelowanpi) which they and their friends would sing around the camp. Some of these songs mentioned the girl's name, although most did not (Deloria ms. 1:107).

Merely touching a girl's privates, or seeing her naked, was enough to violate her virginity, and the only honorable solution in either case was for the girl to marry the man involved (Deloria ms. 3:15; Wissler 1912:72). Because of this, girls sometimes had their legs bound together while they slept, and a girl was not allowed to sleep next to the tipi wall for fear that some enterprising young man might attempt to touch her during the night. Women later boasted that when they were girls their families cared for them so much that they tied their legs at night. One of Ella Deloria's informants told an amusing story about an attempt to touch a girl during her sleep (ms. 3:11); the story of High Horse's courting in Black Elk Speaks (Neihardt 1932:67-76) is another example. In both cases, however, the intention was not to shame the girl, but to put her into a position in which she would have to marry the young man who touched her. The custom is called wot'ant'an, "touching something."

The virginity of unmarried women was highly valued, and special "Virgins' Fires" were held at which girls swore to their virginity. Anyone knowing otherwise was bound to speak up and drive the pretender out. Similar ceremonies were held for married women at which they swore they had been faithful to their husbands. Women were honored if they lived their entire lives having known only one man sexually (Deloria ms. 1:118).

Virginity for men, on the other hand, seems to have been less highly valued. Only the wimnaṡni society insisted on virginity for its members; other young men were apparently expected to have sexual experiences before marriage.

Deloria wrote that the Lakota attitude could be summed up as follows: "It is male nature to trifle. Woman, look out or you could be hurt and it would be your fault" (Deloria ms. 1:105). One of Deloria's informants recalled her aunt's advice when her husband left her for a time (ms. 4:73):

> "Niece, be as though you didn't care, for men are naturally peculiar (o s̆tekape), and there is nothing to do about it. If they notice they are greatly desired, they make themselves unattainable. And if they are ignored, they are wistful in their longing."

If an unmarried girl became pregnant, or if a woman committed adultery, she, not her partner, was held responsible. A married woman's infidelity was publically sung about during the sun dance (Deloria ms. 1:109). It was not expected that a wife would leave her husband if he slept with another woman, but if a wife proved unfaithful, the man was expected to leave her to avoid public ridicule (Deloria ms. 1:143, 367).

If the tensions between the sexes in Lakota culture are perceived as a battle between men and women, the essential point of the complementary duality of male and female is lost. Men were attractive to women and sometimes deceived them and led them astray. This was attributed to elk power possessed by certain men, or to love potions or charmed flutes provided by shamans. According to Tyon (in Walker 1980: 161-163), the Bone Keepers society made special love potions for young men rejected by women. Using a hair from a woman's head, they could cause her to suffer a violent, unceasing nosebleed. Eventually, her father would be forced to ask the Bone Keepers to cure her, promising them in return that she would marry the young man responsible for her affliction.

Of course, women were equally attractive to men and sometimes deceived them and led them astray. Their power was believed to come from deer. It was believed that the white-tail deer might appear to a hunter in the guise of his beloved; after they had intercourse the man would become distracted and might die. Similarly, black-tail deer were believed to seduce hunters and drive them insane, sometimes resulting in death (Tyon in Walker 1980:166-167).

Deloria recorded that Lakotas said of individuals who were particularly attractive to the opposite sex, "He must be an elk," or "She must be a deer," thus invoking a supernatural explanation and doubtless in some sense relieving the individual of full responsibility for his or her actions (ms. 1:110). Metaphorically, if there was a battle between the sexes in Lakota culture, it may be considered a contest between two kinds of power rather than between men and women as individuals.

SEXUALITY

At adolescence both young men and women developed behavioral attitudes referred to by the Lakotas as scu, a shyness or painful awareness of the opposite sex. This was supposed to reflect sexual interest, and was believed to dissipate after marriage, although it would manifest itself again in a person's behavior if he or she developed any sexual interests outside marriage. Roughly comparable to flirtatiousness in American culture, it was contrasted with what Deloria refers to as the "sedate composure" expected of married people (ms. 1:380). Husbands and wives made no public display of their affections, and hugging was appropriate behavior only in private. In public, physical interaction between men and women was minimal. Adults of opposite sexes, even mother and son, would never hug one another under any circumstances (Deloria ms. 1:128, 388).

The extremely restrained behavior between cross-sex respect relatives is a further development of these behavioral patterns. Individuals in these relationships, including brother and sister and son-in-law and mother-in-law, were said to be "shy" (wišteca) toward each other (Bushotter ms. 89, 111). Hence they did not look at one another or speak directly to one another. The respect entailed seems to have had strong sexual overtones. In the brother-in-law/ sister-in-law relationship, sexual tensions were expressed in the opposite manner, through obligatory sexual joking.

In all cases of sexual indiscretion, women--not
men--were held to be responsible. This brings out a
fundamental feature of Lakota sexuality. Women were
considered to be the more insistent in desiring sexual
relations; sexuality seems to have been an important
part of a Lakota woman's self-identity. Men on the
other hand valued continence as proof of their bravery. Bushotter's father told him, "Don't let women
turn your head, but live prudently and fear nothing"
(ms. 101).

In cultural terms, sexual intercourse was valued
only for the creation of children. After a woman
became pregnant, she was supposed to refrain from
further sexual relations. If a baby was born covered
with mucus, it was said that the parents had continued
to engage in sexual relations. It was expected that
the couple would not resume sexual relations until
the baby had stopped nursing; this could be a period
of four or five years. Deloria mentioned that in an
origin story the Lakotas were told that they should
wait for a period of four years between children (ms.
1:58). She wrote that men were supposed to master
their sexual desires by going to war or hunting, by
sweat baths and by prayer. This was a sacrifice that
they made for the benefit of their children. Deloria
says that women were frowned upon if they became
pregnant too frequently because it was not in the best
interests of their children. A child still nursing
when its mother became pregnant again was said to be
"rectum killed" because the mother's milk became
watery and caused diarrhea, forcing the child to be
weaned prematurely. This was considered an offense
against the child and people would say, "Parents
should subordinate their desire for his sake" (Deloria
ms. 1:302). Continence was the usual culturally-
prescribed mechanism for preventing pregnancy,
although medicines were sometimes used for abortion
and for contraception. Some women who were barren
were accused of these practices, as well as of
engaging in excessive sexual activity. In a sample of
seventy-six monogamous marriages, Walker found the
average number of births to be eight; in forty-eight
polygynous marriages, the average was six per wife
(Cook and DeMallie, in press).

The proliferation of stories about adulterous
women and about women's voracious sexual appetites
underscores the importance of this theme in Lakota

culture, but it does not tell us anything about the actual prevalence of adultery. Deloria recorded that she had been unable to collect even a single story of a woman actually having the tip of her nose cut off, even though this was said to be the prescribed punishment for an adulterous wife (ms. 1:136). This may be explained by Walker's observation that although a man might punish his wife for adultery by cutting off her nose or an ear, this only occurred in extreme cases. The most usual punishment, he wrote, was for the husband to cut off one of his wife's braids (1982:42, 56). Bushotter reported gang rape as a technique for punishing a woman who had committed adultery (ms. 225). Quarrels over women seem to have been frequent, to the extent that in the commonly quoted maxim about chiefs it is said that a chief must put the welfare of his people above his own welfare: "If a dog lifts its leg to the chief's tipi, he must not see it," meaning that if a man has illicit sexual relations with the chief's wife he must ignore it. This is a powerful expression of the symbolic importance of adultery in Lakota culture. Only the truly brave man was above caring about it.

It is important to understand sex as a procreative act from the Lakota point of view to see if it reflects the same inequality between the sexes. Sex was not a topic of public discussion for the Lakotas, hence there is little information recorded on the subject. Animal copulation was freely discussed, but human sexual relations were not (Deloria ms. 1:354). The only data on the subject come from Deloria (ms. 1:300). The male element, Deloria writes, was considered to be the essential one in procreation. Nurtured by menstrual blood, the male element begat life. There was no concept of the ovum. It thus seems that even in the biological aspect the male's contribution was considered active and the female's passive.

According to Deloria, the menstrual blood gave a kind of temporary power to a woman, a wakan quality. This was not thought of as polluting but rather as at odds with the wakan power of men; a woman's menstrual power clashed with a medicine man's power. The clash was characterized by the word ohakaya, "to cause to be blocked or tangled" (Deloria ms. 1:375). Hence women had to be secluded from men during their menstrual periods.

Of this _wakan_ quality, Walker wrote (1980:242):

> When a girl is young she is like a boy, but
> when she has her first menstrual flow, a
> _tonwan_ possesses her, which gives her the
> possibility of motherhood and makes her _wakan_
> and this _tonwan_ is in the products of her
> first flow, making it very powerful for either
> good or evil as it may be used.

During this period, Walker continued, the girl should
live alone, not take part in any public activity, and
not talk to men "so that the _wakan tonwan_ of her flow
may harm no one and so that all may know that she is
not with child." The _tonwan_, according to Walker's
informant Finger, "is something that comes from a
living thing, such as the birth of anything or the
growth from a seed" (1917:155). Thus there seems to
be the idea that the menstrual blood had some definite
kind of nurturitive, if not generative, power.

If a man comes near a girl who is menstruating
for the first time, the spirits lurking nearby may
plague him with eruptions, palsy, or with madness.
There is no indication that the woman herself can use
her menstrual power for any other purpose than
nourishing the life-giving substance from the father,
although Walker wrote that certain shamans could use
the discharge of a girl's first menstrual flow to make
a love potion that, mixed with a young man's or a
young woman's food or drink, would cause him or her to
desire the person who administered it (Walker 1980:
242-243). Perhaps as a safeguard against such misuse
of a girl's first menstrual flow, Deloria reported
that the girl was seated over a small hole dug an
arm's length into the earth "so that life-blood and
earth might commingle, both being equally holy and
symbolic of fertility" (ms. 1:373).

Menstruation itself, Walker wrote, was caused by
spirits (1980:243):

> The spirits which take possession of the
> body of a girl when she becomes a woman
> squeeze the blood from her body and cause
> the flow. Each moon they return and do this
> unless she becomes with child, when they
> are pleased and let her alone, except Anog
> Ite [Double Face], who may still plague her

with pains.

Various taboos surrounded women's behavior, particularly while menstruating, to prevent the clash between the women's power and men's power. Thus women were forbidden to ride a fast horse since it was believed that the horse would be slow thereafter. Menstruating women were forbidden from coming near the healing ceremonies of the Bear society, and it was said that if a menstruating woman tanned a bear skin she would turn into a bear; her skin would turn black and her face would become hairy. It was similarly said that if a menstruating woman touched a weasel skin she would become sick and perhaps die (Tyon in Walker 1980:168, 158, 159, 168). In a general sense, menstruating women were prohibited from any contact or even proximity with men's _wakan_ objects and practices.

CONCLUSIONS

The Lakotas have a tradition of four great virtues said to characterize mankind. Walker listed them as bravery, generosity, fortitude and integrity (1917: 62). Hassrick gives them as bravery, fortitude, generosity and wisdom (1964:32). White Bull listed them as bravery, generosity, fortitude and fecundity (Vestal 1934:87). The variations suggest the range of personal characteristics most highly valued by the Lakotas.

A man demonstrated these chracteristics in his youth by hunting and warfare, by joining warrior societies, and in later years by demonstrating his wisdom in council and by playing the role of peace maker within the village. A woman, on the other hand, displayed these virtues largely at home, as a mother, wife and lodge owner. The Lakotas traditionally had a special designation for good women, _slot'a_, "full of grease." This term evoked a woman's buckskin dress, stiff with grease from being worn while tanning hides and preparing meat for drying, a symbol of the wearer's industry and skill (Deloria ms. 1:96). More recently, according to Deloria, the word lost its original connotations and became a designation for women who are skillful, likeable, and of good character. (For some Lakotas today the term has lost its earlier meaning and has taken on the reverse connotation—a woman who is lazy and dirty.)

A Santee woman listed for Deloria the characteristics of a "good woman." She must be faithful to her husband, devoted to her children, industrious and skilled in womanly arts, genuinely hospitable and generous, and a strict follower of kinship etiquette. She should think much but say little, and she should stay at home and occupy herself with her own business. Chastity was of paramount importance. She must not be guilty of any "deeds" (oh'an), meaning indiscretions. "Without chastity all the other fine qualities are not enough to earn the name 'good woman'" (Deloria ms. 1: 366-367).

Thus a man's strength was in his bravery and his devotion to matters outside of home life; a woman's strength was in her chastity and her devotion to matters relating to the home.

Metaphorically, "female" was frequently manipulated as a symbolic foil to "male." Boys were told not to act like women, and for any male to be compared to a woman was the worst possible insult (Deloria ms. 1: 369). Using the same metaphors, Bushotter reported that people said that since the white men had put the Lakotas on reservations, they had made women of them (ms. 118). The meaning here is not that the whites had dominated the Lakotas physically, but that they had taken away the glorious men's pursuits of war and hunting. In Lakota society, women were dominated by men neither in a physical nor a psychological sense. The important social units were the family and the extended family, groups composed of both men and women. What each sex did redounded to the glory of the family as a whole.

The stereotypical portrayal of Lakota society as dominated by males is only correct to the extent that it characterizes a culture in which the activities of men were considered to have greater symbolic value than the activities of women. To describe it as a male-oriented society characterized by psychological warfare between the sexes is to impose on the Lakotas our Western categories and meanings, and our conceptions of the appropriate relationship between the sexes. It perpetuates the same kind of error as that made by the French trader Pierre-Antoine Tabeau who wrote of Lakota women in the first years of the nineteenth century, "they are, in the fullest sense, slaves" (Abel 1939:182). Both evaluations are equally ethno-centric.[3]

Symbolically, the Lakotas believed their society to be no stronger than their women. No better argument can be made for this than to remember that the pipe, the primary means by which Lakota men gained power from the spirits, was the gift of a woman, the White Buffalo Woman. Hence the intense emphasis on the virginity of maidens and the chastity of wives. The purity, industry and goodness of Lakota women were the safeguards of society. Without women to protect and honor, the entire system of warfare lacked justification, for the ultimate aim of all the men's glorious activities in war and hunting that took them far from the comforts of camp was the continuation of society. From the Lakota point of view, the glory was recompense for the suffering required. In a culturally real sense it was men who subordinated themselves to women, resisting sexual temptations and the comforts of home to risk their lives in war and hunting and to humiliate themselves before the powers of the universe to beg for spiritual help to enable them to accomplish their duties as providers and protectors.

NOTES

1. I owe a primary debt to Ella C. Deloria, whose work provided much of the data on which this paper is based. Discussions with Miss Deloria, as well as with many Lakota friends, have shaped my understanding of the issues discussed here. I also owe a special debt to Elaine A. Jahner, Department of English, University of Nebraska--Lincoln, with whom I have discussed most of the ideas presented here. The word "traditional" in the title refers to a reconstruction of the values of nineteenth-century Lakota culture as an ideological system.

2. Contra Hassrick 1964:121.

3. This is not intended as a general evaluation of Hassrick's work. His book is the fullest and best overall survey of Lakota culture and society in the anthropological literature. However, the pervasive psychological perspective that he employs may well mislead the general reader into ethnocentric generalizations.

REFERENCES CITED

Abel, Annie Heloise, ed. (1939) Tabeau's Narrative of Loisel's Expedition to the Upper Missouri. Norman: University of Oklahoma Press.

Buechel, Eugene, S.J. (1970) A Dictionary of the Teton Dakota Sioux Language. Paul Manhart, S.J., ed. Pine Ridge: Red Cloud Indian School.

Bushotter, George (ms.) Lakota Narratives with Interlinear Translation by James Owen Dorsey. 287 texts. 1887. National Anthropological Archives, Smithsonian Institution, ms. No. 4800. Translation by Ella C. Deloria, American Philosophical Society Library, ms. No. 30 (X8c.3).

Cook, Della C., and DeMallie, Raymond J. (in press) Fertility and Family Structure Among the Nineteenth Century Oglala Sioux: A Reappraisal. American Anthropologist.

Deloria, Ella C. (1944) Speaking of Indians. New York: Friendship Press.

_____ ms. 1. The Dakota Way of Life. Copy through the courtesy of Vine Deloria, Jr.

_____ ms. 2. Camp Circle Society. Nebraska Historical Society, Lincoln.

_____ ms. 3. Wot'ant'an wan. American Philosophical Society Library, ms. No. 30 (X8a.10), part II.

_____ ms. 4. Mrs. Andrew Knife's Story. American Philosophical Society Library, ms. No. 30 (X8a.4), part 3.

DeMallie, Raymond J. (ms.) Field Notes from Cheyenne River and Standing Rock Reservations, 1970-71.

Densmore, Frances (1918) Teton Sioux Music. Smithsonian Institution, Bureau of American Ethnology, Bulletin 61. Washington, D.C.: Government Printing Office.

Dorsey, James Owen   (1894)   A Study of Siouan Cults.
    Smithsonian Institution, Bureau of American
    Ethnology, Annual Report 11, pp. 351-544.
    Washington, D.C.: Government Printing Office.

Fletcher, Alice C., and LaFlesche, Francis   (1911)
    The Omaha Tribe. Smithsonian Institution,
    Bureau of American Ethnology, Annual Report 27,
    pp. 15-654. Washington, D.C.: Government
    Printing Office.

Hassrick, Royal B.   (1964)   The Sioux: Life and
    Customs of a Warrior Society. Norman:
    University of Oklahoma Press.

Howard, James H.   (1960) Dakota Winter Counts as a
    Source of Plains History. Smithsonian
    Institution, Bureau of American Ethnology,
    Bulletin 173, Anthropological Papers No. 61,
    pp. 335-416. Washington, D.C.: Government
    Printing Office.

Hyde, George E.   (1957).   Red Cloud's Folk: A History
    of the Oglala Sioux Indians. (Original ed.,
    1937.)   Norman: University of Oklahoma Press.

Laubin, Reginald, and Laubin, Gladys   (1977)   Indian
    Dances of North America: Their Importance to
    Indian Life. Norman: University of Oklahoma
    Press.

Lewis, Thomas H.   (1975)   A Syndrome of Depression
    and Mutism in the Oglala Sioux. American Journal
    of Psychiatry, Vol. 132, pp. 753-755.

Mirsky, Jeanette   (1961)   The Dakota. In: Cooperation
    and Competition Among Primitive Peoples, Margaret
    Mead, ed., pp. 382-427. (Original ed., 1937.)
    Boston: Beacon Press.

Neihardt, John G.   (1932)   Black Elk Speaks: Being
    the Life Story of a Holy Man of the Oglala Sioux.
    New York: William Morrow and Co.

Nicollet, Joseph N. (1976) Nicollet's Notes on the Dakota. Raymond J. DeMallie, trans. and ed. In: Joseph N. Nicollet on the Plains and Prairies: The Expeditions of 1838-39 With Journals, Letters, and Notes on the Dakota Indians, Edmund C. Bray and Martha Coleman Bray, eds., pp. 250-281. St. Paul: Minnesota Historical Society.

Riggs, Stephen Return (1890) A Dakota-English Dictionary. James Owen Dorsey, ed. Contributions to North American Ethnology, Vol. VII. Washington, D.C.: Government Printing Office.

Sword, George (ms.) Manuscript Writings of George Sword. 1 Vol. Ca. 1909. Colorado Historical Society. Translation by Ella C. Deloria, American Philosophical Society Library, ms. No. 30 (X8a.18).

Vestal, Stanley (1934) Warpath: The True Story of the Fighting Sioux Told in a Biography of Chief White Bull. Boston: Houghton Mifflin Co.

_____ (1957) Sitting Bull: Champion of the Sioux. (Original ed., 1932.) Norman: University of Oklahoma Press.

Walker, James R. (1917) The Sun Dance and Other Ceremonies of the Oglala Division of the Teton Dakota. American Museum of Natural History, Anthropological Papers, Vol. 16, Part 2, pp. 51-221.

_____ (1980) Lakota Belief and Ritual. Raymond J. DeMallie and Elaine A. Jahner, eds. Lincoln: University of Nebraska Press.

_____ (1982) Lakota Society. Raymond J. DeMallie, ed. Lincoln: University of Nebraska Press.

Wissler, Clark (1902) Field Notes on the Dakota Indians. Department of Anthropology Archives, American Museum of Natural History.

_____ (1912) Societies and Ceremonial Associations in the Oglala Division of the Teton-Dakota. American Museum of Natural History, Anthropological Papers, Vol. 11, Part 1, pp. 1-99.

CHAPTER 9

"WARRIOR WOMEN" - SEX ROLE ALTERNATIVES
FOR PLAINS INDIAN WOMEN[1]

Beatrice Medicine
University of California - Northridge

In much of the ethnohistorical and ethnographic
literature on Plains Indians, females are characterized as docile human beings and drudges. Such
characterizations serve as a counterpoint to the commonly described male attributes of aggressiveness and
bravery. But when one moves beyond the idealized
generalizations and examines actual descriptions of
individuals and their activities, it becomes apparent
that there was considerable variation in the roles of
women and men.

One role, which apparently was widespread in
North America, is the "warrior woman." Besides
references (Lewis 1941; MacAllester 1941; Seward 1946;
Denig 1961; Landes 1968) to the appearance of this
role among Plains Indians, it has been reported in
such widely separated societies as the Kutenai
(Schaeffer 1965), the Navajo (Topper, field notes),
Tlingit (Knapp and Child 1896), and Ottawa (Duggan's
Journal 1793).[2] The existence of the warrior woman
role not only challenges pervasive ideas about the
passivity of native women, but it also offers an
excellent case example for examining female role
variations in American Indian communities.

The purpose of this paper is to describe and ana-
lyze the Plains Indian warrior women, not as a form of
deviant and idiosyncratic behavior, but as a healthy
and self-actualized role. More specifically, it is

argued that the warrior role for women was institutionalized in Plains Indian communities, and that it
was one of several culturally accepted positions which
accorded women power and prestige in areas typically
identified as "masculine."

BACKGROUND

The subject of sex role reversal has been a popular subject in the literature on Plains Indians. Most
discussions of this subject, however, center around
the role of the male berdache (Jacobs 1968). While
female role reversals have been described in several
sources (Lewis 1941; MacAllester 1941; Seward 1946;
Denig 1961; Schaeffer 1965), there has been a dispro-
portionate emphasis on the berdache.

The usual explanation for the institutionalization of the berdache, and the one originally enumerated by Ruth Benedict (1934), is that certain men
were unable to meet the demands of masculinity and
aggressiveness in the warrior role. From this, it is
also assumed that the berdache--donning the attire of
women, imitating their voices, acquiring their mannerisms, and following their domestic occupations--
provided a necessary outlet for men who did not fit
into the typical male role (Hassrick 1964). And
finally, it is commonly asserted that rejectors of the
masculine warrior role were individuals with unproduc-
tive vision quests.

While it is true that berdache took on behaviors
and activities associated with women in Plains Indian
societies, their role did not exactly correspond with
that of women. Among the Lakota, for example, Winkte
("wishes to be woman"--i.e., womanlike) continued to
engage in masculine activities. They often accompanied war parties, and they could support themselves
through hunting. In addition, they carried on certain
activites that were viewed as normative in their role,
including: the naming of children in a ritual way,
dispensing herbal medicines, and prognosticating the
outcome of war parties. In these and other activities, berdache received a measure of respect and
prestige in their community. And even though their
social position was not enviable, it was better than

that of a man who was a repeated failure as a warrior.

Sue-Ellen Jacobs (1968) has suggested that the warrior woman may have been the female counterpart to the pervasive and widely reported berdache. In so far as many warrior women combined achievements in masculine occupations with traditional female roles, there was a parallel. There was also a similarity in the sanctioning of sex role reversals through supernatural means. Among the Lakota, women changed gender identities through recurrent dreams, while men sanctioned their sex role reversals through vision quests. Yet, in both cases supernatural visitations were interpreted by religious practitioners and accepted by kin and community. Thus, through institutionalized dreams or visions both sexes could assume other roles without seriously damaging their social acceptance and self-esteem. The parallels, however, stop at the level of description. When it comes to customary explanations of sex role reversals, the one commonly applied to the berdache does not appear applicable to the case of warrior women. It seems unlikely that women could not meet the demands required of females in most Plains Indian societies. But then, the whole idea that sex role reversals, for either women or men, constituted deviant forms of escapism from "normal" behavior is open to question.

Instead of looking at sex role reversals as a form of "deviance" derived from "incompetence" in the roles associated with a person's gender, it might be more productive to examine them as normative statuses which permitted individuals to strive for self-actualization, excellence, and social recognition in areas outside their customary sex role assignments. In this light, changing sex role identity becomes an achieved act which individuals pursue as a means for the healthy expression of alternative behaviors.

FEMALE ROLE VARIABILITY

In the nineteenth century, major changes were taking place in the social positions of Plains Indian women. As Oscar Lewis (1942) so carefully demonstrates with the Blackfoot, the involvement of Plains Indians in the Euro-American hide market brought about

269

major changes in the position of women. Among these changes was the growing economic dependency of women. Increasingly female labor was engaged in the processing of hides, a commodity whose acquisition and trade were largely in the hands of men. The economic dependency of women had important consequences on their social positions within their families and in their communities at large. Generally, their status declined, and they became more vulnerable to the interests and machinations of men.

Although Plains Indian women had become more dependent and vulnerable, there were many different avenues through which they could act in independent and decisive ways. These included: socially sanctioned role alternatives, participation in certain female sodalities, as well as many different options of a situational nature.

The most detailed and complete discussions of female role alternatives appear in the literature on the Piegan of Alberta and Montana. Among the Piegan, there was a small group of women, called "manly-hearted women," whose ambition, boldness and eroticism contrasted with the prevailing ideal of female submission and reserve (Lewis 1941). Although the Piegan, along with other Plains groups, put a premium on male dominance, they accorded certain women exceptional privileges and prestige in areas typically associated with men. The manly-hearted women excelled in every important aspect of tribal life—property ownership, ceremonialism, and domestic affairs.

As children, manly-hearted women were often favored with more food, toys, care and attention than other siblings. Such favoritism, which incidentally, was widely distributed among northern Plains groups, must have had a profound impact on a child's sense of self-assurance and independence. Indeed, favorite female children among the Piegan often led in childhood games, played boys' sports, and took for themselves the names of great warriors. Moreover, some indulged in sex play early in life.

As adults, the self-esteem and drive of favored females led to superiority in men's as well as women's work. These women attained wealth by taking on the economic roles typically played by men, and as a consequence, they attained a level of self-

270

sufficiency which permitted them independence in other realms as well. They selected dance partners and cursed when the occasion demanded it. Some dominated their husbands and exposed them to ridicule (Lewis 1941:181). Yet, in spite of this, their position in the household was secure. According to Lewis (1941:181), this security was related to their passionate and unconventional sexuality. They allowed their husbands sex play that other women refused, and they expressed their dominance in assuming the male position in intercourse. Such privilege is especially remarkable in view of the prevailing ideology of male dominance which included wife beating and disfigurement for infidelity. The predominant picture of the manly-hearted women certainly presents an anomaly in the customary view of Plains Indian women as submissive and oppressed.

When the manly-hearted female role is examined in the light of other socially sanctioned status positions for women, it becomes apparent that it is not a "deviation" but one of several alternative female roles. These optional positions can be studied by examining four different native role categories among the Canadian Blackfoot. These are: (1) Ninawaki (manly woman)[3]; (2) Matsaps (crazy woman); (3) Sun Dance woman; and (4) Ninaki (chief woman or favorite wife). (For an interesting diagrammatic representation of these categories, see Seward 1946:120.)

The Ninawaki (manly woman) corresponds to the "manly-hearted" woman of the Piegan. This category identifies a woman in whom aggression was developed to the point where she behaved like a man. (For another interesting discussion of masculine striving among Kaska women, see Honigmann 1954.) Some of these women, though not all of them, engaged in warrior pursuits.

The Ninaki (chief woman) refers to an able and respected female who is capable of doing a job as a chief. This term, however, has a second meaning, which is the favorite wife of a man. John Ewers (1958:100) refers to this favorite wife as a "sits-beside-me-wife." According to Ewers, this woman had the responsibility of carrying the ceremonial equipment of the man (1958:93). She also shared responsibilities with a man in caring for sacred bundles and in conducting certain ceremonies. She also may have been a sexually favored wife. Usually, this woman was exempt from household work, and only a wealthy man could have afforded such a person in his household. It must also be noted that these women appear to have been trained for this role as children, and like the manly-hearted women, they received the kinds of special privileges accorded to a favorite child.

Matsaps designates a "crazy woman" but with special reference to sexual promiscuity. Among the Lakota, a correlate female figure is "Witkowin." Sexual promiscuity exhibited by a witkowin was sanctioned through certain types of dreams. Dreaming of the Anog-Ite, "The Double Face Woman," or dreaming incessantly of the Wakinya (Thunder Beings) released a Lakota woman from her commitments to the cultural ideals of virginity or marital fidelity (Wissler 1912:93). Oral history material suggests that there were incidences where women who had witkowin-like dreams were given away by their husband. This occurred not in the manner of "throwing away the wife," which typified divorce. Instead, the husband, recognizing the affection of his wife for another, dressed her in her finery, painted her face and the part of her hair, and led her on a fine horse to the man she esteemed.

The Sun Dance woman represented in Piegan society, and among the Lakota society as well, the extreme of womanly virtue. Before marriage, she was a virgin. She was never unfaithful to her husband nor did she remarry after his death. These women were rewarded by assuming an honorary position in the Sun Dance. Among the Lakota, there was also the prestigious "Bite-the-Knife" ceremony in which post-menopausal women were honored for their virtuousness.

The female role categories of the Canadian Blackfoot, which also have correlates among other Plains groups, indicate that there was a range of special statuses for women. Although two positions, that of the favorite wife and Sun Dance woman, epitomize the idealized features of femininity, they were no less important and accepted than those which linked women to manly pursuits. These varied role categories also suggest that the idealized behavior of women was not as rigidly defined and followed as has been supposed.

Besides the evidence of female role variability provided by the categorical statuses just mentioned, there is also the well-known diversity of behavior associated with a woman's birth order. Among the Dakota, for instance, birth order positions had a powerful impact upon how children were raised and what behaviors were expected of them. Such differential treatment must have had a major influence on later adult behavior. There was also variation in treatment and expected roles of wives from the first to the last married, and there were differences in how women behaved in their various kinship statuses (i.e., older sister, younger sister, daughter, mother). Unfortunately, the varied social positions of women in Plains Indian societies have not been well-documented, and as a consequence, it is difficult, if not impossible, to make conclusive statements about the dynamics of psychological and behavioral variations among women that correspond with recognized role diversity.

WOMEN AND WARFARE

The fact that there were a range of socially accepted roles for women in Plains Indian societies permits us to understand the role of warrior women as one aspect of this variation.

The most detailed account of a warrior woman comes from the writings of the well-known trader on the Upper Missouri, Edwin Denig (1961:195-200). This woman was a Gros Ventres who was captured by the Crow when she was twelve years old. Already exhibiting manly interests, her adopted father encouraged these inclinactions and trained her in a wide variety of male occupational skills. Although she dressed as a woman throughout her life, she pursued the role of a male in her adult years. She was a proficient hunter and chased big game on horseback and on foot (Denig 1961:196). She was a skilled warrior, leading many successful war parties. In time, she sat on the council and ranked as the third leading warrior in a band of 160 lodges (1961:198). After achieving success in manly pursuits, she took four wives whose hide-processing work brought considerable wealth to her lodge (1961:198-199). Although this woman's

manly-oriented life may have been exceptional, it was
socially recognized and esteemed among the people with
whom she lived.

Other reports of female warriors are not as
complete, and most do not distinguish between women
who pursued warfare as a life occupation and those who
joined war parties on a situational basis. Among the
Blackfeet, there appear to have been women who pursued
warfare as an extension of their manly inclinations
(Lewis 1941; MacAllester 1941). There were also
women, usually childless, who accompanied their
spouses on raiding expeditions and who may (or may
not) have been actively involved in fighting (Ewers
1967:329). And finally, there were women who took on
the role of warrior only for a short time and for a
specific reason (e.g. to avenge the death of a relative, [Lewis 1941]).

Cheyenne women, according to George Grinnell
(1956:157), also engaged in warfare. Although many
appear to have accompanied war parties as "helpers,"
some fought in battle, raided for horses, and counted
coup on the enemy. The participation of women in warfare, however, appears to have been less common in the
late nineteenth century than it was in earlier times.

There were also women warriors among the Dakota.
Ruth Landes (1968:39) indicates that while women were
tacitly barred from joining war parties, many did participate in war for glory as well as revenge, and some
even led war expeditions (1968:49). Women who had
achieved war honors played an important role in the
winoxtca (the female equivalent of the male akicita or
soldiers). These women were called upon to police
other women in the campsite and to punish female
offenders (1968:69). It is noteworthy that while the
female warrior role was apparently common among
eastern Dakota (i.e., Mdewakanton, Sisseton,
Wahpeton), it has not been reported for western Dakota
(Teton).

These are a few examples of women's reported participation in Plains warfare and raiding. The motiva-
tion for women to engage in war can only be
conjectured. First of all, there was the prestige and
glory which accrued to counting coups, obtaining guns,
killing and scalping, and cutting tethered horses
from within a tipi circle. Women who were capable in

274

these activities could achieve prestige and wealth independently, as the case of the Crow female warrior indicates. Secondly, there was the need for women to be assertive and able to fight for reasons of self-defense. In a period of history, when Plains Indian populations were engaged in bitter and unceasing rivalries with neighboring peoples, it was imperative that women were prepared to fight and assert themselves, not only at times when they were alone but also when men were present in the camps. And finally, women were also motivated by revenge and engaged in warfare to avenge a relative's death. Importantly, reasons for female engagement in warfare--defense, glory, and revenge--were not different from those that inspired men to fight.

Even when women did not participate in warfare directly, they played a very important role in supporting the military activity of men. Robert Lowie (1935:106) mentions the importance of women's auxiliaries in the military societies of the Crow, and George Grinnell (1956:10-12, 20-22) discusses the importance of women in the scalp ceremonies and social dances which followed the warriors' return. Besides their participation in formal institutions, women supported military ventures in other ways. Among the Dakota, for instance, women expected their husbands to avenge a brother's death. They also pressured husbands to acquire horses to increase the wealth of their lodges, and they encouraged husbands to obtain co-wives (including women captured in war) to assist in the processing of hides and other domestic duties.

Whether Plains Indian women participated in military activity directly or supported it in an indirect way, it is clear that they saw their own well-being and that of their kin and community in terms of a social system which revolved around warfare. In this system, prestige and wealth centered around success in the warrior role. The typical status configurations of women mirrored this orientation. As a female grew up, her status was typically reflected in the warrior position of her father, then brother, husband, and sons. But it could also be reflected in her own warrior status which, if successful, was achieved and pursued along masculine lines.

CONCLUDING REMARKS

The idea that some Plains Indian women followed masculine roles and behaviors, either on a permanent or situational basis, does not deny the idealized and normative patterns of female passivity and dependence in Plains Indian societies. But even though the general ethnographic picture paints Plains Indian women in a dependent role, it is clear that they had other options which included assertiveness and independence. In social settings where maleness and femaleness were separate and contrasting spheres, as they certainly were in Plains Indian societies, the roles of manly-hearted women and berdache were sources of mediation. They offered men and women opportunities for displaying cross-sex talents in socially approved ways, and in doing so, they were probably essential to the psychological well-being of peoples who lived in societies with highly dichotomized gender expectations.

What is clear from the information presented here is that Plains women and men were able to assume a range of roles that were either consistent with or contrary to their customary gender ascriptions. Unfortunately, such notions as "warrior society," "male dominant," and other male supremacist expressions have set the tone for the analysis of male and female behavior in Plains Indian societies. Consequently, the rich complexity of female gender roles and the variety of relations between women and men has been largely obscured.

In this regard, the shared beliefs and strategies for obtaining status is well-documented for Plains Indian men. Comparatively little information, however, is available on how women pursued alternative roles, how they achieved self-actualization in a male-oriented social system, and how they managed conflicts between personal strivings and societal norms. But it is precisely because many ethnographers of Plains Indian communities assumed, a priori, the existence of a modal and rigid personality profile for females that such questions were not asked. While a new generation of scholars has begun to pursue questions such as these, their answers may never be complete or conclusive. Regrettably, the kinds of data that might illuminate and clarify the nature of female role reversals in Plains Indian societies have not been recorded. At least for the pre-reservation period, it is now too late to uncover such material with any degree of depth. In the end, all that remains on this fascinating subject are cursory references which, while suggestive, are not sufficient to fully reconstruct the nature and dynamics of role variability among Plains Indian women.

1. A different version of this paper was originally presented at the International Congress of Americanists (Rome, Italy, 1973). It was a preliminary statement to call attention to the problem of women's status in the male dominant societies of the Northern Plains. It emphasized the need to re-examine ethnographic data to provide new insights into this issue and to chart courses for future research involving Native American women. I wish to thank Patricia Albers and William James for their considerable assistance in drafting this paper.

2. Dr. Martin Topper records an historical case of a Navajo woman avenging her son's death and leading a Navajo war party on a successful raid against the Hopi. Topper's informants were Percy John and Donald Dejolie (field notes 1971). The reference for the Tlingit is as follows "... it was usual for an old woman of rank to sit in the stern of the canoe and steer, for even in some battles, women were leaders in battles" (Knapp and Child 1896:64). Dr. Christian Feest, Museum fur Volkerkunde, Wien, sent this reference in 1972:

> November 15. An Ottawa sent by Egushewa de Bout Call'd on me in his way to inform me he was sent to acquaint the Ottawas that one of the prisoners a Frenchman taken by the little Otter's part had shot the Indian who owned him, whilst asleep and Tomahawked the Indian wife, Tis a considerable loss to this nation as both the man and woman were leaders of Parties in war, and I greatly fear that all the other prisoners will be sacrificed to avenge this murder. (Extracts from Thomas Duggan's Journal, Detroit, 1793:108).

3. L. M. Hanks, Jr. (personal communication) confirms that the Blackfoot term for manly woman, ninawaki, differs from Lewis' term for manly-heart Ninauposkitzipzpe. These terms need further clarification in use and transcription.

REFERENCES CITED

Benedict, Ruth   (1934)   Anthropology and the Abnormal. Journal of General Psychology 10:59-82.

Denig, Edwin Thompson   (1961)   Five Indian Tribes of the Upper Missouri, John Ewers, ed.   Norman: University of Oklahoma Press.

Duggan's Journal   (1887)   In: Copies of Papers on File in the Dominion Archives at Ottawa, Michigan Pioneer Historical Collections, 12:105-109.

Ewers, John C.   (1958)   The Blackfeet, Raiders of the Northern Plains.   Norman: University of Oklahoma Press.

_____   (1967)   Blackfoot Raiding for Horses and Scalps.   In: Law and Warfare, P. Bohannan, ed. New York: Natural History Press.

Grinnell, G. B.   (1956)   The Fighting Cheyennes. Norman: University of Oklahoma Press.

Hassrick, Royal B.   (1964)   The Sioux: Life and Customs of a Warrior Society.   Norman: University of Oklahoma Press.

Honigmann, J. J.   (1954)   The Kaska Indians: An Ethnographic Reconstruction.   Yale University Publications in Anthropology, Volume 51.

Jacobs, Sue-Ellen   (1968)   Berdache: A Brief Review of the Literature.   Colorado Anthropologist 1:25-40.

Knapp, Frances and Rheta Louise Child   (1896)   The Thlinkets of South East Alaska.   Chicago: Stone and Kimball.

Landes, Ruth   (1968)   The Mystic Lake Sioux.   Madison: University of Wisconsin Press.

Lewis, Oscar   (1941)   Manly-hearted Women among the South Piegan.   American Anthropologist 43:173-187.

279

Lewis, Oscar   (1942)   The Effects of White Contact
     Upon Blackfoot Culture.   Monographs of the
     American Ethnological Society No. 6.

Lowie, R. H.   (1935)   The Crow Indians.   New York:
     Holt, Rinehart and Winston.

MacAllester, H.   (1941)   Water as a Disciplinary
     Agent Among the Crow and Blackfoot.   American
     Anthropologist 43:593-604.

Schaeffer, C.   (1965)   The Kutenai Female Berdache.
     Ethnohistory 13(3):193-236.

Seward, G. H.   (1946)   Sex and the Social Order.
     New York: Macmillan.

Topper, Martin   (1971)   Field Notes.

Wissler, C.   (1912)   Societies and Ceremonial
     Associations in the Oglala Division of the
     Teton Dakota.   American Museum of Natural
     History, Anthropological Papers, Volume 11.